FIVE PERSPECTIVES ON TEACHING
IN ADULT AND HIGHER EDUCATION

FIVE PERSPECTIVES ON TEACHING IN ADULT AND HIGHER EDUCATION

Daniel D. Pratt and Associates
The University of British Columbia

With Foreword by Stephen D. Brookfield

KRIEGER PUBLISHING COMPANY
MALABAR, FLORIDA
1998

Original Edition 1998

Printed and Published by
KRIEGER PUBLISHING COMPANY
KRIEGER DRIVE
MALABAR, FLORIDA 32950

Library of Congress Cataloging-in-Publication Data
Pratt, Daniel D., 1942–
        Five perspectives on teaching in adult & higher education / Daniel
D. Pratt and associates ; with foreword by Stephen D. Brookfield.
        p.   cm.
        Includes bibliographical references and index
        ISBN 0-89464-937-X (hard cover)
        1. Adult education—Cross-cultural studies.   2. Teaching—Cross-
-cultural studies.   3. College teaching—Cross-cultural studies.
        4. Adult learning—Cross-cultural studies.   I. Title.
LC5219.P73   1998
371.7'82—dc21   96–46411

10   9   8   7   6   5   4   3   2   CIP

This book is dedicated to Vivian Goldsmith and Virgil Pratt, two of my most memorable teachers. When I began teaching in 1963, Aunt Vivian said, "Start off firm but fair; then gradually, after awhile, you can be friendly." There is still much wisdom in those words and much fondness in my heart for this dedicated teacher. My mother and friend, Virgil Pratt, continues to teach me how to live, love, and laugh. Amidst the trials of raising a family and working full time, she never lowered her expectations or tempered her love. By example, we learned without knowing we were being taught; and still, in her eighties, she teaches us more than we know.

The Authors

Ric Arseneau is a physician on faculty in The University of British Columbia Medical School and is coordinator of the residency program at a local hospital in Vancouver. In 1992 he received the Teacher of the Year Award for the faculty of medicine.

Arnold Boldt spent much of his career teaching English to adult basic education students. He is currently head of academic programs in Keewatin Community College in northern Manitoba. A large percentage of his students are First Nations People (Canadian Indian), as is Arnold.

Janice Johnson has taught avalanche safety to government personnel for several years before entering graduate school where she is completing her Ph.D. in adult and higher education. Her specialty is the improvement of teaching in a variety of contexts of practice, including classroom instruction and on-the-job training.

Tom Nesbit has worked in labour education in England and as an adult educator in San Francisco. He was a member of the research team that won the 1992 Imogene Okes Award for most outstanding piece of research in adult education (San Francisco State University). He is now director of the Labour Studies Program, and a faculty member at Simon Fraser University, Canada.

Daniel D. Pratt is on faculty in the Department of Educational Studies, The University of British Columbia, Canada. From the Yukon to Arizona, and from Seattle to Shanghai, he has been exploring what teaching means. In 1992 he received the Teacher of the Year Award for the faculty of education.

Dirk Rodenburg has worked as an employment counselor, adult basic educator, and as a multimedia developer in the health sciences. He is pursuing a Ph.D. in adult education and is interested in the application of cognitive science, effective user-modeling, and constructivist and social-situated learning theory as it applies to instructional design.

Caddie T'Kenye has a long-standing interest in nontraditional learners in nonacademic settings. She holds a B.F.A. in creative writing and an M.A. in adult education and works in alternative and conventional health care, as well as the arts.

Contents

SECTION III

Foreword

For three days during early January 1997 I was stranded in a motel room in Sioux Falls, South Dakota. I had come to give a one-day presentation but almost as soon as the plane touched down a blizzard struck that part of the country bringing with it whiteout conditions and wind chill temperatures that dipped to −70 °F. With my usual careful planning I had brought along no topcoat and no computer. My only company was the book you now have in your hands. It was good company. During my three days of enforced solitude I was provoked, intrigued, and challenged to think in new ways about my own practice as a teacher of adults. As I read and re-read the manuscript it struck me, as I had guessed it would, what an important contribution to the literature of teaching adults this book represents.

Most books on teaching adults fall into one of two categories. On the one hand we have autobiographically grounded reflections from which are drawn universally applicable insights. On the other hand we have decontextualized prescriptions of good practice, often drawn from a theory the author favors. *Five Perspectives on Teaching in Adult and Higher Education* is neither of these kinds of work. It is a carefully written, well-researched analysis of five major philosophical and practical orientations to teaching that influence how many of us live our lives as teachers. The book draws equally from theoretical analysis and empirical research. It is not a series of expert proclamations about pedagogy, but rather a thorough exploration of how over 250 teachers live out their different commitments to five honored, and honorable, traditions in the field of adult education. Unlike many other books on teaching which have a polemical axe to grind, favoring one of these traditions over all others, this book presents an even-handed, respectful assessment of the merits and potential shortcomings of each of these five different orientations.

That such a respectful, honest, and provocative account of teaching practices and philosophies should be under the direction of Dan Pratt will come as no surprise to those who know him. For over two decades Dan's questing intelligence has helped many adult educators open themselves to new ways of thinking about, and doing, teaching. His own openness to self-critique, his patience, his concern to integrate theory and practice, and his always overwhelming desire to learn more about teaching, are all evident within this book. As you read through the following chapters you will be struck by the diversity of ideas, perspectives, and voices. This diversity is intentional and revealing. The book has forced me to reexamine many of my own automatic prejudices and allegiances about teaching, particularly regarding perspectives that I assumed were uncongenial, unfamiliar, or misguided. I can think of no greater compliment to pay to a group of writers than to say that they made me productively troubled about some of the easy certainties embedded in my own practice. I know that you, the reader, will be similarly challenged, affirmed, and stimulated by what follows.

Stephen D. Brookfield
Distinguished Professor
University of St. Thomas
St. Paul, Minnesota

Acknowledgments

There are many who should rightfully have their names mentioned here—those who have supported, cajoled, inspired, challenged, and awakened me along the way. First, and foremost, the many teachers that allowed me into the worlds of their teaching and the shadows of their thinking. Without them, this book would never have come to light. In addition, thanks to Knute Buttedahl, for his gentle nudge toward China; the Kellogg Center for Adult Learning at Montana State University, and the Canadian Association for Adult Education, for funding my work in China; Wendy Klein, for her organizational eye; Starbucks coffee, for the closest thing to mainlining caffeine and a place to think and write without so much as an impatient glance; my "children", Todd, Paige, and Sean, who never quite understood why, but always knew where to find me; the other authors, for their feedback and patience as this project unfolded in ways we hadn't fully imagined; and Adrienne Burk, my friend and writing mentor, who led me gently but substantively into a deeper understanding of my own thinking and writing. Finally, thanks to Chris Lovato, my wife and friend, for her endless support and encouragement.

Daniel D. Pratt

Introduction

Daniel D. Pratt

What does it mean "to teach?" Ask a dozen people and you will hear a range of answers that describe guiding, facilitating, telling, showing, planning, helping, directing, and so forth. Some might say teaching is the effective or efficient transmission of information from one person to another. Others might answer that teaching is the socialization of people into a community, for example, helping people learn how to live harmoniously within a particular family or society. Still others might say that teaching is an arrangement of conditions that facilitate someone's learning.

The answers that are given tell something about each person's "perspective" or point-of-view. They also tell something about their experience, as parent, coach, friend, manager, or as learner over many years of formal and informal learning. Some of this experience is received unquestioningly, while other aspects of it have been formed through careful reflection. But overall, a person's perspective is an expression of personal beliefs and values related to learning and teaching.

This book is about five alternative points of view or perspectives on teaching adults. It is the result of several years of teaching and research in Canada, China, Hong Kong, Singapore, and the United States. With the help of several graduate students, I studied 253 teachers of adults, trying to understand what teaching means across vastly different settings. Each teacher was asked what it meant "to teach." Of course, they were asked a great many more questions in addition to that one, including questions about learning, motivation, the goals of education, the nature of the learners they taught, and the influence of context on their teaching. Their responses revealed five qualitatively different perspectives on teaching which form the conceptual backbone of this book. The five perspectives are:

1. Transmission—Effective Delivery of Content

2. Apprenticeship—Modelling Ways of Being

3. Developmental—Cultivating Ways of Thinking

4. Nurturing—Facilitating Self-efficacy

5. Social Reform—Seeking a Better Society

Although this book came from research, it is not about research. It is, instead, an in-depth examination of the intentions and beliefs that give direction and justification to what teachers do and how they think about their teaching. As such, it is intended for teachers of adults, whether in formal, nonformal, or informal settings, and those who wish to explore the deeper structures that define teaching.

These five are not the only perspectives on teaching; others have been explored and described by people such as Apps (1991), Brookfield (1990; 1995), Fenstermacher and Soltis (1986), Joyce and Weil (1986), and Kember (in press) among others. However, the perspectives presented here differ from earlier literature in at least three important ways. First, they are derived from research over several years, in five different countries. Thus, they are empirically derived from practitioners rather than intuitively from scholars. Second, each perspective is portrayed in both theoretical and practical terms. Theoretically, each is examined and analyzed as a cluster of actions, intentions, and beliefs. In addition, each perspective is described in contexts of actual practice, and in the voices of several educators. Finally, much of the research on teaching perspectives (often called conceptions) portrays a range of perspectives, usually along a continuum from less developed to more developed ways of thinking about teaching (e.g., Kember, in press). In presenting them as a hierarchy of more or less developed views, there is an implied valuing of some perspectives over others. This book takes a different approach, presenting each perspective as a legitimate view of teaching, subject only to variations in the quality of implementation, not the nature of their underlying values.

Thus, each perspective is presented as a legitimate form of commitment and valuing in teaching and corresponding ways of thinking, acting, and believing about the instruction of adults. How could it be otherwise, given that they are based on the actual practice of more than 250 teachers around the world? The intention of presenting them in this volume is to describe them robustly, so they coexist as five identifiable perspectives. Presenting each of them not as a "method" of teaching, but rather as a unique constellation of actions, intentions, and beliefs, should provoke critical reflection on issues of evaluation and quality, while also respecting diversity, within adult and higher education.

The presentation of this volume, therefore, proceeds as follows: Section I provides an introduction and overview of a general model of teaching. Following this presentation there is a discussion showing how the model is adaptable to accommodate variations in commitment to particular actions, intentions, and beliefs. The section concludes with a brief introduction to five qualitatively different perspectives on teaching. Section II presents the five perspectives in detail, as described and advocated by authors who self-selected into the perspective about which they write. The five chapters in this section are written in the styles and voices of those authors, rather than the editor of this volume. This allows the passion and conviction associated with each perspective to emerge, unfiltered, through the narration of those who live within each perspective. It is apparent to me, as editor of this volume, that perspectives on teaching reveal themselves in the style of each author's narration as well as in the substance of their writing and educational practice. Finally, Section III, returns to my editorial voice to present an analysis of the perspectives and comment on the difficult matter of evaluating teaching while also respecting a plurality of perspectives on teaching.

REFERENCES

Apps, G. W. (1991). *Mastering the teaching of adults*. Malabar, FL: Krieger Publishing Co.

Brookfield, S. D. (1990). *The skillful teacher*. San Francisco: Jossey-Bass.

Brookfield, S. D. (1995). *Becoming a critically reflective teacher*. San Francisco: Jossey-Bass.

Fenstermacher, G. D., & Soltis, J. F. (1986). *Approaches to teaching*. New York: Teachers College Press.

Joyce, B., & Weil, M. (1986). *Models of teaching* (3rd ed.). Englewood Cliffs, NJ: Prentice-Hall.

Kember, D. (in press). A reconceptualisation of the research into university academics' conceptions of teaching. *Learning and Instruction*. New York: Pergamon Press.

SECTION I

Section I provides an overview to the framework which guided the original research, and the basic structure of five perspectives on teaching that emerged from that research. Chapter 1 introduces a general model of teaching, with five elements and three relationships. This model formed the backbone of the observations and interviews from which the five perspectives emerged. It is the conceptual framework through which teaching was examined and from which perspectives emerged. Chapter 2 looks at three indicators of commitment that helped define perspectives on teaching: actions, intentions, and beliefs. Chapter 3 introduces each perspective as a complex lens through which teachers view the elements and relationships within the general model of teaching. Section I, therefore, provides a conceptual platform that should help you interpret the more visceral descriptions of each perspective in Section II.

CHAPTER 1

THE RESEARCH LENS
A General Model of Teaching

Daniel D. Pratt

DIVERSITY REQUIRES PLURALITY

In much of the research and literature of adult and higher education there is an assumption that educators share perspectives and meanings about teaching. For example, many adult educators assume that andragogy[1] represents the best (and only) way to teach adults, especially when adult education is compared to youth education. Yet, we know there are many people engaged in adult education who do not see themselves as andragogical "facilitators." For some this is due to their own personality and preferences for teaching in a more directive style. Some have no choice, due to the nature of the content they teach (e.g., safety procedures for exiting an airplane in an emergency). For other adult educators, the role of facilitator might be at odds with their cultural traditions for a teacher, as for example, in the case of a Chinese master teaching Tai Chi to Westerners. And in adult basic education (ABE), there is convincing evidence that adult learners and instructors of adults prefer more directive teaching roles when people's primary goal is to pass examinations (Conti, 1985). All of these challenge andragogical assumptions. Indeed, there are many educators who suggest that the usual role of andragogical facilitator reproduces existing forms of power which privilege some people over others.

These examples strongly suggest that there is no basis for assuming a single, universal perspective on teaching adults. Both the philosophical and empirical evidence argues against it. What is needed instead is a plu-

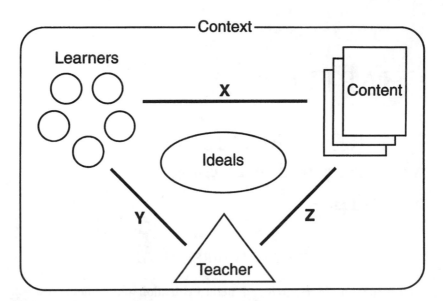

Figure 1.1 A General Model of Teaching

rality of perspectives on teaching adults that recognizes diversity within teachers, learners, content, context, ideals, and purposes. Adult and higher education are pluralistic in purpose and procedure, in context and in content, and in regard for what is considered effective teaching. Such diversity compels us to think broadly when considering what teaching means.

A GENERAL MODEL

While this diversity must be acknowledged, we must also recognize the impasse that would result if we had no commonality or organizing framework for considering how to effectively teach adults. One way to accommodate diversity, within a common frame of reference, is to construct a general model of teaching. Such a model, developed for the initial research that lead to this book, is presented in Figure 1.1.

The model contains five elements (teacher, learners, content, context, and ideals) and three relationships (lines X, Y, and Z). The easiest way to understand how the model works is for you to imagine you are a teacher and are thinking about your own answers to these questions:

Teacher: How do you define your role and responsibility?
What is your primary role and responsibility as an instructor?
If someone were evaluating your (or someone else's) teaching in this situation, what would they expect you to be doing? How would they know if you were doing that?

Learners: How do you describe your learners?
Who are your learners?
What do they bring to the learning situation that might influence their learning or your teaching?
What are some factors, histories, or problems that might impede their learning?

Content: How do you decide what to teach and what should be learned?
What do you want people to learn?
What might be difficult about learning that?
Is there an order or structure to your content that is important to learning it or teaching it?

Context: How do you locate your teaching within a context?
Describe the circumstances that frame your teaching.
Does the context influence either your students' learning or your teaching? How?

Ideals: Can you name any ideals, beliefs, or values that influence your teaching, and which would be important to understand if someone were evaluating your teaching?

In the original research, each element served as a potential avenue for interviewing respondents about their perspectives on teaching. Some teachers more readily talked about their learners, while others were more articulate when talking about subject matter or content. Most people were quite willing and able to talk about each of the elements, although with different degrees of clarity and commitment, with the exception of the element of ideals. It seems that most respondents held their ideals implicitly, as taken-for-granted values, rather than explicitly as well-articulated statements. However, teachers holding a Social Reform Perspective were an exception to this (see Chapter 8).

Relationships between Elements

The relationships between elements provided another avenue for interviewing respondents' about their perspectives (lines X, Y, and Z in Figure 1.1). In the research it was clear that people used different means to engage learners in the content (line X), preferred different kinds of relationships with learners (line Y), and held contrasting beliefs about an instructor's content credibility (line Z). Again, imagining yourself as a teacher, think about the answers to these questions:

Line X: How do you engage learners in the content and assess their learning?
Describe a typical teaching session for you.
How do you actually teach?
How do you evaluate what people have learned?

Line Y: What is the nature of the social contract between the learners and you?
Describe your relationship with the learners.
How do you provide feedback to them?
What kind of learners are most challenging for you? Why?

Line Z: How do you establish your content credibility or expertise?
How do you deal with questions on the content?
How do you deal with a question that you can't answer?
What do you do when people challenge the utility or relevance of what you are teaching?

Once again in the research, educators found that not all the relationships were equally significant for them. Some were more meaningful, others less so. This opened the possibility that perspectives might be anchored in different combinations of elements and relationships. Not one of the 253 people studied, held all the elements and relationships as equally important. Instead, their comments revealed they were committed to uniquely blended combinations of actions, intentions, and beliefs. A study of those commitments led, in turn, to an understanding of the five perspectives presented in this volume.

Figure 1.2 Aspects of Commitment

COMMITMENTS IN TEACHING

Return, for a moment, to the General Model of Teaching (Figure 1.1). As a conceptual framework the model simply identifies elements and relationships that may be important in teaching. It does not suggest relative importance or significance; no element or relationship is pictured as more dominant than others. Yet, the fundamental difference between perspectives rests upon the belief that some elements (and relationships) are more important than others. That is, educators show greater, or lesser, commitment to some elements than others when talking about their teaching.

Commitment is defined here as a sense of loyalty, duty, responsibility, or obligation associated with one or more elements within the General Model of Teaching. It is revealed through the way a person teaches (actions), what a person is trying to accomplish (intentions), and statements of why those actions and intentions are reasonable, important, or justifiable (beliefs) (Figure 1.2). Commitment is, thus, pivotal for understanding perspectives on teaching.

As mentioned above, a teacher's commitment is usually directed more toward one or two elements than others; it is prominent while teachers plan, conduct, evaluate, and reflect upon their teaching. This does not mean they have no regard for the other elements; rather, some elements are more noticeable in teachers' thinking and tend to be the focal point for clarifying intentions and beliefs related to teaching.

Commitment to a particular element focused the respondents' comments markedly in the original research. Those committed to an element spoke vividly about it. To give you an idea of how commitment to an element sharpens a teacher's awareness of it, four elements are re-presented here, with some elaboration from respondents in the original research.

Learners

One form of commitment is directed toward the learner. At the end of the day, teachers with this commitment reflected on the people they taught, not the content, as they made judgments and decisions about whether things went well or how they might be improved. When asked, "What are you trying to accomplish?" they spoke about helping people gain confidence, or getting them back into the workforce, or helping them overcome a sense of failure or instilling in them a sense of self-confidence and self-esteem as learners. For these teachers, the focus was on learners' self-esteem and dignity. As one teacher said,

> I would like my students to think I cared about them. I cared about their learning and I cared about the quality of our work. Most of all, I hope they would believe that they could make a difference in their lives. Why? Because I think these are the best things I can possibly do as a teacher, is care about my students and have them learn to respect themselves.

Still others focused on the learner's intellectual development. They talked about helping people learn to think critically, to solve problems, or to go beyond the obvious and probe the content for its deeper meaning or significance. As one physics teacher at an Oregon community college put it, "I want to teach more about less; I want to help people think, not just about physics, but about the physical world around them." In that statement he was making content the servant of thinking and rejecting institutional pressures to cover the syllabus.

In each case, the subject of these teachers' conversations, and the focus of their commitment, was the learner, not the content. The content was a means; the learner was the end. This is not uncommon in adult education, which has a long history of attracting teachers whose primary commitment is to their students. From adult basic education to graduate school, many of those involved in the teaching of adults think first about the learners as they plan, conduct, evaluate, and reflect on their teaching.

Content

Some of the teachers felt a strong commitment to their content (it could also be called discipline, profession, trade, or field of practice).

Many people involved in higher education were obviously committed to the discipline or content area they teach. They felt passionately about chemistry, forestry, nursing, or literature and they turned to that content when addressing the question, "What are you trying to accomplish?" Watching them teach, one could see evidence of enthusiasm; it was apparent they had strong feelings about their subject matter. Further, they expected learners to be committed to that subject matter or discipline.

I saw a similar dedication in the training of service industry and trades personnel. For example, the director of training for Sheraton Hotels in Singapore expressed a strong sense of responsibility toward the hospitality industry. However, his commitment was not to the industry per se, but to a particular kind of excellence which was defined by his hotel. The Sheraton staff and management prided themselves on setting standards of service and training that went beyond industry standards. They felt, as do many who are committed to content, that education and training is concerned most of all with maintaining high standards of achievement or application.

Context

Other teachers were equally clear about their commitment to context, that is, the need to locate learning in authentic contexts of practice and social relations. They could not imagine significant learning taking place apart from real life and the place where learning was to be applied. Of course, there are many kinds of context—cultural, historical, political, geographical, organizational, and so forth. However, here context refers to the physical and social environment where people learn.

I first became aware of people's strong feelings about context while working with First Nations People (native Canadians) in the Yukon Territory of Canada. The most powerful and important teachers in the communities were the elders. They embodied much of what younger people were expected to learn about life in the North including a range of skills and values. Whether the content was storytelling, hunting and trapping, or sorting out social conflicts, learners learned alongside someone more experienced within a community of people that was interdependent. Learners watched, listened, and gradually participated in the social community of working and living together. Life and learning were one; context was the place where living and learning coincided.

However, it wasn't just the First Nations People of Canada that expressed this sentiment. Trades people in the original study also questioned learning that didn't happen on the job—especially classroom learning. That was seen as artificial and devoid of the realities essential to learning a trade. They, like the elders of the north, saw context as *the* critical element for meaningful learning.

Ideals

Perhaps most emphatic of all were those who defined their teaching in terms of an ideal or principle. These teachers believed, for example, that teaching ought to be governed by a commitment to justice or equality, or the need to redress power or value imbalances within society. Their commitment was more to a set of clearly articulated values or ideals than to content, learners, or context. One woman, teaching automotive maintenance for women, was very clear that her agenda was to help women bring about social change such that there would be no imbalance of power affecting employment and advancement in the workplace based on gender. This principle superseded all the individuals in her classes. Her commitment was clearly to changing society, not just to the immediate employability of women attending her classes.

SUMMARY

The diversity of learners, content, context, and ideals in adult and higher education suggests that a meaningful examination of teaching needs to address types of commitment more than a series of techniques. The General Model of Teaching presented here identifies elements about which practitioners expressed that commitment, in terms of actions, intentions, and beliefs. How these actually coalesce into the five perspectives presented in this book will be detailed in subsequent chapters, although at this point, there are a number of central propositions which warrant stating. They emerged from the original research and also guided the conception and writing of this book.

Perspectives, then, govern what we do as teachers and why we think such actions are worthy or justified. They are indicated by commitment toward one, or more, of the elements and relationships within the General Model of Teaching and expressed through actions, intentions, and beliefs related to those elements. As you progress through the book you will be reading about these perspectives on teaching. This is not to say they are the only perspectives; only that these five represent an understanding of a great many adult educators' perspectives on teaching. In closing this chapter, let me spell out several propositions that emerged from the research and guided the writing of this book.

- Proposition 1: There is no single, universal, best perspective on teaching adults.

Most books, and evaluators of teaching, would have us believe there is an agreed view of how best to teach adults. This volume rests on a different assumption, one that values a pluralistic view of teaching and a diversity of commitments and perspectives.

- Proposition 2: Teaching is guided by one's perspective on teaching, which is defined by actions, intentions, and beliefs regarding: (a) knowledge and learning, (b) the purposes of adult education or training, and (c) appropriate roles, responsibilities, and relationships for instructors of adults.

Many books on teaching adults are concerned, almost exclusively, with techniques of teaching. Yet, most of the research on effective teaching today acknowledges that techniques are only the tip of the iceberg; if we wish to understand and influence people's teaching, we must go beneath the surface to consider the intentions and beliefs related to teaching and learning which inform their assumptions.

- Proposition 3: Some of these beliefs are more central to one's being than others and, therefore, are less open to change.

Some of our beliefs are so rooted in core values that they represent long-held and significant aspects of who we are and how we see ourselves in relation to the world. At the other end of the spectrum, other beliefs are those things which we simply prefer, or find to be more useful today. Although they are a part of our perspective, they are more peripheral than central to our image of self-as-teacher and, therefore, more susceptible to change.

- Proposition 4: Improvements in instruction can focus on actions (e.g., improving lectures), intentions (e.g., clarifying exactly what one wants to accomplish), or beliefs (e.g., articulating what is taken for granted about learning).

Many readers might wonder if it's possible to improve their teaching without actually teaching and receiving feedback on the effects of it. It's an important question and the answer is "yes". There is an increasing body of research that suggests we can improve our teaching through reflection, especially if that reflection considers the underlying beliefs and intentions that guide our teaching. In fact, it is difficult to imagine significant growth in teaching without reflecting on what you are trying to accomplish, how you go about it, and why you think that it's important. As mentioned in the second proposition, teaching is guided by an interrelated set of actions, intentions, and beliefs. Therefore, reflection must go beyond actions, to include intentions and beliefs.

- Proposition 5: Development as an instructor can mean improving current ways of teaching or it can mean challenging fundamental beliefs about instruction and/or learning.

Too often, I believe, people think only of getting better at what they already do or know about teaching. Certainly, that is one important way of improving teaching—learning how to give better lectures, conduct more effective discussion groups, develop a broader means of evaluating what people have learned, and so on. However, there is another important way in which we develop as instructors and that is through critically reflecting on what we believe about teaching and learning. One of the authors in adult education literature that has greatly affected my work is Jack Mezirow, now retired from Teachers' College, Columbia University. He has written extensively on a form of learning called "perspective transformation." This form of learning centers on the fundamental structures of our thinking and perceiving and the ways in which we see ourselves in relation to others and in relation to our work. For me, this is another avenue of growth or development as a teacher. Perspective transformation doesn't happen often, and when it does, it rarely comes quickly. But when we experience this form of learning it is truly profound; it affects every aspect of teaching. It comes from a change in those belief structures that we hold close to our core being and which are normally quite resistant to change.

ENDNOTE

1. Andragogy is "the science and art of teaching adults" (Knowles, 1980). It is built upon two central, defining attributes: First, a conception of learners as self-directed and autonomous; and second, a conception of the role of teacher as facilitator of learning rather than presenter of content. Within North America,

no view of teaching adults is more widely known, or more enthusiastically embraced, than Knowles' description of andragogy.

REFERENCES

Conti, G. (1985). The relationship between teaching style and adult student learning. *Adult Education Quarterly, 35*(4), 220–228.

Knowles, M. (1980). *The modern practice of adult education: From pedagogy to andragogy.* Edgewood Cliff, NJ: Prentice Hall Regents.

CHAPTER 2

INDICATORS OF COMMITMENT
Actions, Intentions, and Beliefs

Daniel D. Pratt

A few years ago I attended a 3-day workshop on teaching. Twenty-five people, from widely different subject areas came together with a common desire to be better teachers. Some taught college students; others taught people from the community. Still others taught patients and worked in homes or at bedsides. We represented a wide range of disciplines and experience. Some were there as a condition of recent employment; others were there out of choice. No one was there because their teaching had been judged problematic.

Over the 3-day weekend we learned how to write behavioral objectives, sequence content, give lectures, write different levels of questions, conduct a discussion, and plan for evaluating learning. All of this was done within a supportive and well-structured environment. The instructors were enthusiastic and well prepared; clearly, this program had been delivered many times before, in several parts of the country. Yet, something seemed fundamentally wrong.

A few days after the workshop I had time to reflect back on it all. We had been led through a particular view of teaching, composed of a set of skills that were assumed to apply regardless of our context, students, content, or personal preferences and beliefs. Not once had we been introduced to an alternative view or asked what we thought effective teaching might mean in the context of our work. There was no mention of beliefs or values, or even any possibility that we might

15

have different notions of what it meant to teach, to learn, or to know
something. These generic skills were assumed to be appropriate
across disciplines, contexts, learners, and even cultures. Effective
teaching had been reduced to a set of value-neutral skills, most of
which could be captured on videotape for review and further prac-
tice. There were two implicit messages in this workshop: First, this
was the only legitimate view of teaching; second, it didn't matter
what, where, or whom you were teaching, these were the essential
skills (Daniel D. Pratt).

This experience is not uncommon. Many people characterize teaching as a set of generic skills or techniques to be mastered. The assumption is that if teachers have sufficient content knowledge, all they need to
learn is a predetermined set of skills to be on the road to effective teaching. Teaching is thus conceived of as a politically neutral, skilled performance—setting objectives, leading discussions, giving lectures, asking
questions, providing feedback, and so forth. Any values, beliefs, and
commitments embedded in those actions, go unexamined. Effectiveness
is equated with doing these things with a degree of skill; the more skilled
the performance, the better the teaching.

This view is evidenced by the proliferation of manuals and texts focusing on teaching techniques. As a consequence, when first asked to
think about different perspectives on teaching, people often confuse
technique with perspective: "Sometimes I teach according to one perspective; other times I take a different perspective. It all depends on the
situation." What they are saying is that they vary their approach or use
of techniques depending on the situation. They may even change their
intent or purpose, along with the approach they take, depending on the
circumstances. The terminology might change, but the implication is the
same—teaching is understood in terms of a flexible set of actions and
intentions, sometimes modified according to the situation. Beliefs and
values are assumed to play a minor role, if any, in teaching.

But, as shown in the last chapter, beliefs and values are not minor,
they are fundamental. They provide the submerged "bulk of the iceberg"
upon which any particular technique rests. To look only at what is visible
(i.e., the performance) is to miss the essence of the argument about perspectives. Still, there are "indicators of commitment" that can be made
visible and do help define the perspectives on teaching: actions, intentions, and beliefs. This chapter considers each of these in turn.

ACTIONS

How do you routinely start an instructional session? Do you have a routine for ending a session? How would you describe yourself as a teacher? What are your preferred techniques? If I observed your teaching, what kinds of activities would I see? How would you describe yourself as a teacher? What do you want to learn to do better?

First attempts at improving teaching often focus on actions—the routines and techniques we use to engage people in content. As you can see from the questions above, they are the most concrete and accessible aspect of a perspective on teaching. We might work on giving lectures, leading discussions, asking questioning, setting objectives, or developing means of assessing learning. These are the ways in which we activate our intentions and beliefs. It is what we do to help people learn. In adult education we refer to these as techniques; within schooling for children and youth they are called methods. In both cases, we are talking about activities that are meant to help people learn—a means of helping them do something with content.

Regardless of their perspective on teaching, teachers use a variety of techniques or methods to help people learn. The choice of techniques usually depends on what they want to accomplish and how familiar or comfortable they are with the technique. It might also depend on the amount of time available. For example, in a 1-hour class that I teach at my university, I might use a 20-minute lecture, followed by small group discussions, and then reconvene the whole class for a debriefing of the small group activity. Throughout each of those techniques, I use questions to probe people's learning and further engage them in particular aspects of the content. Before the close of the hour I ask people to write one question they would like addressed the next time we meet.

For those of you who have taught, this is not an unusual sequence of events; in fact, it is recommended that we vary the stimulus, or the learning activity, every 20–30 minutes, usually by switching instructional techniques or through the use of media. *Techniques, then, are activities which engage learners with the content and which, it is assumed, facilitate learning.* Teachers switch back and forth between techniques, sometimes as often as every 20 minutes, in an attempt to take people more deeply into the content.

Certainly, the teacher's actions are important to understanding any view of teaching. Yet, unless we understand what a person is trying to accomplish (intentions) and why they think that is important or reasonable (beliefs) we are very likely to misunderstand the meaning of their actions. It is also unlikely we will have any meaningful way to evaluate or improve those actions.

INTENTIONS

What are you trying to accomplish? Do you have an agenda or mission that guides your instruction? What would you say is the overall purpose of this course, program, workshop, etc.? What is your role and responsibility in this process?

Intentions are general statements that point toward an overall agenda or sense of purpose. They are an expression of what a person is trying to accomplish and, usually, an indication of role and responsibility in pursuit of that. *Intent, then, is the teacher's statement of purpose, responsibility, and commitment directed towards learners, content, context, ideals, or some combination of these.*

A Note on Objectives vs. Intentions

Within much of adult and higher education, instructional objectives are equated with instructional intent. It is assumed that an effective teacher should be able to specify what the learner will be able to do at the end of a teaching session. Instructional objectives, it is argued, accomplish three things: first, they articulate the goals of a curriculum so that colleagues and learners can compare what is expected across different courses or programs; second, once clearly stated, objectives facilitate the selection and organization of content; and third, if objectives are clearly specified, they make it possible to evaluate learning and assess the effectiveness of teaching. For many, this may appear to be a rational and convincing argument for writing instructional objectives as a means of clarifying instructional intent.

However, objectives are not the same as instructional intent. Objectives are precise statements that indicate what specific behavior will stand as evidence of learning. They are usually written in behavioral form, that is, they use verbs to clearly indicate what kind of behavioral change would be accepted as evidence of learning. The implication is that learning outcomes must be both predictable and observable.

Furthermore, even when trained to write objectives, many educators do not use them. In our research, teachers seldom mentioned using behavioral objectives. Here are some of the reasons they gave for not using instructional objectives:

- learning within complicated environments (e.g., emergency medicine) is so complex as to require an exhaustive number of objectives
- the nature of the content or subject (e.g., creative writing) is trivialized if reduced to behavioral indicators
- it is impossible to predict with any accuracy the most important forms of learning that would result from their teaching (e.g., attitude changes toward safe driving)
- it is feared that objectives could inadvertently cause learners to take a superficial approach to learning, that is, simply learn to fulfill the objectives (e.g., learning to work in teams)
- the most important learning is situated in contexts of application and, therefore, it is difficult to specify in advance what might be the best evidence of learning (e.g., patient education following heart surgery)
- objectives are thought to restrict teachers' ability to be flexible and responsive to the dynamic nature of teaching and the complex mix of learners (e.g., retraining for the workforce)

Thus, although objectives may be useful to some teachers as a means of stating their expectations for learners, they are not as useful in determining a teacher's sense of commitment and perspective on teaching. In fact, teachers studied in the original research, for the most part, found it difficult to use objectives as a means of indicating what they were trying to accomplish, yet they had no difficulty articulating their intent. They quite readily answered the question, "What are you trying to accomplish?" with responses that were natural, easily expressed, and coherent. They had an agenda, a game plan, or a set of aspirations. Further, it was apparent that they planned for, and reflected on, their teaching using intentions, not instructional objectives.

Intentions Are (Part of) Commitment

Intentions are general statements of the instructor's agenda or overall sense of direction. They are an indication of the instructor's commitment. Whereas objectives are specific and may be distant from a teacher's sense of commitment and purpose, intentions are held with intensity and conviction. For example, a teacher of literacy talked about her intentions and aims in the following terms:

> As an advocate of feminist, antiracist pedagogy, I want to develop a sense of community in which speaking, listening, reading, and writing [are] not limited to school, but will spill over into the larger community . . . Their [the students] ability to liberate themselves from illiteracy and related social oppression depends on changing individual and group ways of thinking [as well as] opening the doors of public institutions previously considered as inaccessible . . . [this is part of] wanting to promote attitudinal growth leading to social change . . . it is an educator's moral obligation to contest ideological presumptions that inscribe systemic inequities.

As you can see, her intentions are an important indicator of her commitment and very likely an essential part of her perspective on teaching. In another, less passionate example, an instructor teaching a course on evaluation said her intention was to provide people with sufficient knowledge about evaluation theory and practice so that they had a choice of perspectives when conducting evaluations. She held this intention with clarity and conviction; it was quick to come forth in our conversation and clear in its articulation. The fact that it was general allowed her to be flexible in the attainment of that intention; she was able to adjust the course as she went along, to take advantage of unanticipated turns and events in the journey. Furthermore, evidence of the students' attainment of this choice manifested in ways she couldn't have predicted. For example, one student told her about attending a presentation on evaluation that was clearly from only one perspective, and how meaningful it was to be able to ask about other possible views and approaches to evaluation.

It is also apparent that intentions are an extension of commitment; teachers feel passionate and firm in their statements of intent. This is not the case with objectives. In over 20 years of teaching, I can't recall anyone speaking passionately about an instructional objective! Not only is it a distant and microcosmic representation of intent, it is also expressed in a form that doesn't feel natural to most teachers. The behavioral straight-jacket of objectives is not at all like the flexible and passionate statement of intent I heard educators express. Intentions, therefore, are clearly more than the collection of one's objectives. *They are an enthusiastic statement of commitment and an indication of one's role and responsibility.* They are what gives meaning to actions, and a necessary part of understanding someone's perspective on teaching. However, they too are only part of the structure of commitment. Although intentions are a more direct statement of commitment than actions, there is a third, even more crucial, indicator—beliefs.

BELIEFS

How have you changed, as a teacher, over the years? What is the most important aspect of your content? How do you know when someone has truly learned what you are teaching? What does it mean, to learn? Can you think of a motto or metaphor that guides you in your teaching? Do you have a particular conviction or set of beliefs that are important to your teaching?

Beliefs are the third aspect of commitment in teaching and, along with actions and intentions, another defining attribute of perspectives. They are the most abstract and the most important aspect because they represent underlying values. As such, they are held with varying degrees of clarity, confidence, and centrality. Some are vague and implicit; others are clear and readily explained. Some are held tentatively; others are considered incontestable. Some are marginal to the way a person thinks; others are central and even dominant.

The measure of centrality of a belief is not necessarily a matter of logic or rationality but, more often, the extent to which the belief itself is not in question. When a belief is held without question it acts as arbiter in determining whether intentions, actions, or even other beliefs are reasonable and acceptable. Most teachers are able to accommodate a variety of changes in circumstances—including changes in what they teach, whom they teach, and under what conditions—as long as those changes do not challenge their core beliefs, e.g., those most central to their values. *Beliefs, therefore, represent the most stable and least flexible aspect of a person's perspective on teaching.*

Beliefs regarding knowledge and learning are, usually, the most central of all beliefs related to teaching. Our beliefs about knowledge determine what we will teach and what we will accept as evidence that people have learned. Our beliefs about learning determine how we will engage people in that knowledge and what roles and responsibilities we will assume as teachers. Yet, what is meant by knowledge and learning is usually taken for granted. It is either assumed that educators are in agreement on what they mean, or that these concepts are not particularly relevant to the question of how to teach. My view is that it would be impossible to adequately understand someone's perspective on teaching without understanding his or her personal beliefs about knowledge and learning.

Beliefs about Knowledge

It is not possible to talk about teaching without, at least implicitly, adopting some belief about knowledge or "personal epistemology." Yet, as Candy says, "When authors advocate a particular approach to teaching (or learning), only rarely do they make explicit their view of what constitutes valid knowledge, of how it is created, shared, or reproduced" (1991, p. 262).

There are two fundamentally different views of knowledge related to perspectives on teaching. One conceives of knowledge as existing independent of the learners' interest in it, or awareness of it (objectivism); the other conceives of knowledge as something that is intimately determined by the learner (subjectivism). Objectivism is based on a logic of discovery; subjectivism is based on a logic of interpretation. They are presented here as the ends of a continuum of personal beliefs about knowledge. Although I will discuss them as bipolar opposites, they are more accurately represented as a continuum (Figure 2.1), suggesting that not everyone is completely objectivist or subjectivist in their beliefs about knowledge.

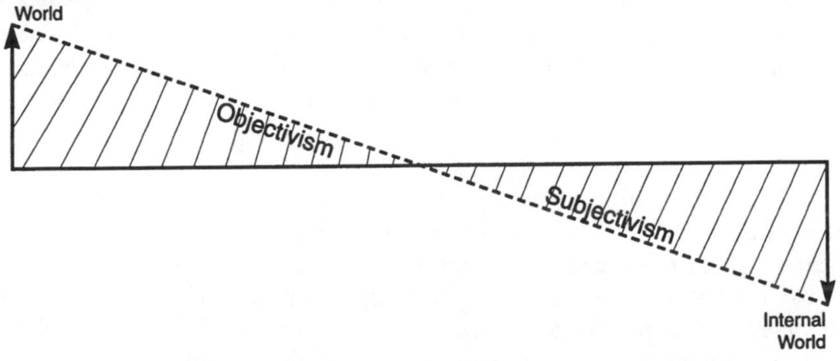

Figure 2.1 Continuum of Beliefs about Knowledge

Objectivism

One of the most basic beliefs of objectivism is that people can rationally come to know the world as it really is; the facts of the world are essentially there for study. The object, therefore, of teaching is to provide a literal account of what the world is like.

Knowledge, or what people learn, exists independent of their knowing it; learner and content are distinctly separate entities. Indeed, the objectivist believes that basic theories, principles, and rules which govern our lives and world exist quite separately from our experience of them; knowledge about the world exists "out there," waiting to be discovered. And, because it is assumed there is an external world out there waiting to be discovered, only questions pertaining to that "real world" are truly scientific; other questions, such as those concerning morality and aesthetics, fall outside the realm of legitimate scientific inquiry (Guba & Lincoln, 1994). This is the classic subject-object dualism wherein knower (learner) and knowledge (content) are deemed to be separate.

From an objectivist point of view, truth is a matter of the "goodness of fit," or correspondence, between observation and description. Therefore, whether one is a scientist, journalist, teacher, or a citizen testifying at a trial, observations are expected to be neutral and represent no particular interests or purposes; descriptions, likewise, are to be an objective or detached report of what happened. To demonstrate one knows reality (or subject content) one must accurately describe it or reproduce it. A statement is true when it corresponds to reality as empirically validated, and false when it does not. In other words, truth is a matter of the accuracy of reproduction (in language or action) of reality as judged by some authority.

Authority is highly correlated to how much expert knowledge one possesses. The more one has knowledge or expertise validated through experience, observation, and experimentation, the more authority one holds over those who wish to have that knowledge. Therefore, to be a teacher one must be an experienced expert in the content area. Further, one must hold and present that content objectively. Objective knowledge is that which is not distorted due to the influence of particular interests and values. The opposite, of course, is subjective knowledge, which by definition (within this conception of knowledge) is distorted through the bias of values and personal interests or interpretation. To objectivists, facts and values can and should be kept separate.

There is within objectivism another, slightly softer, belief about the separation of facts and values. It acknowledges that they are not actually separate, but interdependent, yet claims objectivity may still be achievable as long as values are allowed to dictate problems (what we examine) but not prejudge solutions (what we find). Therefore, we may allow that values will influence what we decide to teach, but we must guard against values distorting the content or influencing our decisions as to whether the content has been correctly learned.

Subjectivism

Subjectivists are committed to quite different beliefs about knowledge and truth. Indeed, from this point of view reality is understood to be both pluralistic and plastic—pluralistic in the sense that any reality is expressible in a variety of symbol and language systems (e.g., societies and cultures); plastic in the sense that reality is stretched and shaped to fit the purposes and intentions of the people involved (Schwandt, 1994). Therefore, knowledge (and truth) is dependent upon what individuals bring to the moment of perception. Knowledge and truth are created, not discovered; the world is only knowable through people's interpretations of it.

Social reality, more particularly the world of teaching, "is a constructed reality, the product of the meanings people give to their interactions with others . . ." (Smith, 1989, p. 8). Imagine a stump of a tree that was seen by different people in the dark of night. The first, a thief, was certain it was a policeman; the second, a young man arriving late for an appointment, thought it was his friend patiently waiting for him; and, third, a young boy walking home from a scary movie, was certain it was something to be feared. But all the time it was the stump of a tree. For subjectivists, we see the world as we are; that which we have inside, we see outside. Therefore, knowledge is neither a copy nor a mirror of some external reality but, rather, a construction of the individual experiencing it. People (learners) do not merely respond to the world; they impose meaning and value upon it and interpret it in ways that fit, or make sense to them.

Rather than look for correspondence with the outside world, subjectivism looks for correspondence with the inner world, the observer's particular interests, prior knowledge, purposes, and values. Suddenly the criterion of detachment makes no sense; why would one want to be detached from one's prior knowledge or purposes for observing in the first place? Thus, to subjectivists, it is not the action that is important as much as the meaning of the action, to both the actor and the observer. To them, intentions infuse actions with meaning.

What constitutes knowledge, therefore, is believed to be dependent upon ways of perceiving and understanding. Our perception and interpretation of the world is intimately tied to our cognitive structures, our ways of thinking and valuing. From this point of view, we can never know the world as it is because our perceptions are determined by our values; that is, we can only know the world through the lens of our beliefs. Nor can we detach our experience from the purposes and values that bring us to that experience. Whereas the motto of objectivism might be "seeing is believing," the motto of subjectivism might be "believing determines what is seen." Therefore, to subjectivists, the separation of mind and world, observer and observed, subject and object, or even learner and content must be rejected.

So, how do subjectivists see objectivity? To them, objectivity means consensual agreement between observers, rather than detachment from an observer's place, purpose, or values. The process of arriving at truth is not one of striving for a correspondence between observation and description, but one of negotiation about the meaning of observations. Subjectivists assume that we all observe the world from a particular place of interest and purpose. Therefore, truth is based on the "goodness of fit" between various interpretations, not on the reproduction of a static observation, faithfully described. This is true for subjectivists in all concerns about truth whether it involves deciding someone's guilt or innocence, or evaluating teaching. Subjectivists ask different questions about truth: "How believable is the interpretation?" "How widely held is this interpretation?" "How well does it correspond with the interpretation of others that might have more experience?"

Indeed, this view of knowledge holds that one cannot observe in any reproducible way without a conceptual or theoretical framework. There can be no value-free observations; what counts as data, that is, what we then report from our observations, is influenced by the interests, purposes, and social practices of those doing the observing. This is similar to the Cree and Ojibwa belief that "to tell the truth" means "I will tell it as I know it," which allows for each observer to tell a different version of what happened. Through this process, truth is arrived at not by seeking correspondence, but by seeking consensus; not by looking for a perfect match, but by finding a reasonable fit; not by assuming detachment but by assuming commitment. Truth, therefore, is relative rather than absolute; it depends upon time and place, purpose and interests.

Conceptions of Learning

Both objectivists and subjectivists agree that learning is the primary aim of all teaching. Yet, teachers (and learners) differ in their beliefs about what it means to learn, and what influences learning.

Some of the most influential research on beliefs about learning was done in Sweden where university students were asked, "What does it mean, to learn? What do you actually mean by learning?" (Saljo, 1988) Saljo's work was subsequently replicated with a number of adults studying at the Open University of Britain. The results consistently showed that people held one of five different conceptions of learning. All conceptions represent a belief that learning means a change in something. However, they differ most significantly in their belief about what changes. Essentially, there were three dominant views about what changes when we learn: *quantitative* and *qualitative* changes in knowledge, with a bridging conception between those extremes. They are presented here, slightly modified from the original research, in order to illustrate the relationship between beliefs about knowledge and beliefs about learning.

Quantitative Changes in Knowledge

The first two conceptions of learning rest upon a belief that learning is a change in the amount of knowledge or skill one has. These are additive conceptions of learning because they portray learning as a process of expanding one's existing store of knowledge or improving one's performance; all learning is therefore to be built upon a platform of what already exists. Yet, there is no suggestion that one's existing knowledge might interact with the new knowledge; new knowledge is simply added to, or mapped upon, old knowledge.

1. *Learning is an increase in knowledge.* People holding this conception think of learning as simply an increase in the amount of information they can recall. They liken it to filling a container with discrete items; information or knowledge need not be related to anything. It is simply an increase in the quantity of information that signifies learning.

2. *Learning is memorization, usually for recall or recognition on tests.* Here, as with the previous conception, there is an assumption of learning equating to an increase in the amount of information one has. However, the purpose for learning is related to testing. Knowledge resides in the authority of the text or teacher, and is to be transferred from that authority to the learner. Learning has occurred when

the learner can accurately reproduce the content to the satisfaction of the authority (e.g., teacher).

These two conceptions of learning are based on an objectivist epistemology, sometimes referred to as a received view of knowledge. The content to be taught (and learned) is thought of as an accumulated body of facts, principles, rules, theories, and procedures which have been verified through experience, observation, and experimentation. Authorities, such as teachers, are assumed to have more experience with the content and, therefore, to have accumulated a greater body of knowledge which can then be passed on to learners. Thus, these conceptions tacitly assume that learners will be the receivers and teachers the transmitters of knowledge.

These conceptions reify authority as text and/or teacher, and rest on a received view of knowledge. Learning is the accurate and efficient reproduction of knowledge (information, procedures, skills, attitudes, etc.) in a form that resembles the knowledge of their texts and/or teachers.

This is not an uncommon understanding of learning. Much of formal education is directed toward a nonproblematic, additive view of learning, that is, one which either increases how much someone knows, or fine-tunes knowledge or skill to increase a person's speed or efficiency in using the information.

Bridging Conception

The third conception of learning is something of a bridge between the views on quantitative and qualitative changes in knowledge understood as learning. This third conception is still anchored in a belief that learning is a process of adding greater amounts of knowledge, but it assumes that knowledge is only useful to the extent it can be applied in a practical setting, as opposed to memorized for tests. The dominant belief about knowledge behind such a view is still objectivist: knowledge is believed to exist "out there" and is to be reproduced by the learner in forms that resemble the knowledge of those more experienced or more knowledgeable. However, learning, in this conception, adds the dimension of context to existing ways of knowing and acting.

3. *Learning is the acquisition of information and procedures so they can be used or applied in practice.* The difference between this conception and the preceding two is in the context, and consequently, the kind of knowledge that is valued. Knowledge that is immediately applica-

ble is seen to be more valid. Learning is a process of acquiring such knowledge as is necessary and appropriate to practical applications. A sense of purpose, beyond testing is, in this conception, an integral part of learning. The learner is placed in a slightly more interactive role with knowledge, making judgments about what is useful content. However, the learner is not as important as the context in understanding either the process or product of learning.

As in the first two conceptions, learning is associated with the accumulation and application of knowledge; that knowledge is received without challenge or modification. New learning, as before, is mapped onto existing cognitive structures of the learner and accepted in forms represented by an authority. Furthermore, learning relies on the unquestioning acceptance of both the knowledge and the authority of teachers and texts; there is little or no assumption of authority by the learner to alter the knowledge before it is applied. However, an important difference between this conception and the previous two is the emergence of context into the meaning of learning. Learning is believed to be dependent on context; that is, what is learned is determined, in part, by the context in which it is learned and applied.

Qualitative Changes in Knowledge

In the final two conceptions of learning, there is a shift from objectivism to subjectivism regarding their underlying beliefs about knowledge. In these conceptions, learning is understood to be an interpretive process, not an additive one. Learning means making sense out of something, not just accumulating information. Conceptions four and five move the learner from a position of passive, unquestioning receptivity of knowledge and authority, to active interpretation and interrogation of content in an effort to "make knowledge their own." The person enters the picture as an influence on both the process and product of learning.

4. *Learning is the abstraction of meaning.* In this view there is a significant shift away from merely satisfying an external authority by reproducing content as taught, to reconstructing it in ways that are personally meaningful to the learner. The learner moves from background to foreground in the learning process, as judge and interpreter of that which is to be learned. The content to be learned is viewed as changeable, tentative, and adaptable material from which the learner can extract meaning, not as stable, unquestionable truth.

5. *Learning is a complex interpretive process aimed at understanding reality and self as co-determinant.* This belief about learning emphasizes the interdependent relationships between individual, social, historical, and cultural ways of knowing. The individual, as learner, is believed to be situated within a set of values that influence both the process and product of learning. From within this conception, the meaning of any subject matter is dependent upon cultural, historical, and personal factors. For example, when learners are asked to critically reflect on the relationship between gender and learning, if they hold this conception of learning, they must consider the social, cultural, and historical meanings of such concepts as "girl," "boy," "woman," "man," and "learning." Therefore, the interpretive process (learning) involves the interaction of individual, cultural, and historical factors.

With conceptions four and five, learning is more than simply mapping knowledge onto existing structures. It involves the learner in actively making, or revising, cognitive maps into which knowledge and experience can fit. Furthermore, it is the learner who constructs his or her own cognitive maps, not the teacher; the person has now entered the process of learning as an arbiter of meaning. In these conceptions, trying to replicate an authority's interpretation of knowledge, or performing exactly like a teacher, is understood to be impossible; instead, learning necessitates an interpretation of the content, not a reproduction of it. Therefore, the object of learning has shifted from the content, per se, to the ways in which learners construe or understand the content. Learning is, thus, understood to involve a dynamic relationship between purpose, context, and person.

As you can see, the two major views of learning, quantitative and qualitative, are highly related to the two major views of knowledge, objectivism and subjectivism, (Figure 2.2).

Quantitative views of learning position the learner in the background, as a receiver of objective knowledge. Knowledge is believed to exist independent of the learner; therefore, teaching is a matter of efficiently moving it from outside to inside. Once that process is complete, the learner either (a) knows more or (b) performs better; the test of learning in these conceptions is the ability to reproduce the knowledge of the authorities in more accurate and efficient forms. Learners are positioned as receivers of knowledge from authorities.

Qualitative views of learning position the learner squarely in the

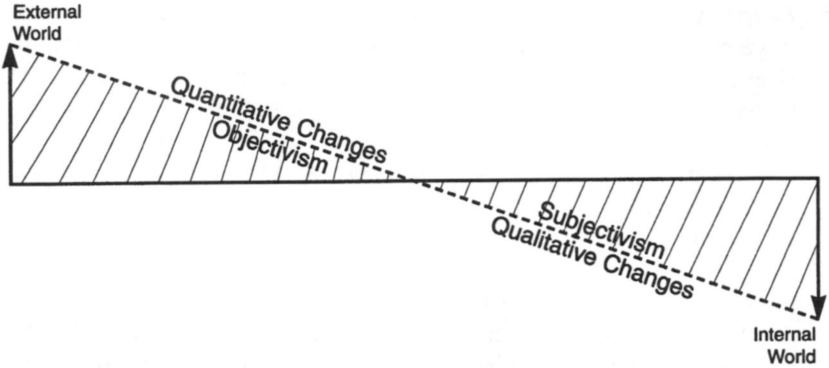

Figure 2.2 Conceptions of Knowledge and Learning

foreground, with content subject to the learner's interpretation. Knowledge, or what is learned, is understood to be influenced by the purposes, values, and interests of the learner, within cultural and historical contexts. Teaching and learning, therefore, are subjective processes involving the negotiation of meaning. Conception three is a bridge between the two views of knowledge, suggesting a transition from objectivism to subjectivism.

Some readers might disparage conceptions one and two, thinking they cannot possibly represent an informed view of learning. Indeed, we might assume that all teachers should hold beliefs about learning that resemble conceptions four and five. Yet, even if we could agree that some of these views of learning are more appropriate than others, we must acknowledge that learners come with their own beliefs about what constitutes learning. Curiously, it is learners' beliefs, even more than the beliefs of their teachers, which significantly influence the approach they take to learning as well as what they ultimately learn.

What is most important, for our purposes, is to recognize the interrelationship between personal epistemologies and conceptions of learning. Each of these is part of an elaborate and coherent system of beliefs that forms a perspective on teaching. Our beliefs about knowledge and learning are part of a larger system of beliefs and intentions that have significant implications for how we understand the process of teaching and the purposes of education. For example, if we understand learning as a quantitative increase in knowledge, we would very likely teach our content and evaluate students' learning quite differently than someone who believes learning means examining what we know from several different points of view. Consequently, our assumptions about appropriate roles and responsibilities would also be quite different.

The problem is that most of us go about teaching without articulating what we believe or why we do what we do as teachers. Yet, based on over twenty years of teaching, I am convinced that all teachers act within a system of personal intentions and beliefs about what is to be learned, how and why it should be learned, and what their roles will be in that process. As we gain experience, we should be more able to state those intentions and beliefs, and there should be more agreement between all three—actions, intentions, and beliefs.

I do not mean to imply that there will always be a consistent and logical relationship between actions, intentions, and beliefs. Indeed, I suspect that this is often not the case. Faculty in higher education, for example, often believe their courses are developing critical thinking in learners. Yet, many of them teach in ways that discourage these noble aims; their actions are inconsistent with their espoused intentions and beliefs. As a result, some of the best work in faculty development today is attempting to help professors bring their actions in line with their intentions and beliefs (Kember, in press).

When it is well articulated, this interrelated web of actions, intentions, and beliefs ultimately forms the back bone for a sense of commitment in teaching. In turn, commitment forms the basis for a point of view or perspective on what teaching means and how it should be carried out. The next chapter moves from evidence and indicators of commitment to their broader consequences, that is, five qualitatively different perspectives on teaching.

REFERENCES

Candy, P. C. (1991). *Self-Direction for lifelong learning: A comprehensive guide to theory and practice.* San Francisco: Jossey-Bass.

Guba, E. G., and Lincoln, Y. S. (1994). Competing paradigms in qualitative research. In N. K. Denzin & Y. S. Lincoln (Eds.), *Handbook of qualitative research* (pp. 105–117). Thousand Oaks, CA: Sage Publications, Inc.

Kember, D. (in press). A reconceptualisation of the research into university academics' conceptions of teaching. *Learning and Instruction.* New York: Pergamon Press.

Saljo, R. (1988). Learning in educational settings: Methods of inquiry. In P. Ramsden, (Ed.), *Improving learning: New perspectives* (pp. 32–48). London: Kogan Page, Ltd.

Schwandt, T. A. (1994). Constructivist, interpretivist approaches to human inquiry. In N. K. Denzin & Y. S. Lincoln (Eds.), *Handbook of qualitative research* (pp. 118–137). Thousand Oaks, CA: Sage Publications, Inc.

Smith, J. (1989). *The nature of social and educational inquiry: Empiricism versus interpretation.* New Jersey: Ablex Publishing Company.

CHAPTER 3

ALTERNATIVE FRAMES OF UNDERSTANDING
Introduction to Five Perspectives

Daniel D. Pratt

When people ask, "What's your perspective on this?", what are they asking? Chances are, they are asking where you stand on an issue? What is your view, outlook, position, or stance? Can you put into words your commitments—your thoughts and beliefs related to a specific issue? They might just as well have asked, "What is your own bias on this?", for each perspective is really a particular bias, based on how you "see" the issue and what vested interests are most important to you.

When we speak of a perspective on teaching, we are speaking of much the same thing; an interrelated set of beliefs and intentions which give meaning and justification for our actions. Thus, although perspectives are enacted through activities, they are far more than the activities or even the specific commitments we hold. They are a lens through which we view the world of teaching and learning. We may not be aware of a perspective because it is usually something we look through, rather than look at, when teaching. As we shall see in later chapters, it becomes the object of our attention only when we reflect upon our beliefs, intentions, and actions as a whole.

For the most part, each person's initial perspective on teaching was received without question or challenge. It was the result of years of being a learner, in the home, at school, in the community, on sports teams, and in a thousand other moments responding to someone acting as teacher. From watching others teach, we form impressions about what teachers do, what learners do, and how the process of teaching works and doesn't work. Eventually, within an individual, a set of conceptions related to learning and teaching evolves and is carried forward until it is challenged, perhaps because it no longer works, or because an alternative perspective emerges and seems to work better.

But until we change a perspective consciously, how does it operate? How does it affect what and how we see? The German philosopher Nietzsche claimed that it is a fiction to assume we can take a pure, objective stance toward knowing anything. Knowing from such a posture requires,

> an eye [that is] turned in no particular direction, in which the active and interpreting forces, through which alone seeing becomes seeing something . . . these always demand of the eye an absurdity and a nonsense. There is only a perspective seeing, only a perspective "knowing"; and the more affects we allow to speak about one thing, the more eyes, different eyes, we use to observe one thing, the more complete will our "concept" of this thing, our "objectivity", be. (Nietzsche, translated by Kaufman & Hollingdale, 1969, p. 119)

The same is true for perspectives on teaching. If we know only one perspective on teaching, it will dominate our perceptions and interpretations of all that goes on, yet remain hidden from view. Just as the world above the pond is invisible to a fish, so too are other perspectives invisible to those who know only one perspective on teaching. Thus, if we are to understand our personal perspectives on teaching, we must consider other ways of thinking and believing about teaching, alternative ways of constructing learning, knowledge or skill, and multiple roles for instructors.

The account of the teaching workshop presented at the beginning of Chapter 2 showed how the workshop involved an implicit denial of perspective and, consequently, denial of alternative ways of thinking about teaching. That is, the workshop portrayed a unidimensional view of teaching, characterized by generic skills and behavioral objectives, and devoid of variation in context, content, learners, beliefs, and commitment. Knowledge, learning, and our roles as teachers could only be interpreted within the prevailing, but invisible, perspective; alternative views did not exist.

What happens, then, when we behave as though all teachers do share the same perspective, the same criteria for effective teaching?

PERSPECTIVE AS JUDGMENT

Each perspective on teaching is a complex web of actions, intentions, and beliefs; each, in turn, creates its own criteria for judging or evaluating right and wrong, true and false, effective and ineffective. Perspectives determine our roles and idealized self-images as teachers as well as the basis for reflecting on practice. When you talk with another teacher who believes as you do, there is an immediacy of communication and the feeling of being understood. However, just the opposite holds true when there are disagreements between people holding different perspectives on teaching. It is as if each is from a different culture, where values and meanings are different.

This commonality or disparity in perspective becomes even more apparent and significant when one's teaching is being evaluated. Evaluation makes more sense and is less disturbing if it is done by someone from the same perspective as your own. It is easier to understand and agree upon criteria and judgments of what is "effective" when like-minds negotiate these things. On the other hand, evaluation that crosses perspectives can be problematic, to say the least.

For example, a friend's teaching was being evaluated for his promotion. The evaluation process called for two colleagues to review his teaching syllabus and observe at least three consecutive hours of instruction. This is how he told his story to me:

On the evening of their observation I was leading a discussion of learning styles and approaches and their implications for research on adult learning. In the session, which ran from 4:30 to 7:00 p.m., I had set out several questions and put people into buzz groups to discuss the questions. After about 40 minutes of this I reconvened the large group of 18 graduate students to talk about their small group discussions. Through all of this, my evaluators sat silent and observed from the back of the room. At the coffee break they both explained they had to leave but would meet with me in the next few days to discuss their observations and report.

Three days later one of the evaluators met with me at a coffee shop on campus and, after polite exchanges, opened the conversation with the question, "Do you think your students are getting their money's worth?" I was stunned. Everything I had experienced to that point suggested my teaching was not only adequate but, in some regards,

exemplary. I was so shocked I could only ask, "What do you mean?"
The response was, "Well, you didn't answer their questions; they
asked several questions and you just turned the questions back to the
group. In fact, they left that evening with more questions than an-
swers. I expect you know the answers to their questions and they de-
serve answers."

No amount of explaining would answer this charge. Two very different perspectives on teaching were about to collide. My friend held the
view that graduate seminars were a forum for exploration and inquiry;
his colleague was of the opinion that the role of a professor was to provide information, not questions; to act as authority, not co-learner. It was
as if people from two different cultures were speaking past each other,
even though discussing the same episode. Unfortunately, one person was
in a more powerful position than the other. Evaluation presents problems
of power imbalance, which conflicting perspectives can exacerbate.

As mentioned earlier, perspectives are enacted through techniques,
but they are far more than simply the actions or techniques of teaching.
In the example just given, the educators' disagreement went well beyond
the issue of lecturing versus questioning. It included different conceptions of knowledge, and how knowledge is learned, different conceptions
of graduate school and the purposes that are most central to that enterprise, and different conceptions of roles and responsibilities for a professor leading a graduate seminar. In other words, each of them brought to
this transaction a set of meanings and values that "framed" the events
and people in particular ways.

Each of their personal "frames" consisted of a set of interrelated conceptions. From within each of their perspectives, conclusions made sense.
Each one could have written an evaluation of the teaching and justified
his conclusions on the basis of his observations. Each evaluation would
have been internally consistent, that is, coherent and logical, based upon
the ways in which key elements and processes were interpreted. Internal
consistency is quite natural in long-held perspectives.

A similar process may have happened to you if you have ever left
your home culture to travel or work in another culture. Back home, your
understanding of what's done is intact and solid, your worldview is internally coherent and logical. And yet, walking around that first street,
encountering that first social situation in a market square or a post office,
it becomes obvious that your logic is not shared! At that moment, that

which was invisible and taken for granted becomes visible and, as a result, becomes the object of awareness and open to scrutiny and examination for the first time.

In 1984, I was getting ready to teach my first course in Hong Kong. As you can imagine, I was excited to learn about Hong Kong and shared that excitement with a friend. To my surprise, he dismissed this as naive and said that I would very likely learn more about Canada than about Hong Kong. I dismissed that, thinking that he really didn't understand what I had said. But, after 10 years of teaching there I believe he was right; I learned a great deal more about my own culture than I did about the culture of Hong Kong. I had a basis of comparison and, for the first time, my own culture was visible to me.

In much the same way, perspectives on teaching are cultural views of teaching, powerful but largely invisible frames of reference through which all of us make meaning of our worlds. They limit our perceptions in much the same way; until we encounter a basis for comparison, our own assumptions remain invisible. It isn't possible to forget our perspective, any more than it's possible to forget our cultural upbringing; but still, it is possible to engage meaningfully with new perspectives.

ACCEPTING VS. ADOPTING NEW PERSPECTIVES

Just as it's quite common to judge a new cultural experience on the basis of our own logic, it's also quite common to judge another's teaching in terms of one's own perspective. This is especially true within institutions where evaluation of teaching crosses disciplinary or programmatic boundaries (e.g., colleges and universities). In such instances, evaluation focuses on the technical or skill-based activities of the teacher, more than any underlying beliefs or intentionality. It is assumed that effective teaching is similar regardless of variations in context, learners, content, and teachers. This approach is justified on the assumption it is more objective and expedient. It may be more expedient, but it is neither objective nor impartial.

This doesn't mean people have to adopt another's perspective before they can evaluate his or her teaching. People can learn about other perspectives without adopting the commitments and beliefs of those perspectives. It is much like the distinction between learning a culture and becoming enculturated. To learn a culture is to learn about, or acquire,

its propositions or statements of meaning and value; to become enculturated is to internalize them as personal beliefs, that is, as beliefs, meanings, and propositions that are thought to be appropriate, significant, or
true for you!

In much the same manner, we can learn about other perspectives on
teaching, and acknowledge their appropriateness for other people and
circumstances, without taking them on as our own. That is, we can learn
about a different perspective, as opposed to committing to a different
perspective. This is the most common result of reading a book on teaching. Most people find ways to confirm what they already believe rather
than change the more central beliefs they hold regarding teaching.

The remainder of this chapter is given over to briefly introducing five
perspectives on teaching. However, before reading about alternative perspectives, try the exercise in Figure 3.1 as a way of exploring your own
perspective. It is important that you do this before reading about other
perspectives if you want to have some indication of what you believe before exploring other beliefs about teaching.

As you look over your list of responses you might see a pattern or
trend that suggests underlying beliefs and commitments about knowledge, learning, and/or your role as teacher. The list of sentences is best
used as a point of departure for exploring beliefs and commitments. Although you may see some trend or pattern in your responses, the list is
not very revealing in and of itself. However, it is a useful place from
which to begin a conversation about beliefs and commitments related to
teaching, learning, and knowledge.

INTRODUCING FIVE PERSPECTIVES ON TEACHING

A Transmission Perspective: Delivering Content

*My job is twofold: First, I have a lot of people that have to learn this
math so they can go on to something else, whether it's some application of it or the next course in algebra, or calculus. For them, I need
to be really clear about the sequence of what comes next and what
they need now. I mean, math really is quite simple, if it's presented
clearly and you do each day's work. So, I need to be clear about what
it is they need to learn and then be sure they do the assignments. If I
do that, they should have no trouble when they go on from my class*

Think about a subject that you teach. It can be any subject or content. Then identify a typical set of learners engaged in learning that content. Once you have identified a subject matter and can visualize or imagine a group of learners, complete the sentence below ten times.

I know my teaching has been effective when . . .

1.

2.

3.

4.

5.

6.

7.

8.

9.

10.

Figure 3.1 Exploring Personal Intentions and Beliefs

to the next one. My second job, although no one tells me this, is something I got from my professors at university . . . I represent math. I really do! And if I didn't like math, they [the students] wouldn't like it either. So I let my enthusiasm show. I do like it. It's beautiful. How many things in this world are so straightforward and organized? So, I try to show people that math isn't the "baddy" that everyone says it is. They don't need to be afraid of it. I did it, and I'm no Einstein. (community college math instructor)

This is, perhaps, the most "traditional" and long-standing perspective on teaching. It is based on the belief that a relatively stable body of

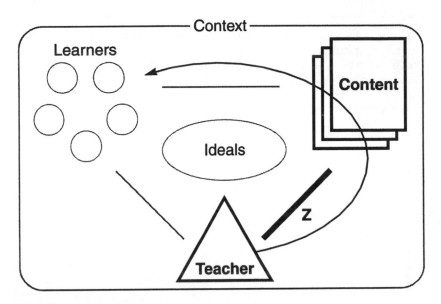

Figure 3.2 A Transmission Perspective

knowledge and/or procedures can be efficiently transmitted to learners. The primary focus is on efficient and accurate delivery of that body of knowledge to learners. Thus, teachers with this as their dominant perspective feel obliged to adequately cover the content, regardless of time constraints. The dominant elements are the teacher and the content; and the dominant relationship between elements is represented by line Z (content credibility), that is, the teacher's concern for and authority over that which is to be learned (Figure 3.2).

The arrow's path and direction illustrate the instructional process, which has first regard for adequate representation and efficient presentation of content. Notice that the process arrow goes through the content to the learners, suggesting the name of this perspective, that is, the transmission or delivery of content from teacher (or other resources) to learners. Therefore, the primary responsibility of a teacher is to accurately present content and help learners accurately reproduce that same content.

With this rather substantial respect for the content, teachers are expected to be an "expert" in what they teach. Good teachers are expected to be knowledgeable in their subject areas and should be, first and foremost, experienced in their fields. They are expected to know their content well enough to answer most questions, provide multiple examples, give clear and detailed explanations, and specify with authority and precision just what people are expected to learn. Therefore, content credibility (line Z) is of paramount importance.

Compared to other perspectives, this one is primarily "teacher centered" with an emphasis on first, what the teacher does in the process of teaching and second, how well the content has been planned, organized, represented, and transmitted. Very often teachers from this perspective are concerned about adequately covering the content within constraints, such as a limited amount of time. They also speak about the integration and coordination of their material or course with other parts of a program or curriculum, thus, implying assumptions about the hierarchical nature of the knowledge they teach. That is, what they teach is understood to be dependent upon what has come before and, in turn, forms a necessary basis for the mastery of subsequent courses and content.

Teachers holding this as their dominant perspective often end up teaching well-defined content, that is, material where there is clear agreement about right answers and where new content fits hierarchically into or upon prior knowledge. This kind of knowledge can then be managed and presented in a step-by-step fashion. Content that is traditionally thought to be well defined includes safety procedures, plumbing, grammar, math, electronics, military training, most competency-based programs, and so forth. However, as Boldt notes in Chapter 4, no matter what the content, teachers from this perspective either find or impose structure on their subject matter.

> In fact, to regard most content areas as well-structured is not a difficult task for transmission teachers. This is especially so for the initial teaching stages where basic concepts or techniques are introduced in presentation, applied in practice, and then built upon step-by-step as a subject matter becomes increasingly complex.

Thus, most often it is not the content itself that determines how it is taught, but the teacher. A most convincing example of this is found in Nesbit's chapter on teaching mathematics from a Social Reform Perspective (Chapter 8).

As you read Chapter 4, notice the poor reputation that characterizes this perspective. As Boldt notes, we all seem to have had a great deal of negative experience with this perspective. Recalling those experiences very likely conjures up images of conceptions one and two of learning (Chapter 2). Many teachers from this perspective believe learning is a matter of accumulating a body of information and reproducing it on tests or assignments. This received view of knowledge, and reproductive view of learning, typifies much of what has been found in research on conceptions of teaching in higher education (e.g., Fox, 1983; Prosser, Trigwell, & Taylor, 1994; Samuelowicz & Bain, 1992). Furthermore, the work of Gow and Kember suggests that this perspective is associated with surface approaches to learning. (Gow & Kember, 1993; Kember & Gow, 1994)

This evidence, along with the experience of many readers, might lead one to conclude that all teaching within the Transmission Perspective results in rather superficial learning. Yet, it is my contention that this is the result of its implementation, rather than its underlying structure. Even though we may be able to cite more examples of negative, rather than positive, learning within the Transmission Perspective, we should not use that as grounds for dismissing it as a potentially legitimate view of teaching. There are too many examples of effective teaching that fall within the Transmission Perspective to say it is categorically, and unequivocally, ineffective. The Transmission Perspective can be an exciting, engaging, effective source of learning, as illustrated in Chapter 4.

An Apprenticeship Perspective: Modeling Ways of Being

For me, teaching means helping this guy [his apprentice] get beyond the stuff they taught him at school and learn how to work a job. There's a big difference between nailing 2 x 4s in a class project and working with a bunch of guys on a construction site that are never sure about the next job . . . There's more to carpentry than pounding nails . . . I mean, first of all, I have to be good at this, not just talk about it [carpentry]. There's no way I could teach him if I wasn't a pretty good carpenter myself. But it's more than that. I mean, this is a way of life, not just a job . . . Sure, I have to know what he can do and what he can't do. When he started he couldn't do much of anything besides the most basic stuff. And that's what you do when you start. It's scut work but it has to be done . . . Now, he's doing more than hauling stuff up to us on the roof; he's actually doing most of what we do. But still, there's so much more, you know? (carpentry instructor)

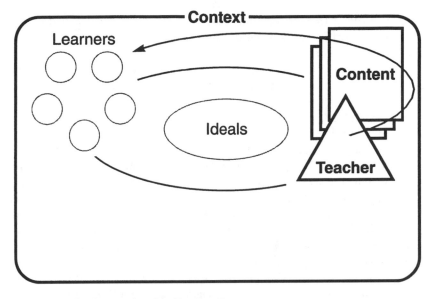

Figure 3.3 An Apprenticeship Perspective

While the Transmission Perspective is the stereotypical view of teachers in classrooms, the Apprenticeship Perspective represents a long-standing view of teaching outside classrooms. Within this perspective, teaching is the process of enculturating learners into a specific community. By community, I mean a group of people with a common sense of identity and purpose, and clearly defined roles, usually suggesting levels of authority and responsibility. Community can refer to a family, a trade or vocation, a profession, one of the marital arts, or even a cultural grouping such as the First Nations People of Canada. In each of these "communities" the process of enculturation results from intensive, diversified, and prolonged participation in the work and social relations of the community.

The dominant elements in the General Model of Teaching are the teacher, content, and context. However, in this perspective, the content and teacher are fused as one, signifying the inseparability of teacher and content, within context (Figure 3.3).

In this perspective, teachers are expected to embody the knowledge and values of their community of practice. They are an extension of the values and knowledge as lived or practiced within that community.

Therefore, what they know (and wish to teach) cannot be learned in any authentic way if it is abstracted or removed from the place of its application, that is, its context.

Therefore, what one learns, and can then do, is "textured" with the context and situation within which it was learned. Learning something in one context for application in another is believed to be fraught with problems. Indeed, if we consider the difficulty people have transferring and applying what they learn at short, intensive training sessions, there is justification for this belief. Practicing the skill of listening and paraphrasing within a 2-day workshop on communication skills is not the same as learning to listen to someone under the press of an argument; practicing soccer drills is not the same as playing in an important game; learning to do math problems from a textbook is not the same as figuring out which groceries to buy with a limited amount of money; and practicing first aid in the classroom is not the same as applying what you know at the scene of an accident.

Furthermore, from this perspective what we learn is not only textured by the context in which it is learned, it is also indexed by that context. That is, we are dependent upon similar cues, from the context, to retrieve and use that knowledge. An everyday example of the situated and indexed nature of knowledge comes from recognizing people and knowing who they are. Outside the usual context of our local neighborhood we may recognize the grocery clerk as someone we know but can't quite place. We know she is familiar, but can't remember who she is because she is out of context, not indexed (Arseneau, 1994, p. 34).

A convincing example of this argument comes from the director of a self-defense program for women in Vancouver, called *Model Mugging*. The program is based on the principle that one must practice self-defense under conditions that come as close as possible to the real thing. It was started by a woman who was attacked and raped, even though she had earned a third degree black belt in karate. When she most needed them, her considerable skills in self-defense were nearly useless. Why? Because she had trained in contexts devoid of the flood of emotions that accompanies a real attack. She had practiced and learned a great deal about self-defense in the dojo, or training center, but, when confronted with the shock and fear of a real attack, she froze. Something was terribly wrong with her learning that it was so completely unavailable when she most needed it.

Finally, this view of teaching is committed to learning a role and identity as well as a set of skills or body of knowledge. Learning is directed as much at learning to be someone, as learning to do or know something. Through guided practice, and success on real tasks, this perspective professes that people begin to believe they have a legitimate role in relation to others, whether as a negotiator, as a member of a soccer team, as a responsible and capable shopper, as a first-aid attendant, or as a woman trying to regain a sense of confidence and control.

Chapter 5 will give more details. For now, it is enough to know that this view of teaching is fundamentally committed to locating teaching and learning within contexts that are as authentic as possible. In that context, one learns not just a set of skills or body of knowledge, but an identity within, or in relation to, a social group. Consequently, teachers try to move learners from the periphery to more central roles, from low risk to high risk procedures, and from simple to complex ways of understanding, in an attempt to have learners take on ways of thinking and problem solving that are necessary for membership in a community of practice.

A Developmental Perspective: Cultivating Ways of Thinking

What am I trying to accomplish? That's simple—help these people learn how be good family physicians. But, in addition to that, I want them to learn how to continue learning beyond the supervision of someone like me. You can't survive on the knowledge you get in medical school and residency training . . . my job is to take them beyond that, to think like seasoned physicians. So, I tend to ask a lot of questions. I ask a LOT of questions. Rarely do I provide an answer. I don't mean I ignore questions. But when they ask a question, I have to be sure not to provide an answer that they could find out for themselves. When I do, it seems to interrupt learning rather than move it along . . . I also show them how to find the answer to their questions and I'm not afraid to say I don't know . . . Mostly, it's getting out of the way and resisting the natural tendency to give them the answer and show them how smart I am. That really stops learning! (family physician)

This is the emerging dominant perspective in North American "schooling" today, particularly in science education, but increasingly in other disciplines. It is based on a view of learning derived from cognitive psychology wherein each learner is assumed to have developed a personal cognitive map to guide his or her interpretation of the world. As learners encounter new information or situations, they first try using their exist-

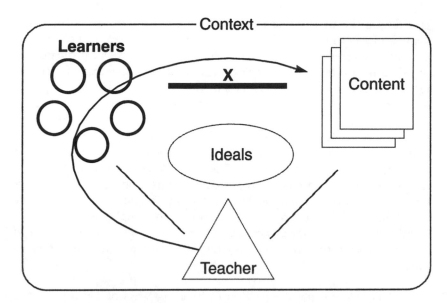

Figure 3.4 A Developmental Perspective

ing map; if that doesn't quite work they are confronted with a dissonant situation where they must either revise their map or reject it and construct a new one. Either way, prior knowledge and ways of thinking form the basis of each learner's approach to any new content and provide a window into their thinking.

It is this process of constantly revising one's map of the terrain that gives this perspective its focus. Learners are perceived to be in a state of balance or equilibrium as long as their map fits the terrain. When they are confronted with new information that doesn't fit, it causes a moment of imbalance or disequilibrium until they can either dismiss the new information or revise their cognitive map. Thus, the teacher's role is to challenge and disturb that equilibrium, causing learners to reestablish it through reconstructing their understanding of something.

Within this perspective content moves to the background and learners come to the foreground, making it a "learner-centered" philosophy of teaching (Figure 3.4).

Whereas in Transmission and Apprenticeship perspectives commitment centered on authentic forms of representing the content, here teachers are committed to developing particular ways of thinking or problem solving. Most often this is expressed as helping learners think and problem solve in ways that resemble expert thinking or problem solving. The teacher's task, therefore, is to help learners think like experts (in a discipline, profession, vocation, etc.). Content is the means through which preferred ways of thinking are developed.

Learning, therefore, is the process of considering new knowledge, skills, or attitudes with existing cognitive structures and revising or replacing those structures. The product of learning is the emergence of new or enhanced understanding and cognitive structures that allow learners to move beyond their previous ways of thinking. Stated somewhat differently, learning is a change in the quality of one's thinking rather than a change in the quantity of one's knowledge. Thus, learning is not simply a process of adding more to what is already there; it is, initially, a search for meaning and an attempt to link the new with the familiar. Ultimately, it is a qualitative change in both understanding and thinking.

Effective teachers, therefore, must be able to build bridges between learners' present ways of thinking and more desirable ways of thinking within a discipline or area of practice. Bridging between these two forms of knowledge means teachers must be able to identify and then reconstruct essential concepts in language and at levels of meaning that can be understood by learners. In addition, learners' conceptions of knowledge and ways of thinking must be respected as legitimate, though incomplete, ways of knowing. Thus, instead of working to pass along information or "get information across," these teachers try to introduce learners to the "essence" of their content in ways that engage what they already know and expand their ways of knowing.

Thus, within this perspective, it is necessary for teachers to explore learners' current conceptions of content and then challenge those conceptions to help learners move to more sophisticated levels of thinking and reasoning. This is not always easy. A common tendency for beginning teachers within this perspective is to fall back into the role of "expert" and provide more answers than challenging questions. But perhaps the most difficult challenge for teachers in this perspective is to develop means of assessing learning that are congruent with the beliefs and intentions of this perspective. While teachers may be able to bridge from the learner's prior knowledge to more desirable ways of understanding and thinking, they may not be able to develop tests, assignments, and means of assessment that allow learners to demonstrate how their thinking has changed to more resemble that of a professional.

As you might have already guessed, teachers holding this as their dominant perspective on teaching have a profound respect for learners' thinking and prior knowledge. Indeed, they take that as the starting point for their work, proceeding from the known (learners' prior knowledge) to the unknown (more sophisticated forms of understanding and thinking). Therefore, teaching must take its direction from the learners' knowledge, not the teacher's. This is a significant shift from more traditional, especially transmission, perspectives on teaching. Arseneau & Rodenburg (Chapter 6) set out seven guiding principles, the first of which is that prior knowledge is the key to learning. From this principle, they move on to explain how a teacher can activate prior knowledge so learners can bridge between new content and what they already know.

A Nurturing Perspective: Facilitating Personal Agency

Most people, at least here in the West, think outdoor recreation means developing some kind of skills. For example, in kayaking that would mean boat-handling skills, pre-trip planning and management skills, understanding tides and river currents, or any other tasks that focus on the activity of kayaking. The essence of my work, and of recreation in general, is the development of a person's sense of well-being. Not just their physical well-being, but their whole being. I try to provide physical, intellectual, and emotional challenges to people; that means I have to attend to their whole being, not just to their physical ability or their physical accomplishments. (outdoor recreation instructor)

Philosophically, the Nurturing Perspective has been the most prevalent view of teaching for adult educators within North America for at least 25 years, as represented in the work of Malcolm Knowles (1980, 1984, 1986). Yet, it is not confined to the cultural norms of the United States and Canada. The original research for this study found variations of this perspective in Singapore, China, and Hong Kong as well as the United States and Canada.

As with each perspective, this one is characterized by a fundamental belief about what influences learning and gives direction to teaching. In the Transmission Perspective it was the belief that effective teaching depends, first and foremost, on the content expertise of the teacher; in the Apprenticeship Perspective it was the belief that learning must be located in authentic social situations related to the application of knowledge; with the Developmental Perspective it was the belief that prior knowledge and ways of thinking are the essential determinants of what people will subsequently learn. In the Nurturing Perspective, it is the be-

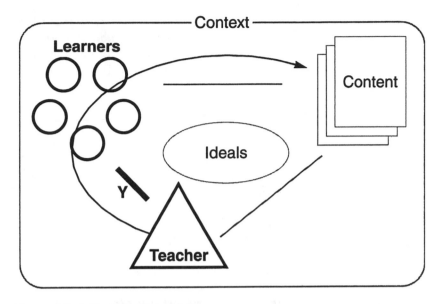

Figure 3.5 A Nurturing Perspective

lief that learning is most affected by a learner's self-concept and self-efficacy. That is, learners must be confident that they can learn the material and that learning the material will be useful and relevant to their lives. Thus, in Figure 3.5, the dominant elements are the teacher, the learner, and particularly the relationship (line Y) between them.

A nurturing relationship is neither permissive nor possessive. It is, in its own way, professional and demanding, characterized by a high degree of reciprocal trust and respect, and always seeks a balance between caring and challenging. Caring means empathizing with learners while providing support and encouragement as they attempt to learn; challenging means holding to expectations that are both achievable and meaningful for learners. The statistics instructor, Jackson, that T'Kenye describes in Chapter 7 is a good example of how someone can achieve a balance between challenge and caring.

The goal is to help people become more confident and self-sufficient learners. To achieve this, it is believed that learners must not only be successful, they must also attribute success to their own effort and ability, rather than the benevolence of their teacher or the serendipity of circumstance. This perspective is, therefore, fundamentally concerned with the development of each learner's concept of self as learner per se. Thus, once again, content becomes a means rather than an end; it is the means through which individuals achieve certain goals and, more importantly, learn that they are capable and self-reliant learners. From this perspective, a learner's self-esteem must never be sacrificed to professional or institutional standards.

A Social Reform Perspective: Seeking a Better Society

Teaching, for me, is more about changing society than repairing cars. When these women are wrestling with a wrench that's heavy and trying to reach down into the engine, I want them to think about why it's so difficult. It's not accidental that the wrench is heavy and the bolt a long reach away. Who do they think designed the tools and the engine? Who were they intended for? What does that say about being a mechanic? Or even repairing your own car? That kind of discrimination is what I'm out to change. Sure, I want them to be able to maintain their car; I don't want them dependent on someone else for that. But, my teaching is just as much about changing society as it is about repairing cars. If they can keep their car running but have no idea they've been excluded from certain occupations . . . what's the point? (automotive repair instructor)

As with the Developmental Perspective, this view of teaching is gaining popularity and prominence around the world, most notably in movements that espouse a clear and articulate vision for social reform. From the feminist movement to fundamentalist religious movements, this perspective is distinctive for the presence of an explicitly stated ideal or set of principles which are linked to a vision of a better society. Each ideal is based on a core or central system of beliefs, usually derived from an ethical code (such as the sanctity of human rights), a religious doctrine (such as the sanctity of God's law), or a political or social ideal (such as the need to redistribute power and privilege in society).

Although some readers may not agree, I take the position that all teaching is ideological. Every teacher represents an underlying "political" stance toward the individual, society, and the role of education within society. In turn, one's ideology gives rise to ideals, that is, one's conception of what might approximate "the good," or "the just." Yet, many teachers claim a personal and epistemic neutrality in terms of their ideals and ideology, denying that they, and that which they teach, represent certain interests and exclude others. This is not the case with social reform teachers. In the Social Reform Perspective, ideals emerge from an am-

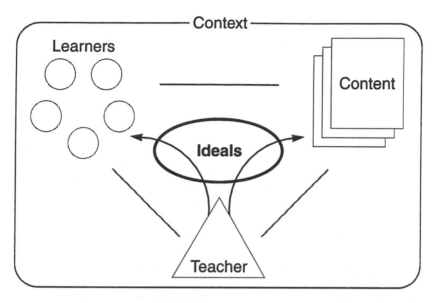

Figure 3.6 A Social Reform Perspective

biguous and covert position of influence to occupy a clear and prominent place of significance in thinking about one's role and responsibility in teaching. They become the focal point of a teacher's beliefs and commitment (Figure 3.6).

The dominance of ideals overshadows all other elements within the General Model of Teaching. Emphasis is on social, cultural, political, or moral imperatives that determine, to a great extent, how each of the other elements and relationships are understood. The focus of commitment, and therefore of teaching, shifts from micro to macro concerns, from finding better technologies of instruction, ways of knowing, and means of facilitating cognitive or personal development to issues of a moral or political nature. Learners and content are secondary to a broader agenda as the commitment and agenda shifts its focus from the individual to the collective.

No single ideology characterizes this perspective; consequently, there is no unifying view of knowledge, learning, or learners. Within this perspective, there are multiple views of knowledge, ranging from objectivist views based on the immutable truth of God's word, to subjectivist views based on the need to understand what it means to have choice over matters concerning one's own body. For example, one individual, teaching in the People's Republic of China, spoke of how he was guided by the Communist Party's teachings regarding obedience to authority and the need to maintain harmony and order in society. For him, these were "first principles" which were necessary for China and for himself. Another person, a woman teaching other women in a work reentry program in Canada, expressed the view that knowledge and authority were socially constructed and relative, and, as part of the learning process, were to be challenged.

One fundamental difference between perspectives can be found in the nature of the means and ends of each perspective. The nature of the ends they seek and the means they choose, depends on the beliefs which comprise them. As you read Chapter 8 notice that within the Social Reform Perspective the ends (goals) of the other perspectives (e.g., mastering content, moving from the periphery to more active and central roles in a community, developing ways of thinking, and enhancing self-efficacy) become the means toward the accomplishment of social changes beyond the bounds of the participants and learning environment. Thus, while Social Reform teachers may be pleased with their students' learning, it is not sufficient; they must have an impact on society to accomplish their teaching mission. That is the "end" and all else the "means" by which they seek their teaching goals.

SUMMARY

As mentioned in the introduction, the five patterns I call Perspectives came from interviews with over 250 people teaching adults a variety of subjects, in a variety of contexts. Their experience represents years of choices, reflection, and refinement of actions, intentions, and beliefs. It is impossible to capture the richness of that diversity, particularly the cultural and social nuances that are not easily understood by outsiders such as myself.

Ideally, this volume would present accounts of the perspectives layered with dimensions of those cultural nuances and the myriad applications that made the evidence of these five patterns so striking. But the publication and linguistic constraints of the book, and the desire for authored chapters by colleagues whom I could regularly encounter have necessitated a North American bias for the detailed contextual descriptions of the perspectives. These are contained in Section II.

REFERENCES

Arseneau, R. (1994). *A study of the impact of a resident teacher education program on teaching self-efficacy, beliefs about teaching, and self-reported teaching behaviours.* Unpublished master's thesis, The University of British Columbia, Vancouver, Canada.

Fox, D. (1983). Personal theories of teaching. *Studies in Higher Education,* 8(2), 151–163.

Gow, L., & Kember, D. (1993). Conceptions of teaching and their relationship to student learning. *British Journal of Educational Psychology,* 63, 20–33.

Kember, D., & Gow, L. (1994). Orientations to teaching and their effect on the quality of student learning. *Journal of Higher Education,* 65(1), 58–74.

Knowles, M. S. (1980). *The modern practice of adult education: From pedagogy to andragogy* (pp. 40–62). Chicago: Association Press, Follett Publishing Co.

Knowles, M. S. (1986). *Using learning contracts: Practical approaches to individualizing and structuring learning.* San Francisco: Jossey-Bass.

Knowles, M. S., & Associates (1984). *Andragogy in action.* San Francisco: Jossey-Bass.

Nietzsche, F. (1969). *On the genealogy of morals* (W. Kaufman & R. J. Hollingdale, Trans.). New York: Vintage Books.

Prosser, M., Trigwell, K., & Taylor, P. (1994). A phenomenographic study of academics' conceptions of science learning and teaching. *Learning and Instruction,* 4, 217–231.

Samuelowicz, K., & Bain, J. D. (1992). Conceptions of teaching held by academic teachers. *Higher Education,* 24, 93–111.

SECTION II

Section II presents a glimpse of the richness of detail and emotion that was evident during the original research. Each chapter features a colleague who responded to my request to write from within a perspective about a personal philosophy and approach to teaching. These individuals were asked to tell their stories, that is, to represent their views on teaching, in a way that would be faithful to the original research, while also revealing their own personal beliefs and commitments. None of the six authors was involved in the original research, neither as coresearcher nor as respondent. They did, however, self-select into one dominant perspective after studying all five perspectives.

The six authors and I met four times over the course of a year to review drafts of chapters and provide feedback, while allowing each other the right to speak in our own voices and write in styles that reflect personal values and commitments related to teaching.

As editor, I was surprised by their responses: some chose to write in the first person and some in the third; some are more academic and others more personal; some chose to follow the general model, while others took an entirely independent form of representing their perspectives; and, some are more strident in their advocacy of a particular perspective than are others. These differences, along with the lengths of chapters, are simply a reflection of the authors' choices and narrative style.

Each chapter is a personal elaboration of one perspective, as if I had asked, "What does it mean, to "teach" from this perspective? Thus, each of the chapters in Section II represents a "mirror" for readers to look into and see if they find an image of themselves. Of course, as mentioned before, you may see reflections of your beliefs and commitments in more than one perspective, as did the authors who wrote these chapters.

In Section III, I will return to present an analysis of the perspectives and revisit the difficult matter of evaluating teaching while respecting the diversity you are about to encounter in the next five chapters.

CHAPTER 4

THE TRANSMISSION PERSPECTIVE
Effective Delivery of Content

Arnold Boldt

PROFILE OF A COMMUNITY COLLEGE INSTRUCTOR

When the reality of having accepted an instructor position at the local community college became more concrete, Paul began feeling somewhat apprehensive. Like many college instructors, Paul lacked a formal background in teaching. He graduated from the public school system, went straight into university and then spent a few years in the business world as a public relations consultant. He was confident about his practical experiences and theoretical knowledge of the subject matter, but his knowledge of teaching and learning came only from his experiences as a student.

Paul's employment interview had focused primarily on his knowledge base, his theoretical and practical business experience, and on his organizational and time management skills. Secondary emphases were directed to Paul's ability to communicate his knowledge and experiences to students and on his interpersonal skills.

The first few days of preparation at the college diminished some of Paul's anxiety. All courses offered in the program already had well-detailed objectives in place. Reviewing outlines for the courses he was scheduled to teach, he realized that he could structure course material to meet the desired course ends.

Paul now teaches a course in the Business Administration diploma program called Business Communications II. It is the second in a se-

ries of three communications courses offered in the program. By the end of this course, it is expected that students will be fluent in the processes and techniques of letter, memorandum, and informal report writing necessary for success in the business world.

The behavioral objectives and competencies for each course are clearly laid out; the skill and knowledge base required of graduates by employers are explicit. All programs at the college are approved first in concept and then course by course through program advisory committees. Committee members come from the community, usually work in the program-related field and ultimately employ or supervise graduates of the program. Instructors can recommend course objectives, but advisory committees have the final word in amending, deleting, and ratifying objectives and competencies according to their projected human resource needs. Paul's responsibility in this context is twofold: to plan the content so that it matches the course's objectives; and to efficiently deliver the content to the students within the allotted course time. His task is to take his students from their present skill or knowledge level to the competency levels defined by the course objectives.

After several years' teaching experience, consulting with colleagues, and receiving feedback from students, Paul has created what he considers to be a pretty good curriculum. It is structured into three general subdivisions. The first subdivision focuses on the macro level of written communication. It provides students with an overview of how writing can be used to achieve a number of different business objectives, what constitutes effective and ineffective written communication, how a template can be used and adapted to any situation related to business, and what formats and styles contemporary correspondence take. The second and third subdivisions focus on the micro level, on different kinds of business correspondence: letters, memorandums, and short, informal reports. In turn, these are divided into three types: letters and memos that either inform or persuade; reports that describe incidents, work progress or completion; and trip or field assignments.

Paul set up the course so that students have an assigned reading for every topic. These readings, then, form the basis for the class lecture, demonstration, question or discussion time, and practical assignment (group or individual).

A typical 50-minute class begins with Paul's returning assignments and briefly reviewing previous material relevant to the session's topic. He then continues with a 15- to 20-minute lecture, presentation, or discussion session. If the topic is "request letters," he lectures on typical situations in which request letters are used, shows on the overhead a writing plan template used to frame request letters, discusses and critiques a sample request letter, and uses a case study which the class collectively brainstorms, organizes, and writes out in rough form on transparency paper. To round off the session, a second case study is assigned to allow students to independently practice and apply their writing skills. During the last part of the session, Paul walks around the class checking student progress and fielding questions.

The students in Paul's course vary in age from eighteen to forty. Their backgrounds and motivations are equally varied. Some were recently graduated from high school, some had worked in business a few years before entering college and others are looking for a career change. The students' diverse backgrounds make for interesting, often lively discussions and brainstorming sessions. Overall, the students are very comfortable with the course structure. The detailed outline specifies exactly what material will be covered in class and what is expected of them with regard to their participation, assignments, and evaluation. They know where they going and how they will get there.

INTRODUCTION

For many readers, first reactions to the Transmission Perspective on teaching may be negative. Your reaction might stem from the fact that the primary focus of this perspective is the content and that the central relationship is that of teacher-to-content (see the General Model of Teaching in Chapter 1). You might also react cautiously, if not negatively, to the assumption in this perspective that there is a relatively well-defined, stable body of knowledge and skills (content) that can be competently transmitted to learners. Of course, this implies that the primary responsibility of the instructor is to structure or organize the content and create educational materials that can be efficiently delivered within the allotted course time. But why do these things engender negative reaction?

When the authors of this text were asked for personal examples of effective learning experiences emerging from transmission teaching, most of us had little difficulty doing so. We listed examples of masterful teaching of music, accounting, English literature, computer applications, nursing, cabinetmaking, and many other subjects. It became clear during the discussion that what made these experiences positive was the teacher's mastery of subject knowledge or skills and ability to organize for and explain, demonstrate, and problem solve at the students' level of understanding. Of course, we also came up with many examples of ineffective transmission-oriented teaching. My colleagues' adverse reactions to this teaching perspective were influenced by their negative experiences with it. Most often cited were examples of poorly organized teachers who jumped without connection from topic to topic, overwhelmed students with facts, offered convoluted explanations and responses to student questioning, or mismatched what they taught (usually by lectures) and what they based their evaluations on (usually in tests).

Why is there such a love-hate relationship with the Transmission Perspective of teaching? Part of the reason for this perspective's popularity—and notoriety—can be attributed to its extensive use within public schools and other institutional settings. It is understandable that if, first as children and then adults, we experienced transmission teaching throughout our formal education, we would then embrace it as a perspective on teaching for ourselves when we become teachers. And when we now find ourselves in teaching positions but lack other teaching perspectives with which to compare and contrast, we draw on this perspective since it is the only one with which we have familiarity. Since we have experienced its use extensively, or perhaps exclusively, it becomes a part of our perspective of what it means to teach. Furthermore, if we have experienced only bad examples of transmission teaching, we will be tempted to reject it outright when we encounter a different and seemingly more appealing teaching perspective rather than reflect on why it was ineffective. Regardless of the teaching perspective used, there will always be examples of both effective and ineffective use.

Various labels have been used by educational researchers to describe or conceptualize some aspects of what we are calling transmission teaching. Fenstermacher and Soltis (1986) describe it as the "executive approach" to teaching. This approach places primary emphasis on process, on the teacher's ability to effectively transmit knowledge or skills from a source (teacher or text) to the student. In other research by Fox (1983), the Transmission Perspective is partially described by combining his "transfer" and "shaping" theories of teaching. The essence of these theories is that the teacher controls what is delivered and what it looks like after delivery. Samuelowicz and Bain's (1992) research described similar teaching perspectives in their "imparting information" and "transmitting knowledge" conceptualizations. The central emphases of these descriptors rests on the primary relation of the teacher-to-content and the efficient delivery of content—two defining attributes of the Transmission Perspective of teaching.

Is this teaching perspective applicable across contexts? Is it applicable across subject matter? What does effective teaching look like from this perspective? What distinguishes this perspective from the other perspectives? What aspects of this perspective remain constant and which ones might change, across differing contexts, content, ideals, and learners? How is knowledge viewed from this perspective? In a somewhat systematic, yet exploratory way, this chapter attempts to respond to these questions. To achieve this, I try to elicit some of the underlying beliefs, assumptions and values held implicitly and explicitly by transmission teachers. Additionally, I direct attention to some difficulties faced by teachers using this teaching perspective.

RELATION OF ELEMENTS TO TEACHING IN TRANSMISSION PERSPECTIVE

In any teaching situation there are several different elements that combine to influence the perspective from which teachers teach. Teacher's actions and intentions are influenced in varying degrees by learners, content, context, and their own ideals, and each of these elements in some way influence and interact with each other. To better understand the Transmission Perspective of teaching, we will use the profile of a college instructor (Paul) as a means of exploring and elaborating upon the elements in the General Model of Teaching (see Chapter 1).

Teacher

How are the roles and responsibilities of a transmission teacher defined? Paul initially drew his normative beliefs of role and responsibility from two sources: his experiences as a student and the job interview at the college. Reflecting on his student experiences, Paul believed that he learned best when the teachers knew their subject matter well, structured the course in logical, easy-to-follow steps, and communicated ideas in ways he could easily follow and understand. From the job interview, with its emphases on his knowledge base and organizational and time management skills, Paul understood that the college expected him to be well versed in content matters and able to organize and deliver courses within allotted time frames.

Paul's initial weakness lay in having no teaching experience—a procedural weakness. But after several years of trying different methods and taking student feedback seriously, he concluded that his teaching was most effective when he used several techniques within a 50-minute class. A typical class begins with a short presentation followed by a short writing assignment done in small groups. While the groups draft their work on transparencies, Paul circulates among groups to field questions and provide feedback on the work in progress. About 15 minutes before class ends, each group presents its assignment on the overhead while the other groups first compare it with their own work and then critique the work projected on the screen.

Paul's rationale for using this delivery style is based on his belief that theory (lecture or presentation) needs to be applied (assignment) quickly to a situation if it is to take hold and make sense to his learners. Thus the short presentation at the start of the class is immediately followed by an assignment, often done in groups. The group work has two functions. First, it diminishes the students' stress levels of having to listen to and concentrate on the teacher's presentation for a prolonged period. Secondly, group work enables students to pool their resources and to apply immediately what they have only just been exposed to in concept. Furthermore, presenting their work and then discussing it with the teacher offers students immediate feedback on their interpretation and application of the concept. If students have difficulties with or misunderstandings of the topic, this is immediately apparent in their work or questions. The teacher can then take steps to provide clarification, reteaching, or reviewing of the material.

One assumption that Brown and Atkins (1987) explicitly make in their discussion of teaching in higher education is "that effective teaching consists of a set of skills that can be acquired, improved, and extended" (p.1). These skills include lecturing, small group teaching, laboratory teaching, and research and project supervision among others. They implicitly suggest, however, that these skills will be of little value if the teacher is not a content expert. Teachers also require deep subject knowledge so they will be able to "think and problem-solve, to analyse a topic, to reflect upon what is an appropriate approach, to select key strategies and material, and to organize and structure ideas, information, and tasks for students" (p. 1). Without content mastery, teachers will not be able to present a wide range of examples, answer student questions well, provide useful resources, or design assignments that reinforce course objectives. These summarize some of the key responsibilities of the transmission teacher. Without mastery of the subject matter he needed to teach (and some familiarity with his students' abilities), Paul would not have been able to structure his class as confidently as he did.

Learners

Transmission teaching recognizes that student learning and personal issues affect one another. However, in contrast to the Nurturing Perspective (see Chapter 7) where student physical and mental well-being are a priority, the Transmission Perspective clearly places personal student issues second to efficient course delivery. One reason for this is that formal educational institutions usually define the roles of teacher and counselor as separate functions. In this way education institutions and industrial training centers actually encourage transmission teaching. Teachers are hired for their content expertise, not counseling skills. Being able to organize and structure content is how teachers are most useful, how they play their role. Paul, for instance, expresses concern for his students and tries to address their learning needs as best he can, but his personal relationship with them is not his primary responsibility. If he feels that certain personal issues interfering with student learning are beyond his competence to counsel, he refers them to the counseling department. Transmission teachers do not have to become involved in areas beyond their competence. Especially in formal settings, there are other experts whose role it is to deal with individual difficulties.

As mentioned earlier, Paul's students vary widely in age and experience, though all would have met the college's prerequisites for program entry. They all will have completed Grade 12, had equivalent upgrading, or been granted college entrance based on mature student status. They also will have successfully completed Communications I, a course dealing with grammar, punctuation, and usage. It is commonly assumed by program planners in formal education settings that screening students by using prerequisites leads to a relatively uniform academic base among students. This assumption gives transmission teachers a particular starting point from which they can organize and structure course content. When Paul teaches Business Communications II, for example, he assumes students have mastered grammar, punctuation, and usage: he constructs his lectures, assignments, and evaluations on the basis of this assumption.

However, the reality of this assumption is challenged by significant individual differences among his students. These divergences in age and life experiences means that Paul works hard at structuring the course to keep everyone interested and actively involved with the subject matter. Some of his students have significant recent writing experience; for example, those coming straight from high school or from a job where writing skills were required. To keep these students interested, Paul uses an in-class group assignment and critique teaching technique. The experienced members of a group, he reasons, balance the inexperienced writers: they can serve as the "experts" in the groups as they work on writing projects. For those students having great difficulty, Paul may refer them to a learning or resource center for remedial work.

Transmission teachers must be prepared for the fact of diverse learner motivations. While many students simply want to get through a program or course and on to other things, others are very stimulated by the educational process. Paul, for example, is well aware that some students are interested primarily in passing his course, the program, and getting a "real" job. Nevertheless, he tries hard to express and generate enthusiasm in his teaching and the students' learning. By varying teaching methods within each class and from class to class, Paul is better able to keep learner attention on the task than by using a single teaching method, like the lecture, in all his classes.

This teaching perspective is concerned with effectively transmitting knowledge and skills to students. Accounting for individual differences by giving individual attention and scheduling extra sessions better ensures that knowledge and skills are effectively transmitted. Since there are always a number of students in courses who have young children or work part time to finance their education, many teachers feel the need to somehow acknowledge and address the times that students miss class because of their life situations. Paul, for example, knows that he cannot slow down course delivery as long as he is responsible for covering the whole syllabus within his allotted 60 hours. But how does he account for the problem of individual student academic difficulties or life situation differences? For students willing and able to attend, he offers extra class or tutorial sessions several times a week. Other formal education institutions often acknowledge that their strict time allotments for course delivery do not account for all student life situations. So they openly support and encourage teachers to make themselves available beyond regularly scheduled class time.

The purpose of teaching, from a Transmission Perspective, is to move knowledge or skills from a content expert (teacher or text) to the learner. The teacher's function is to show learners the right or better path to the knowledge or skills they seek to apply in future careers. Teachers assume that learners are there for a purpose: to learn skills and pick up the knowledge base needed to gain entry-level job positions in careers of their choice. The ideal learners in a transmission teaching setting are those who know exactly why they are there and what they want to do with the skills they learn. With a broad overview of what they want to be and do following their education, they will be more motivated and knowledgeable of the small steps taken to achieve their goal. They will be willing to actively participate in and follow through with assignments when required by the teacher. Moreover, the ideal learners will have relatively stable personal lives. They will be comfortable with their life situations and able to deal with personal problems in a way that does not distract them too much from their learning.

Content

To be effective, transmission teachers must have a well-organized presentation of subject matter that is easily structured. Rosenshine and Stevens (1986) argue that "explicit teaching" (transmission teaching) is most effective for content areas that are hierarchical; that is, where new learning builds upon an established base of prior learning: "where the objective is to master a body of knowledge or learn a skill which can be taught in a step-by-step manner" (p. 377). Mathematics, grammar, music, plumbing, and electronics are examples of well-structured content areas. In fact, regarding most content areas as being well-structured is not difficult for transmission teachers. This is especially so for the initial teaching stages where basic concepts or techniques are introduced in presentation, applied in practice, and then built upon step by step as subject matter becomes increasingly complex.

It is important to realize, however, that although different teachers structure their content area differently, they may well be equally effective. It is not a specific structure that matters. Rather, what is central here is simply that teachers identify a structure, and then reduce it into "bite-sized" pieces for teaching. These bite-sized pieces are then translated into various methods used to transmit course content, among them are lectures, demonstrations, group discussions, assignments, readings, guided practices, reviews, and objective evaluations. For example, breaking grammar and punctuation into bite-sized pieces to teach to secretarial students who need good proofreading skills is easily done: first, an overview and definition of the sentence; second, an overview and then detailed breakdown of the eight parts of speech; third, a look at the grammar of the sentence; and fourth, a breakdown of punctuation. Following structural breakdown of the content, the next step is to decide on a method of transmitting the knowledge and skills to the students so they can perform better and ultimately reproduce the knowledge and skills taught. When teaching an introductory section on comma usage, for example, a presentation on linking independent clauses with commas will be followed by students first practicing their recognition of these clauses and ultimately writing their own sentences using commas to link one or more clauses.

Program and course goals and objectives are usually clearly defined in formal education. The objective of Paul's communications course is that students will be able to compose well-written business documents (i.e., they letters, memos, or various types of reports). Since writing longer reports is more difficult than writing short memos for most people, Paul structures his course to progress in a step-by-step manner from simple to more complex writing skills. First, he provides an overview of what makes for effective business writing by providing comments on examples of skilled writing. He then breaks the course down to teach writing in a step-by-step technique, from short, simple messages meant to inform readers to longer, more complex messages or reports designed to persuade readers. Since the students in his course intend to work in business after graduation, Paul simulates a business environment in all assignments. This entails setting up case studies from which students first sort and organize the essential information and then begin the writing process. At the beginning of the course, students are given the background and organizational charts for several imagined companies. All assignments come from typical business situations: students write interdepartmental memos informing staff of new company policies, letters to customers denying credit applications, project progress reports, proposals for building renovations and reports detailing a market analysis.

Due to the centrality of content structuring in transmission teaching, this perspective may be unsuitable in some content areas. For instance, in foreign language conversation, where spontaneity and self-expression are essential to fluency, there are no steps into which the lesson can be divided. Other examples of such areas are counselling skills, art or music appreciation, and poetry writing. In such cases, transmission teaching could inhibit skill development. Rosenshine and Stevens (1986) suggest that there are "ill-structured" content areas, especially when teaching becomes more deeply involved in subject matter. Thus, in areas where steps are difficult to contrive or skills do not require repeated application, this teaching perspective may not be effective.

The line between ill- and well-structured content areas is not easily drawn. Where some teachers may see no structure, others may find it possible to imagine a content structure and thereby find an efficient means to deliver it. When I presented a case study of an instructor teaching ethics in a formal setting to my colleagues, many at first resisted the idea that it could be taught effectively using transmission teaching. However, I believe that when they saw how ethics could be given a structure and subdivided into various types and theories, it became more difficult to imagine content areas that could not be structured.

Let us imagine what a short ethics course might look like from a transmission teaching perspective. Instructor X teaches introductory ethics at a community college. The course objective is for students to be able to take amoral dilemma and resolve it from a number of different ethical perspectives. The course is set up so that students have assigned readings for each class. These readings form the basis for the class lecture, discussion time and assignment. The course is broken into two subdivisions. The first focuses on "teleological ethics" (ethics of ends) and some of its manifestations such as egoism, act- and rule-utilitarianism and Kierkegaard's teleological suspension of the ethical. The second subdivision focuses on "deontological ethics" (ethics of duty) and its manifestations such as Kant's formalism, rights-based theories and social-contract theories. The instructor begins class with a brief overview of previously covered material, returns assignments and reviews last class's assignment. The instructor then lectures and opens the floor to questions about the ethical theory under consideration for that class. Halfway through each class, the instructor takes up the issue of capital punishment and demonstrates how it would be justified using the just-presented theory. Following, students are given an assignment wherein they must work out (either in groups or individually) how the issue of abortion would be viewed from the perspective just presented.

An example of how a course can be created, designed, structured, and taught follows:

Step 1:   Define student entry levels and course goals and objectives.

Step 2:   Define course content to meet objectives.

Step 3:   Break content and structure it into logical step-by-step pieces that build on each other, from simple to increasingly complex skills and concepts.

Step 4:   Organize pieces to fit into allocated class time.

Step 5:   Create assignments, applied practice, to reinforce and complement skill and conceptual knowledge.

Step 6:   Define standards of achievement and create formal evaluation procedures that measure learning and reflect course content and objectives.

Step 7:   Define appropriate method(s) of skill and knowledge transmission and organization of class time. For example, begin a 50-minute class with a review of the last session (5 minutes); return assignments (5 minutes); present a new topic by lecture (15 minutes); discuss topic as a group (10 minutes); reinforce presentation with assignment (15 minutes).

One of the equivocal aspects involved in transmission teaching is when the teacher, as a content expert, becomes an opaque substitute for the content. That is, the teacher's presentation and charisma overwhelm the learners' experience of the subject being taught. This is particularly troublesome for performance-oriented teachers—those whose performance is both the medium and the message. I am sure all of us have experienced highly energized teachers whose passion for their subject matter is clearly evident in their lectures. As students (or audience) we are mesmerized by their performance. Yet when we leave the lecture to reflect on the experience, it is very difficult for us to pin down exactly what has been learned

Northrup Frye (1980) provides a solution to the problem of performance-oriented presentations when he explores the question "How do I teach literature?" Frye argues that the ultimate aim in teaching literature (and all other subject areas) is for the teacher's abolition of self, or the turning of self "into a transparent medium" for the subject, so that the authority of the "subject may be supreme over both teacher and students" (p. 20). To achieve subject supremacy over teacher and students, Frye recommends teaching literature by its structure and the content by means of the structure.

Transmission teaching is also troublesome for teachers who succumb to the temptation to teach everything they know about a subject. With its emphasis on teachers as "content experts," it is easy for many teachers to overwhelm students with their expertise. I am sure we have all had teachers whose content area knowledge is vast and ability to draw from a multitude of sources is impressive. Unfortunately, the presentation of an idea that draws on too many sources and illustrates too many points of view usually leaves us as students more bewildered rather than more knowledgeable. Effective transmission teaching requires teachers to plan content delivery in steps easily digested by students.

Context

Teachers' choice of teaching perspectives is highly influenced by the context in which they work. Within formal education settings such as universities, colleges, and industrial training centers, teachers function as a part of a larger whole. Teachers in these settings do not act in a void where they have complete freedom to choose the teaching method which most appeals to them. In fact, the context in which most teachers teach is structured in such a way as to encourage the use of transmission teaching. In Paul's college, for example, most courses are part of larger programs which are subject to approval by various advisory committees, professional boards, or certification agencies. The time and location of his courses are scheduled by others. The length and goals of his courses are approved by planners and advisory committees. Paul's career as a teacher is dependent on his ability to match the content he teaches to the objectives set by others and to deliver the content within the allotted time. It is management (instructional supervisors) who, within these parameters, determine and define what is successful or poor teaching.

The hierarchy of control within established educational institutions leaves little room for interpretation of what it means to teach. A number of factors that foster a transmission teaching environment converge in institutional settings: the articulation of programs with professions and one course with another course; predetermined standards of achievement; traditions within disciplines; historical patterns of course objectives and goals; employer demands. This culture of demand is well known to us and well reflected in the rules and regulations (the annual academic calendar) that govern how teaching and learning occur in institutions. Although not the world of work, educational institutions attempt to mirror the world of work and thereby become an enculturation process for the world of work. For example, there are deadlines for assignments as there are deadlines for work projects. Few personal issues can be used to exempt students from institutional regulations or workers from the work site. Often students enrolled in skills training programs are paid hourly rates by sponsors for class attendance. Missing classes ensures an equal deduction from students' living allowance. Transmission teaching, with its emphasis on efficient (time allotted) content delivery, fits well into this environment.

Furthermore, Paul is encouraged to focus on course content and efficient delivery by the fact that the college has other programs and personnel to address various facets of students' needs. When Paul feels that certain types of learner needs are beyond his competence to deal with or beyond his role as content expert, he directs them to the other support systems available to them on campus. For example, if students' academic skills are lacking, and he cannot address them in class and during extra tutorial sessions, he refers them to a learning assistance or resource center. This doesn't mean, however, that Paul doesn't care about his students: it's simply that the institution provides a compartmentalization of expertise. Different types of student needs are met by different kinds of experts.

By contrast, however, in nonformal or informal education settings the roles and responsibilities of teachers may be defined differently simply because the student support systems found in larger educational institutions are not available. Teachers in nontraditional educational settings may be compelled by their situation to define their teaching role more broadly. For example, when an adult upgrading or ABE program is being delivered in a small town geographically isolated from a larger center, only one teacher may be hired to teach and run the whole program. Often these teachers will not have access to the usual student services available in large institutions. In these instances, teachers invariably assume a much broader role that includes personal, career, and academic counseling.

Student motivations are also a significant part of the context that influence the nature of transmission teaching. Many of Paul's students are in his courses simply because they are required for the program in which they are enrolled. Their interest is motivated primarily by a desire to pass his course and move on to complete the requirements for graduation. Their aim is to get into the working world. Their goals include Paul's courses but are focused beyond as well. To hold their interest while they are in his courses, Paul structures two kinds of experiences for his students. First, he creates case studies and assignments that simulate as closely as possible the business world they hope to enter. Secondly, he brings in guest speakers from the business world to talk about the various issues in and relevancy of business communications.

Ideal/Ideology

Unless the subject matter being taught explicitly has to do with "creating a better society" (see Social Reform Perspective) or challenging commonly held societal values, transmission teachers usually assume the ideology of their employing authority. Shearon and Tollefson (1989), for example, refer to community colleges in Canada and the United States as being "mirrors of their local communities and of the larger society surrounding them" (p. 316). Mirroring implies an acceptance of status quo societal values and ideology. As a result, when institutions hire teachers, they look for those who espouse similar ideals.

Since the mission statements of many colleges include references to economic development and skills training relevant to employers in the community (Shearon and Tollefson, 1989), the onus is on colleges to hire those who do not radically challenge the status quo. In this environment of institutional accountability, the focus is on employing teachers who can competently deliver content aimed at predefined objectives. Though the relevance of ideology may be highlighted in the initial hiring process, it is backgrounded, implicitly present and assumed, when it comes to teaching functions. This situation fosters a very linear teaching milieu wherein teachers' efforts center on structuring content and using delivery techniques that efficiently achieve program goals. Thus, although ideology may vary from institution to institution, teaching functions converge on ways to deliver content within the context of institutional ideology.

Teachers must not only buy into institutional ideology initially upon hiring but often also throughout their careers. Since content experts, like Paul, frequently lack a formal education background, they are often required by their collective agreements to take a number of courses or attain certification from institution-sanctioned programs. If not required, they are usually strongly encouraged. The courses offered in these programs normally focus on teaching techniques and skills: lecturing, small

group work, discussion groups, laboratory work, and classroom management among others. The institutional assumption, like the assumption of
transmission teaching, is that there exists a direct correlation between
teaching skills and student learning.

BELIEFS, ASSUMPTIONS, AND VALUES

For adult educators in both formal and informal settings, understanding the beliefs that frame their teaching practice is fundamental.
Thornton (1989, cited in Johnson, 1993, pp. 2–3) argues that "within a
societal and institutional context, teachers serve as curricular-instruc-
tional gatekeepers. Their beliefs about curriculum, how they plan, and
how they teach, in large measure, determine both the subject matter and
experiences to which students have access. . . ." However, understanding
beliefs is not a simple task. It "requires making inferences about individuals' underlying states, inferences fraught with difficulty because individuals are often unable or unwilling, for many reasons, to accurately
represent their beliefs. For this reason, beliefs cannot be directly observed
or measured but must be inferred from what people say, intend, and do"
(Pajares, 1992, p. 314).

In the following section I look at the actions and intentions underlying transmission teaching practice. My intention is to clarify the *epistemic, normative,* and *procedural* (Chapter 9) beliefs of transmission
teaching.

Epistemic Beliefs

Every perspective on teaching stems from an epistemology—a philosophy of knowledge—that is either implicitly or explicitly presup-
posed. Epistemic beliefs have to do with assumptions about the nature
and use of knowledge and its validation, how it is reproduced. These assumptions will significantly shape, define, and limit a given perspective
of teaching. For example, a teaching perspective that holds knowledge to
be objective, outside the learner, will likely have little difficulty with
evaluation of learning since there are right and wrong or better and
worse answers. Since there is usually a high degree of agreement among
content experts within a specific field on the nature of its particular realities, evaluation of learning becomes a matter of judging how well a
student has re-presented or reproduced those realities. On the other

hand, a teaching perspective that holds knowledge to be subjective, constructed individually, will use different methods of evaluating learning, for reality will differ from individual to individual. The degree to which a teaching perspective is epistemologically explicit or implicit may well mirror the degree to which it is coherent, efficacious and worthwhile for adult educators and, ultimately, adult learners. Three aspects of epistemic beliefs will be considered: knowledge, learning, and evaluation (Pratt 1992).

As discussed earlier, the Transmission Perspective of teaching is fundamentally content driven with an emphasis on efficient delivery. It implies that knowledge can be broken into chunks, structured and transferred to the learner within an allocated course time. Emphasized in this way, it is possible to see that knowledge is more likely to be viewed as objective—that is, independent of human perspective—and easily manipulable by the teacher, for it needs to serve the teacher who is a content expert and deliverer.

In their research on direct instruction, Rosenshine and Stevens (1986) imply that knowledge is objectifiable when they discuss teaching well-structured content areas in a "step-by-step manner" or "small-step approach" (p. 377). They emphasize correcting student errors—the assumption being that there is a right and a wrong answer, with the right answer measured by some objective or easily accessible transcendental criteria. The evidence from Pratt's (1992) study concurs: "[k]nowledge was believed to be relatively stable and external to the learner and teachers were expected to possess the knowledge that learners needed. Content was to be reduced, broken down, and organized for efficient delivery and testing" (p. 210). Therefore, knowledge is viewed as "out there," external to both the teacher and learner. (See Figure 4.1 for a graphic representation.) The teacher's primary role, then, is to master that content and structure its delivery such that learners are able to demonstrate mastery of it following teaching.

Just as knowledge is perceived to be objective, so too are both learning and evaluation. Learning is often spoken of as a student's being able "to master a body of knowledge" or being "taught a general rule which is then applied to new situations" (Rosenshine and Stevens, 1986, p. 377). The inference that knowledge is an objective commodity that can be transferred by the act of teaching is clear. Describing the transfer theory of teaching, Fox (1983) represents one extreme that maintains successful "learning is seen to be the result of well-prepared material, effectively organised and imparted. Unsuccessful learning is seen to be the

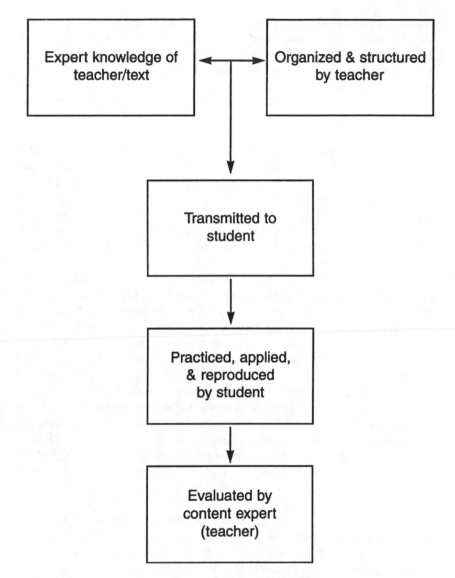

Figure 4.1 Transmission of Expert Knowledge and Skills

consequence of poorly motivated, unintelligent, lazy, forgetful students" (p. 152). From our perspective of transmission teaching, unsuccessful learning can be seen as the result of at least four poor practices. First, the content may have been delivered in too large chunks. Too many facts or skills presented in too brief a time are difficult for learners to digest. If this is the case, the content needs to be "rechunked," presented in smaller pieces. Second, there may have been a lack of sufficient guided and independent practice. In this case, more time should be allowed for practical application of skills and concepts. Third, having been taught only once, some subject matter may still cause difficulty for student comprehension. In this case, the material needs to be retaught, perhaps using another method or from a different point of view. Fourth, the learners may not have been participating to the degree expected of them; for example, by not completing reading or other assignments (designed to reinforce learning) in preparation for class.

Learning, moreover, is thought to occur in predictable and verifiable ways. If students appear to be having difficulty with certain material, proceeding in smaller steps may be helpful; that is, the learning environment needs to be managed or manipulated differently so the student can better process the pieces of knowledge or skills to be learned. Conversely, if learning proceeds more quickly than anticipated, the instructor can control the learning environment by taking bigger steps, providing less teacher-guided practice or undertaking more covert (as opposed to overt) reviewing (Rosenshine & Stevens, 1986). Learning, then, is viewed as something that can be efficiently controlled by the teacher through manipulation of variables external to the learners.

Evaluation from the transmission perspective of teaching is straightforward. If the teacher accurately matches course structure and content to the course objectives, learning and knowledge can be easily measured and validated with regard to the objectives. Of course, the learning outcomes—often called behavioral objectives—of a course must be predetermined, and efficient delivery of content must always aim toward the specific competencies sought. The absence of clearly defined objectives and competencies can lead to ineffective programs. The absence suggests poor program planning or course design. Mismatching content delivery and evaluation confuse the students and clearly suggest ineffective teaching.

Fenstermacher and Soltis (1986) succinctly summarize the significance of correlating teaching objectives and evaluation:

Matching curriculum and evaluation is another aspect, wherein attention is given to the nature of what is taught in relation to what is assessed by tests. It sometimes turns out that students score poorly on tests, not because they failed to master what was taught, but because they were never taught what the tests measured. The teacher who is a good executive will seek a clear match between what is taught and what is assessed by tests. (p. 14)

Tests and exams are not the only means of evaluating teaching (and learning). Returning to the instructor profile, we see that assessment of learning can also be measured through a series of assignments or skill demonstrations intended to simulate the learners' future work environment. What is essential is that the assignments directly match course objectives and content presentation. With measurable outcomes toward which all teaching is directed and with evaluation assumed to accurately measure learning, reality is clearly perceived to be objective, manipulable, and transferable.

In summary, the epistemic beliefs underlying transmission teaching reveal an objectively oriented perspective of knowledge, learning, and evaluation. That learning, knowledge, and evaluation can be so clearly described and designed reinforces the "view that the facts of the world are essentially *there* for study. They exist independently of us as observer, and if we are rational we will come to know the facts as they are" (Schwandt, 1994, p. 125). What are the implications of this? Knowledge and learning gained incidentally during the structured teaching process but beyond the scope of the evaluation and course objectives are of little immediate relevance for either the teacher or learner.

Normative Beliefs

Normative beliefs are the prescriptive or "what ought to be" aspects of teaching. They are the ideals by which teachers measure themselves. By holding up the norms to which teachers aspire, we will see more clearly the values and beliefs implicit in transmission teaching. In the section that follows, we will look at the normative beliefs associated with the roles, responsibilities, and relationships of the teacher.

From the Transmission Perspective of teaching, the primary role of the teacher is that of a content expert. Teachers must be thoroughly familiar with and informed about the subject matter they teach. Some teachers may argue that if they are good at organizing and breaking systems into components, why should they need to be content experts? The assumption of transmission teaching is that if teachers are not experts in their field, it is doubtful that they will be able to structure a course in such a way as to make it comprehensible to their students. If teachers cannot see the whole of a content area, they will have difficulty breaking it down into steps that build upon each other in a logical manner. Since knowledge and learning are viewed as objective, teachers need to master their subject matter in order to first transmit that knowledge to students and then evaluate their learning. Furthermore, in order to check for student understanding (or misunderstanding) and to correct errors, it is imperative that teachers are experts in their subject areas. Without deep subject knowledge, it will be difficult for teachers to probe student understanding or provide a second or third approach to a topic when errors in student thinking hinder successful transmission of knowledge and skills.

Although content expertise is undeniably of primary importance to transmission teaching, this perspective also focuses on transmitting knowledge and skills. Thus organizational strategies of delivery are also key to effective teaching. The other dimensions of teaching such as techniques, teaching strategies, and student/teacher relationships are of a closely related yet secondary importance; that is, they are defined in relation to or in interaction with the content. Discussing attributes of effective teachers, Apps (1991) emphasizes first keeping up to date in their content area, organizing it, and delivering it efficiently. Samuelowicz and Bain (1992, p. 121), when analyzing the "teaching as imparting information" model of teaching, observe that it is essential to have "good knowledge" or "wide knowledge" of the subject. Davis (1993, p. xix) argues that the "heart of teaching is the instructor's understanding of the material." Of course, the argument is not that content mastery is the sole role of the teacher. The assumption of role here is that without content mastery the teacher will not be able to employ effectively the techniques needed to move the content from the source (teacher or text) to the student and thereby fulfill course objectives. Effective teaching also includes selecting appropriate teaching techniques, gauging student comprehension, reteaching where students have difficulty, and making content relevant to student experiences.

The dominant relationship between the elements of teaching referred to in the General Model of Teaching is that of teacher-to-content. That is, teachers must be well versed and up to date in their subject area if they are to enjoy any credibility with their students. The teacher is a content authority. The pivotal premise is that if teachers have mastered the content then all other aspects of teaching will fall into place more naturally and fluidly. Without content mastery, chances of effective teaching are substantially reduced. Correlatively then, the primary responsibility of the teacher is to regulate, systematize, and engineer the content so that it can be delivered in the most efficient manner possible.

Learners play a secondary role in their relationship to the teacher. The degree to which they are distanced from the teacher may vary from teacher to teacher and context to context. At one end of the spectrum teachers may simply argue that if they have made a good effort to organize and deliver the content, then the rest is up to the motivated student (Fox, 1983, p. 153). On the other end, teachers may argue that organization and efficient delivery must be closely combined with consideration for students' prior experiences and current difficulties with the material (Davis, 1993; Draves, 1984; Lowman, 1984). If, when checking for understanding or through evaluation, it appears that the content is not being learned, this is considered a problem related to the way in which the content has been organized or delivered. Perhaps the material was not broken down adequately or the assignments did not mesh well with content presentation. To solve the problem the instructor should first attempt modifications to the design or presentation of instructional materials.

For transmission teachers there is, thus, assumed to be a very direct link between the actions of the teacher and students' learning. Transmission teaching is very linear. As we have seen earlier, there are logical steps that can be taken to design and deliver courses within time-limited educational settings. Fenstermacher and Soltis (1986) formulate this link between teaching and learning in what they call the "executive approach" as "$T\emptyset Sxy$," wherein the "teacher (T) uses certain organizational and management skills $(\emptyset)$ to impart to students (S) specific facts, concepts, skills, and ideas (x) so that these students are most likely to acquire and retain this specified knowledge (y)" (p. 15). In this model, if students do not satisfactorily manage "y," then "x" needs to be manipulated differently through changing the structure of "$\emptyset$."

What do the responsibilities of the teacher look like on a day-to-day basis? Rosenshine and Stevens (1986) relate a number of responsibilities that provide for effective teacher performance. Among others they include these: setting course objectives and standards of student performance; correcting errors and misunderstandings; providing feedback and answers; developing well-organized lectures, group work, or guided studies; directing readings, studies, and reviews; creating assessment tools; and providing summaries, active practice opportunities, and assignments. Underlying these responsibilities are the decisions that teachers need to make regarding what content will be dealt with, how content will be arranged into manageable and sensible steps, and which techniques of content transmission or presentation will be most efficacious for each step. The normative belief elemental to these emphases is that there exists a direct link between teaching responsibilities and the effects that cause learning.

Procedural Beliefs

Procedural beliefs inform the actions and intentions of teachers when they plan and execute content delivery to their students. Procedural beliefs will be discussed with regard to the actions and intentions that emerge from the routines, strategies, and techniques of execution advocated by those who employ a transmission perspective of teaching.

Rosenshine and Stevens (1986, p. 378) provide a general model comprising six functions or routines of effective instruction:

1. Review, check previous day's work (and reteach, if necessary)

2. Present new content/skills

3. Guided student practice (and check for understanding)

4. Feedback and correctives (and reteach, if necessary)

5. Independent student practice

6. Weekly and monthly reviews

This model clearly reflects the dominant relationship of teacher-to-content and links it to efficient content coverage. The routine focuses on manipulation of content and technique. Based on the percentage of correct answers and level of student understanding, the teacher decides when and if to continue or to reteach material. This implies that learning is effected by teacher authority over both content and technique and can be adapted to all learners. Moreover, it reflects the belief of transmission teaching that repetition—presenting, reviewing, applying—is central to knowledge and skill acquisition (of moving it from short-term to long-term memory) and therefore a key function of the teaching process.

Support for learners is discussed in terms of strategies to be employed by the teacher. These strategies are consistent with and elaborate on the above-mentioned routines of effective instruction. Rosenshine and Stevens (1986, pp. 378–379) note that when giving instructional support, the teacher would exercise the following strategies:

a. break the material into small steps in order to reduce confusion,

b. give the learner practice in each step before increasing complexity by adding another step,

c. provide for elaboration and enhancement in order to help the learner move the material from working memory into long-term memory, and

d. provide for additional practice and overlearning of basic material and skills so that the learners are fluent and automatic in using them.

Others describe the effective teacher as a blend of well-organized content deliverer and developer of positive rapport in students (Lowman, 1984) or as a strategist who combines instructional systems with positive reinforcement theory to shape appropriate student behavior (Redwine, 1989).

Both Lowman (1984) and Redwine (1989) emphasize the primacy of implementing strategies that include finding sources of objectives, formatting course outlines, writing course descriptions, interrelating content and objectives, designing relevant evaluations, and fulfilling course objectives through the use of various techniques such as discussions, readings, lectures, and inside/outside classroom assignments. Strategies for transmitting content and pacing of delivery are key to effective teaching. The significant focus placed on incorporating various strategies to transmit knowledge and skills indicates that much of what teachers actually do is done outside the classroom, in preparation for students. Learners play a secondary role; they are the recipients of the various intentional actions of teachers.

Thus, the epistemological assumption or belief that knowledge can be defined as objective is connected to procedural beliefs. Transmission teachers place great emphasis on routines, techniques, and strategies that demonstrate teacher control over subject matter and that show learning to be a function of how well or how logically the content material is organized and developed. The credibility of teachers then rests on their ability to productively and efficiently deliver the content. If this is done well, all learners will benefit.

SUMMARY

Effective transmission teaching is defined as teacher mastery over content combined with expertise at incorporating various teaching skills to deliver that content. Within institutional educational settings, effective transmission teaching is furthermore defined as delivering content efficiently—within the time constraints and other parameters set by the institution and individual program or course sponsors. As long as the lecture remains the main or only perceived manifestation of transmission teaching, the less likely it will be considered a viable teaching perspective and the less likely it can be effective. Creating a structure for content areas, breaking the structure into bite-sized pieces, organizing concepts and practical applications from simple to more complex, and delivering content using a variety of techniques—all combine to make an effective teaching practice and learning environment. Especially within institutional settings, where a myriad of forces converge to define teaching before the teacher actually enters the classroom, transmission teaching is a viable option.

REFERENCES

Apps, J. W. (1991). *Mastering the teaching of adults.* Malabar, FL: Krieger Publishing Co.

Brown, G., & Atkins, M. (1987). *Effective teaching in higher education.* London: Methuen.

Davis, B. G. (1993). *Tools for teaching.* San Francisco: Jossey-Bass.

Draves, W. A. (1984). *How to teach adults.* Manhattan, KS: Learning Resources Network.

Fenstermacher, G. D., & Soltis, J. F. (1986). *Approaches to teaching.* New York: Teachers College Press.

Fox, D. (1983). Personal theories of teaching. *Studies in higher education, 8*(2), 151–163.

Frye, N. (1980). The beginning of the word & on teaching literature. In N. Frye (Ed.), *On education* (pp. 9–21 & 109–137 respectively). Markham, ON: Fitzhenry & Whiteside.

Johnson, J. B. (1993). Beliefs and belief systems. Unpublished paper distributed in ADED 519 seminar, The University of British Columbia, Vancouver, Canada.

Lowman, J. (1984). *Mastering the techniques of teaching*. San Francisco: Jossey-Bass.

Pajares, M. F. (1992). Teachers' beliefs and educational research: Cleaning up a messy construct. *Review of Educational Research*, 62(3), 307–332.

Pratt, D. D. (1992). Conceptions of teaching. *Adult Education Quarterly*, 42(4), 203–220.

Pratt, D. D. (1994). Lecture notes for ADED 519, University of British Columbia.

Redwine, J. A. (1989). Professional teaching strategies. In D. Grieve (Ed.), *Teaching in college: A resource for college teachers* (Rev. ed., pp. 59–81). Cleveland: Info-Tec.

Rosenshine, B., & Stevens, R. (1986). Teaching functions. In M. C. Wittrock (Ed.), *Handbook of research on teaching* (3rd ed., pp. 376–391). New York: Macmillan.

Samuelowicz, K., & Bain, J. D. (1992). Conceptions of teaching held by academic teachers. *Higher Education*, 24, 93–111.

Schwandt, T. A. (1994). Constructivist, interpretivist approaches to human inquiry. In N. K. Denzin & Y. S. Lincoln (Eds.), *Handbook of qualitative research* (pp. 118-137). Thousand Oaks, CA: Sage Publications, Inc.

Shearon, R. W., & Tollefson, T. A. (1989). Community colleges. In S. B. Merriam & P. M. Cunningham (Eds.), *Handbook of adult and continuing education* (pp. 316–331). San Francisco: Jossey-Bass.

CHAPTER 5

THE APPRENTICESHIP PERSPECTIVE
Modelling Ways of Being

Janice Johnson and Daniel D. Pratt

While the transmission perspective may seem overwhelmingly familiar in education, by contrast, the Apprenticeship Perspective is so common outside formal education that it is nearly invisible as a way to explicitly teach and learn (Coy, 1989). When it is used explicitly in teaching, it is applied most often in the traditional sense—to teach procedures (tying a shoe, building a fire, taking blood). But it is also increasingly used in "intellectual apprenticeships" to develop master practitioners in disciplines and practices characterized by great complexity, multiple procedures, and dynamic environments (such as medicine, police work, and professional development).

Unfortunately, because this presentation about the Apprenticeship Perspective must necessarily use a book, this chapter has to violate the core tenet of apprenticeship: it must "tell you about" rather than "involve you within" an actual, physical context of practice. Try to bear this in mind as you find yourself reflecting on discussions here; unfortunately you will be attempting to grasp the difference between this perspective and the last while subject to a technology which favors transmission!

In order to explain the Apprenticeship Perspective from this rather ironic vantage point, two conceptual understandings are fundamental. First, it's crucial to identify how learning itself is understood within this perspective. How is learning created, developed, and manifested? Second, it's important to detail characteristics of actual practice. What are the noteworthy aspects of "mastery" in real contexts of practice? (Master is used here in a gender neutral sense, referring to a person who has acquired a thorough knowledge and skill in a particular area of practice.) Once you have a mental picture of these two conceptual foundations, it's useful to illustrate them in an example. In the first example, we hope the context is authentic and familiar enough to somewhat "pierce" the medium of text and engage you in a bit more visceral, and less abstract, understanding of apprenticeship.

However, to complete an understanding of this perspective, it is also important to trace a second example, of an intellectual rather than traditional apprenticeship. The context of this second example, as it is likely less familiar to you, will require a bit more theoretical discussion comparing the types of apprenticeships. The chapter will end with a summary of the key points about this perspective.

UNDERSTANDING LEARNING FROM AN APPRENTICESHIP PERSPECTIVE

Learning As Changing Schemas

When we enter a new world, whether traveling to a foreign country, or starting a new job, we are confronted with a buzzing, confusing environment filled with new and shifting patterns that don't make sense to us. To deal with our initial confusion we often impose our familiar world upon the new, and in doing so, misinterpret or oversimplify the situation.

For example, imagine a group of tourists that have just returned from 3 weeks of touring China. They were very likely shuttled about in an air-conditioned bus, ensconced in luxury hotels, taken to see the usual tourist attractions, and shown how China is making huge strides in the Four Modernizations, particularly on the economic front. From these experiences our imaginary tourists might have a very simple, romanticized picture of that complex country and its people. If this is their first visit, their understanding of China will likely not only be simplistic and romanticized, but interpreted through the ways in which they live their own lives. They will have placed a template of their own life over the landscape and people of China and from this extracted patterns and meanings that will form the basis for many stories about China. As they tell their stories over and over, their picture of China will become reified, that is, fixed and, consequently, resistant to change. The next time they return to China, or are confronted with a new experience about China, this simplified characterization will frame their understanding.

If they subsequently spend time in China, experiencing the people and the culture from a vantage point not framed by the tourist map, they would, very likely, gradually find new meanings and discover complex patterns that challenged their prior understanding. Eventually, they may even think differently about their own culture and identity. The same process occurs whether encountering a new city, strange customs, or a complicated set of procedures; once we find new patterns, our thinking changes fundamentally.

But what has changed? Cognitive psychologists say our *schemas* have changed, that is, the cognitive maps we build that help us organize and interpret the world. Schemas are the forms in which we summarize our general knowledge, beliefs, attitudes, and experience about people, places, events, objects, and ideas. When entering a new experience, or encountering a new piece of equipment, we project our existing schemas on the new situation, framing and interpreting it according to what we already know. We then use our schemas as mini-theories to predict how we should react in the new the situation.

Initially, we develop simple maps or schemas. Like a child's early drawings, our schemas are oversimplified and contain only the bare essentials. Indeed, they must be simple if we are to cope with the whirling complexity of most novel situations. Yet, as we gain experience our representations or schemas of the situation become more elaborate and more connected to other schemas in our heads. When this happens, our personal theories expand and increase our ability to handle related problems and situations with greater confidence.

Simplistic, individual schemas are like molecules that combine to form larger understandings. For example, a child may have an initial schema about food preparation that begins with simply making sandwiches for friends. As the child grows, and gains experience working alongside a parent, that schema may expand to include more people and a greater variety of food. Eventually, his or her knowledge of food preparation may include more complex schemas that require following recipes and even adjusting recipes to different size groups. Perhaps over time that knowledge of food preparation would develop into a larger schema of catering and involve much more complex coordination of special events, budgeting, settings, and even additional employees. As the person's knowledge of food preparation reached a further level of sophistication, he or she would have many related and complex schemas, each dependent on the others for their meaning and utility in the preparation of food.

Thus, schemas are the building blocks of our understanding. We start with simple schemas, gradually expanding, revising, and linking them with other schemas. With each use, the organization and the content of schemas evolves as we build more complex representations of our work, our relationships, and our knowledge of the world around us. Inevitably, through more and more experience, the process of elaborating, revising, and integrating schemas leads to more developed bodies of knowledge and expertise. Eventually, we have a complexly woven web of information and beliefs that guide our thinking and actions in a particular domain of practice or expertise.

It stands to reason, therefore, that a person with more experience, particularly if they critically reflect on that experience, would have a more complex, elaborate, and comprehensive set of schema than a novice (Brown et al., 1989; Sherman et al., 1987). For everyone, though, according to the psychologists, having schemas is fundamental. Rumelhart (1980, p. 37) puts it succintly:

> [schemas are] a kind of informal, private, unarticulated theory about the nature of events, objects, or situations that we face. The total set of schema[s] we have available for interpreting our world in a sense constitutes our private theory of the nature of reality.

Individual schemas, then, provide us with the first insight into how learning is understood within this perspective. However, an essential component of the Apprenticeship Perspective is the social and relational contexts within which schemas are constructed. Within the Apprenticeship Perspective, learning is understood as a blend of both a product and a process. The product is a change in the quality of our understanding or schemas. The process is the testing, building, revising, and integrating of schemas within contexts of application; the schema we take away from a learning episode, that is, our comprehension of something, is dependent upon the context within which we learned it. It is as if the new schema is textured, or given added meaning and signficance, by the the social circumstances within which it was learned. This is highly significant for effective education. The transfer of learning (i.e., the application of schemas in circumstances outside the classroom) is a serious problem for much of higher education. It isn't that learners don't comprehend what they study, but rather that their learning is incomplete; it is not textured or indexed with the nuances, complexities, and relationships that are a part of situations of application.

Within this perspective there is no separation of the process and the product. What is learned is intimately linked to where, when, how, and with whom it is learned. Thus, context and content, process and product, interact to form the concept of "situated learning."

Situated Learning

Although the phrase sounds new, the idea is not. Traditional apprenticeships have been based on this notion of learning in situations of application for centuries. Recently, the idea has been expanded to give us new insights into old problems, such as why people who fail high school math are able to calculate price savings and best-buy bargains at the grocery store, or why medical students who receive good grades on basic sciences must re-learn that same content for application in clinical settings, or why, as mentioned earlier, a woman with a third degree black belt in karate was unable to defend herself against rape.

Situated learning moves our focus from schemas (inside the heads of individuals) to the social contexts of participation and learning which are rich and complex with meaning. Within situated learning there is a reciprocity between individuals and social groups. Learners do build, revise, and integrate their schemas related to the tasks and relations of their work or communities; but, simultaneously, the community of people also changes. The knowledge, skills, and network of relationships being learned change as each learner leaves behind the yoke of apprenticeship and moves toward becoming a master practitioner; and, eventually, the very nature of a profession's work, or a family's traditions, or the larger community changes. Thus, a central idea embedded in situated learning is that the product of learning cannot be reduced to cognitive structures (schemas), but must acknowledge the larger changes in the social order and work of a community. As Hanks said in his introduction to Lave and Wenger's book (1991):

> The challenge, it would seem, is to rethink action in such a way that structure and process, mental representation and skillful execution, interpenetrate one another profoundly . . . The activity of understanding, in such a view, comes down to recognizing and implementing instances of structure, filling them in with an overlay of

situational particulars, and relating them to a "context" (which is in turn structured). [Learning is located] not in the acquisition of structure, but in the increased access of learners to participating roles in expert performances. (pp. 16–17)

Thus, schemas that result from situated learning are more than simple maps of a terrain or body of knowledge. They are richly textured webs of meaning that involve role, relationship, and legitimate participation in a community's work. The ultimate product of situated learning is knowledge that is embedded in, rather than extracted from, contexts of its application. It is, very often, knowledge that is hidden from view, or tacit, but absolutely key to intelligent action. It is the knowledge one needs to succeed. Unfortunately, it is very often the knowledge that is not explicitly taught, but essential to becoming a skillful practitioner. However, as Sternberg and Horvath (1995) point out, tacit knowledge is crucial to understanding expertise as it develops and as it operates in contexts of application and practice.

Research has shown that tacit knowledge generally (a) increases with experience on the job, (b) is unrelated to IQ, (c) predicts job performance better than does IQ, (d) provides a significant increment in prediction above that provided by traditional tests of intelligence, personality, and cognitive style, and (e) overlaps across field, though only partially. In a typical test of tacit knowledge, subjects are given a scenario relating to a situation they might encounter on the job and are asked to rate the quality of different courses of action as responses to the situation. Every study in this [their own] program of research—investigating the tacit knowledge of business executives, professors of psychology, sales people, and college students—has shown that tacit knowledge is important to expertise on the job. (p. 12)

Thus, a most important outcome in situated learning is tacit knowledge that results in a skillful practitioner. Skillful practitioners have an extensive body of organized and relevant content knowledge that is readily accessible; they are able to take on a variety of roles, anticipate what is feasibly going to occur within specific realms of practice, are able to function effectively in ways that go beyond present schemas, and are able to improvise new schemas based on changing circumstances. Much of that cannot be learned outside contexts of practice. None of that can be learned solely in classrooms. So, how is it learned?

Legitimate Peripheral Participation

This process of acquiring knowledge in the setting where it is applied comes about through a process called legitimate peripheral participation (Lave & Wenger, 1991). In this process, novices enter a community of practice (a workplace, institution, or association), and work alongside more seasoned practitioners, within roles which gradually become more complex; in this way, they acquire situated knowledge. According to Lave and Wenger (1991), this is a natural outcome to peripheral participation; through a process of absorbing, contributing, and reflecting, a novice gradually assumes (or is given) more legitimate influence and responsibility within the workplace or community. Their schemas, and their legitimate experience become of increasing value and trustworthiness in the larger situation of practice.

There are three key factors which aid in successful learning and progression toward mastery. Such a process must be *active*, not passive, *social*, cooperative, collaborative; and *authentic*, enculturated (Brown et al., 1989). Let's consider each of these aspects in turn.

How many of us have some kind of tool in our basements, workshops, sewing rooms, or gardening sheds that we cannot use? Perhaps we saw it advertised, and thought "Wow, that would be a good tool," and yet, when we got it home and tried it, it didn't quite work the way we thought it should. So there it sits, a mute reminder to us of something that might be useful, if we could ever figure out what to do with it. Yet, perhaps what we need to do is simply try using it again, or talk about it with others, or re-evaluate its original purpose. Often, the second or third time we use a tool its function becomes easier to grasp, because our understanding of the tool and the world in which we are using that tool grows, through our active investigations of it. In other words, our internal schemas may have developed, or our experience may have deepened, or, most likely, both have occurred. This is true not only for shiny metal objects in the workshop, but also for concepts that function as ideational tools (e.g., computer training in kindergarten, or block parent programs).

Social interactions also, obviously, affect our internal schemas about tools, but can also lead to a more refined understanding about the appropriate use of, and even the meaning of, particular tools. Thus, two professional communities may use an apparently similar tool, but the social process of negotiating distinct meaning and appropriate use of that tool will ultimately determine its application. For example, both teachers and counselors act as facilitators, but the meaning of their actions and the uses they have for the tool of facilitation differ noticeably.

Finally, the necessity for successful learning to involve authentic content and process means that they must reflect what ordinarily occurs within the culture—the accepted practices and customs of members of the community (Brown et al., 1989). Members of any culture, or community of practitioners, are connected by the tasks that they do and the beliefs that they hold (Geertz, 1983). The ordinary practices of a community are those that are socially constructed through negotiation among past and present members. They are therefore coherent, meaningful, and purposeful to those members, although they may not be so to nonmembers. For example, some orchardists thin their fruit, others do not. Yet all orchardists understand the purpose behind thinning. Nonorchardists often do not.

In sum, novices enter situations of practice, and engage in active, social, and authentic participation. As a result, they gradually acquire identities and perform in roles which are regarded as valuable and essential to the practice. For instance, over time, a medical student ceases to be only a medical student; she becomes a skilled interviewer, a lab technician, an assistant at surgery, etc. We know that this is accomplished through working alongside more experienced practitioners and peers, but what are other aspects of how this process works?

First, the authentic practice itself creates the curriculum for novices. Because legitimate peripheral participants have access to and can observe all aspects of practice, they develop a broad and evolving view of what constitutes the practice, how community members interact, and what there is to be learned. The "curriculum" unfolds as opportunities develop for learners to become engaged in practice, as for example, the way in which new university teachers have the opportunity to teach different classes to different groups of students at different levels of mastery.

Second, for novices to become full members of a community of practice, they require access to a wide range of activities, and to members of the community with differing levels of expertise. They also need access to information, technology, resources, and opportunities for participation. Different communities organize this access in different ways, with varying consequences. The way in which access is organized significantly affects how learners understand the importance and the relationships of the activities, members, and resources within and to the community. For example, bank manager trainees who are only given opportunities to work in a limited number of bank departments will develop a distorted view of the banking community.

Third, in becoming a full member of a community of practice, novices learn how and when to talk, and to be silent, as full participants do. They develop the ability to talk "within" a practice—the discourse of practice—rather than to talk "about" the practice from the outside. Talking within includes both exchanging information necessary to the activities of the practice, and telling stories about problematic and difficult situations of practice in order to aid reflection and decision making, and to signal membership. As novices are accepted by master practitioners, they begin to know that there is a field for their own mature practice. They thus develop a sense of the value of participation to the community and are motivated to learn as a function of their own increasing sense of identity (or identities) as community members.

Finally, as a function of chronology as well as situated practice, within any community of practice, novices ultimately become full participants, replacing those who were the full participants when the novices joined the community. Conflict exists in the ways in which novices and full participants establish and maintain identities, and generate competing viewpoints on the practice and its development over time. Power relations influence these conflicts, which are experienced and resolved through the interplay of differing viewpoints and common stakes within a shared everyday practice. As such, change is a fundamental and inevitable property of communities of practice.

Let us summarize the last few points. Although learning can be described as internalized schemas—which vary both between and within individuals given that they constantly change and evolve—learning is also inherently social and dynamic in nature. The social processes of negotiation, cooperation, and participation fundamentally affect (a) what is considered legitimate learning content, (b) understanding of appropriate use of that content, (c) identities of individual members of a community of practice, and (d) how that community of practice collectively renews itself. Further, successful learning is understood to be active, social, and authentic in nature. Thus, when we think about learning from this perspective, conceptual knowledge (knowing) and problem-framing and -solving skills (doing) are not seen as independent of the situations within which they are to be used. Rather, they are understood to be created and given meaning by the context and activities through which they are learned (Prestine & LeGrand, 1991).

The situation of authentic practice is thus, itself, the domain where learning both occurs and manifests. It changes as novices participate, make mistakes, learn, and contribute on their way to mastery, even as the nature of the practice iteself changes because of new participants and other external influences. In this perspective, true learning cannot occur soley within a classroom or solely by discourse; it demands actual physical engagement within a community. Given that, it's time to look more closely at what characterizes actual practice. What are the realities of situations of practice? What are the discernable traits of master practitioners?

MASTERY IN PRACTICE

Characteristics of Situations of Practice

For many years, educators and professionals have thought of situations of practice as collections of problems to be solved. Moreover, these collections were seen to contain well-defined problems which practitioners simply had to identify and subsequently address with the appropriate solution. Since problems were seen as primarily well defined, this process of identifying and applying solutions was not considered particularly problematic, given that practitioners had adequate conceptual knowledge, or tools.

However, recent studies have revealed that situations of practice are far more frequently ill-defined and problematic, and characterized by vagueness, uncertainty, and disorder (Schon, 1983). These difficult situations often have unique aspects or are unique events, for which there is no standard response. Further, they often include conflicts of values, goals, and interests. For example, in avalanche work, forecasters charged with the responsibility to avert highway avalanche hazards must deal with conflicting pressures to maintain the safety of members of the public, to maintain the safety of maintenance contractor staff, and to minimize interruptions to traffic (and thus the economic and emotional impacts of road closures). As with most situations of practice, it is seldom possible to meet all competing objectives simultaneously. In sum, situations of practice are not straightforward and uncomplicated. They contain few simple solutions, and often involve virtually "first-time" solutions arising from conflicting elements.

Characteristics of Master Practitioners

Master practitioners exist in a huge variety of disciplines, communities, workplaces, and situations. As mentioned earlier, master is used here in a gender neutral sense, to refer to a person who has acquired a thorough knowledge of and/or is especially skilled in a particular area of practice. In an attempt to identify some common characteristics across this diversity, Schon (1983) and Weinstein and Hamman (1994) identified the following criteria:

1. Master practitioners possess great amounts of knowledge in their areas of expertise, and are able to apply that knowledge in difficult practice settings.

2. Master practitioners have well-organized, readily accessible schemas which facilitate the acquisition of new information.

3. Master practitioners have well-developed repertoires of strategies for acquiring new knowledge, integrating and organizing their schemas, and applying their knowledge and skills in a variety of contexts. They are often distinguished by the complexity and sophistication of their schemas. Because they learn and apply their strategies in the contexts of particular practices, they make meaning in their application of these strategies in ways unique to those practices, whether they are university professors, electricians, or native elders.

4. Master practitioners have a mastery orientation to their areas of expertise. They are motivated to learn as part of the process of developing their identities in their communities of practice. They are not motivated to learn simply to reach some external performance goal or reward.

5. Master practitioners frequently display a tacit "knowing-in-practice," a phenomenon with three distinct properties. Masters appear to be able to access actions, recognitions, and judgements spontaneously during their performance of duty. Second, they are often unaware of having learned to do these things, and simply find themselves doing them. And finally, although some masters were once aware and others were never aware of the understandings which were subsequently internalized in "feeling for the stuff of action," all masters are usually unable to describe the knowing which their actions reveal.

Thus, masters not only act from extensive knowledge and elaborately textured schemas, they are also able to adapt successfully to unusual and problematic situations of practice. That is, they can transcend the limits of a single situational context and bring to practice a tacit knowing in new situations. Some of this may be related to how masters remember their knowledge. When it accretes slowly, over multiple applications, it appears that masters remember in an indexed way, which allows for an effective cross-referencing of concepts, data, and situational subtleties.

PUTTING THESE CONCEPTUAL FOUNDATIONS TOGETHER

The realities of situations of practice, added to ideas about learning in this perspective, provide some general insights into what is expected of novices working to develop identities as skilled and knowledgeable practitioners. While doing this, they will often be learning within situations, characterized by complexity, uncertainty, instability, uniqueness, and value conflict. Such situations also have few simple solutions.

Master practitioners are those who possess significant, well-organized and accessible schemas and skills in their areas of expertise. They have well-developed repertoires of strategies for acquiring, integrating and applying their knowledge and skills in practice. They are motivated to develop their knowledge and skills through their participation in, and sense of belonging to, a community of practice. They frequently display a tacit knowing-in-practice—knowledge and understanding of actions which they may not be able to articulate.

Communities of practice come into existence, change, and reproduce themselves through the practice and interrelationships of their members. Conflicts within such communties are negotiated in the context of differing viewpoints, common stakes, and shared everyday experience. Novices are motivated to learn through their increasing participation in the curriculum of the authentic practice itself. The ways in which communities organize access to activities, members, information, technology, resources, and opportunities for participation can enhance or hinder the learning of novices. Eventually, novices' participation results in mastering multiple identities useful to, and valued by, the community, as well as a facility for engaging with the "discourse" of the practice.

As mentioned right at the outset of this chapter, all of us have countless examples of the whole gestalt of the Apprenticeship Perspective, as both teachers and learners. To bring all the foregoing theory and discussion into focus, let's highlight all their elements in two situations of practice—one so enmeshed in daily life as to be nearly invisible as a process, and one in an explictly educational forum. We extend thanks to Adrienne Burk for her help in articulating the first example.

An Everday Example

These days, it's easy to imagine that nearly every child, and certainly virtually every child with urban experience in North America, has some experience with cars. Perhaps it starts as early as the first ride home from the hospital, or across a landscape to the grandparents' house. There is sensation, colour, sound, the beginnings of a schema about movement, and soon, even of a vehicle. Perhaps the child is given a toy car, and, ignorantly leaving it in the dog dish or on the bottom stair, is sternly informed that cars belong on roads, or at least in particular places. The schema spirals up one level of sophistication. Let us suppose the child grows a little, and begins to identify cars in books, in visual media, from sounds on the radio, and even begins to differentiate between Dad's and the neighbor's car.

This child begins to travel as a matter of course—whether by bus, snow- mobile, or Jaguar—and a notion of traffic develops. Mom lets the child insert the car keys; Dad talks through the various ways of watching traffic flow. Perhaps the child rests her hand on the gear lever while a parent shifts, perhaps another cranes his little neck outside the window to help an adult check the curb.

Years pass. Every automotive errand, incident, or accident moderates and elaborates the child's schema about cars, and, via peripheral participation, adds to the child's notions of the situation of practice, e.g., driving a car. The day arrives, and the child decides no longer to be a novice, but a master; she signs up for lessons at a driving school. What happens? Does the instructor take her onto a spaghetti junction of highways at night in the rain?

No. He sits alongside her, in a shut-off car with dual steering wheels and brake systems, and talks to her for several minutes. He talks about assumptions, ground rules, rhythms to driving. He then drives her to a parking lot, a deserted road, the quietest street in town, and turns off the motor again. He asks her to check her mirrors, adjust her seat, notice the way she is holding the steering wheel. Finally, he asks her turn the key in the ignition, feel the proper level of idle, and drive to that little shed 300 yards ahead, at a specific speed, and stop. What's he doing?

The instructor is beginning by offering the novice a simple, skeletal, conceptual map. The elements in it are authentically weighted (e.g., the dimensions of the real community of practice are acknowledged by the initial talk, as well as the drive through traffic to the practice area), but the novice's first, focused task is easy, and straightforward, and emphasizes successful completion. Such a task serves to increase the novice's sense of confidence, and a sense of actively joining an authentic practice community. She is situated, here, not as an observer, but as a participant.

Gradually, with each lesson, each successful completion of tasks, complexity is added, and the novice's learning becomes textured and remembered in an indexed way within her schema about driving so that it is accessible for increasingly less controlled driving situations. During this time, the instructor parallels, coaches, and protects the novice by operating alongside (and potentially controlling) the driving situations in the event of too much complexity. As the novice increases in mastery, she begins to think of herself less as a "student driver" and more a "driver". She learns the highway code, and passes the driver's test first time.

With practice, and over time, she becomes a commuter. In a few years, maybe she's a trucker, a highway cop, or maybe she's switched to being a motorcyclist or a van driver. A decade after that, she finds herself amazed to be where she never imagined she would be—a teacher sitting alongside her teenage son in a parking lot in an idling car telling him to check his mirrors, adjust his seat, and drive to that little shed 300 yards away, and stop. Our novice has become a master. Now, she effortlessly and unconciously adjusts to changes in weather, to weight and length of rental vehicles, to unfamiliar roads, tight parking spaces, speed limits, and habits of her fellow drivers. She knows how to anticipate hazards and when to start talking about them. Since she started to drive, all sorts of practices have changed, and traffic has altered dramatically; all of this she takes in stride. No longer novice, now she models for and influences those who are the new novices; she, together with the drivers around her, is evidence that the community of drivers has transformed.

TRADITIONAL APPRENTICESHIPS

This example embodies a traditional apprenticeship experience— learning a procedure and gradually developing mastery. In it, learners and teachers go through several key stages, most of which are self-evident by their names: observation, modelling, scaffolding, fading, and coaching.

Observation, both of the master demonstrating tasks and of other apprentices and practitioners with differing levels of proficiency, helps novices develop an overall conceptual model of the practice and its many skills. This provides novices with an advanced organizer for their initial attempts at performing skills. It also provides an interpretive structure to help learners make sense of the feedback and suggestions they receive from the master during interactive coaching sessions (Collins et al., 1991; Schon, 1983). In addition, it provides learners with an internalized guide or standard for use when they later work more independently. Of course, observation includes the social context in which the learning occurs. Seeing various models of expertise-in-use against which to measure their growing understanding, novices understand that there may be multiple ways of carrying out a task. Furthermore, it becomes obvious that knowledge and expertise reside within the organization of the community of practice, and is not embodied solely within any one individual. Finally, as novices observe learners with varying degrees of skill, they also come to see learning as an incremental process.

Modelling occurs when the learners observe the master demonstrating how to perform different tasks, often explicitly showing learners what to do. The learners then model their efforts on those of the master.

Scaffolding is the support the master provides to learners as they work on a task. As they begin, this may entail doing much of the task for them; as they become more adept, the master may provide only occasional hints. Slowly removing the support, and encouraging learners to take more and more responsibility for the task, is known as *fading.*

Coaching occurs throughout the apprenticeship, and consists of overseeing the students' learning. It may include choosing tasks, scaffolding and fading, evaluating work and diagnosing problems, challenging and encouraging, working on particular weaknesses, and providing feedback.

INTELLECTUAL OR COGNITIVE APPRENTICESHIP

By contrast, when an intellectual or cognitive apprenticeship is called for, a slightly different relationship must emerge between master and learner. The focus for this type of apprenticeship is on cognitive, or intellectual tasks, which are less easily observable than the tasks of traditional apprenticeship. This approach differs from traditional apprenticeship in three ways.

First, because of the kinds of tasks involved, teachers must expressly articulate their thinking to learners in order to make it visible to them, and learners' thinking must also be made visible to teachers. This means that both teachers and learners must say what they are thinking during their demonstrations of the application of knowledge and skills. Such explicitness ensures that learners can observe and practice the relevant thinking processes, and that teachers and other learners can provide useful help.

Second, the context for these kinds of tasks—the community of practice—is often not as immediately apparent as it is in traditional apprenticeships. Because of this, teachers must explicitly place the tasks in contexts that make sense to the learners, and for which they can see some value. They must help learners answer the questions "What's in it for me? Why should I learn this? How will I ever be able to use this knowledge?"

Third, the challenge for teachers is to help novices learn when a knowledgeable skill is and is not applicable across contexts—to help them generalize the skill. This requires that teachers help them identify when to use existing knowledge in new situations.

As with the traditional apprenticeship model, cognitive apprenticeship consists of five phases, with distinctive roles for the teachers (models) and the learners (see Figure 5.1). These phases include modelling, approximating, fading, self-directed learning, and generalizing.

Remember how many masters show tacit knowing in practice, but neither know how they learned nor how to articulate it? All of us have run into teachers who cannot easily bring us into their own understanding of practice. For our second example, let's take a novice professor, newly appointed to a university. If we apply the key features of this

	Role of Learner	Role of Teacher	Key Concepts
Phase I Modelling	Observe performance of total activity, not merely the individual steps. Develop a mental model (schema) of what the real thing looks like.	Model real-life handling of complex, ill-defined and/or risky problem of practice that learner wants to perform satisfactorily.	• *articulation* • *subject specific heuristics* • *situated knowledge* • *schema*
		States aloud the essence of the activity. Includes tricks of the trade and relevant shortcuts.	
Phase II Approximating	Approximate doing the real thing in protected situations and articulate its essence.	Provide coaching to the learner. Provide support when needed.	• *scaffolding*
	Reflect on the teacher's performance. Use self-monitoring and self-correction.		• *coaching*
Phase III Fading	Continue to approximate the real thing, operating in more complex, risky, and/or ill-defined situations. Work individually or in groups.	Decrease coaching and scaffolding.	• *fading*
Phase IV Self-directed Learning	Practice doing the real thing on his/her own, amending as necessary. Do so within specified limits acceptable to profession and society.	Provide assistance only when requested.	• *self-directed learning*
Phase V Generalizing	Discuss the generalizability of what has been learned to similar ill-defined, risky, or complex problems	Discuss the generalizability of what has been learned to similar ill-defined, risky, or complex problems.	• *generalizability*

(Adapted from Farmer, 1992)

Figure 5.1 Cognitive Apprenticeship for Adults

chapter, perhaps we can design an ideal cognitive apprenticeship to help our novice professor become a "master" professor.

Example Two: An Emerging Master at University

These days, master practitioners at universities have multiple responsibilities and identities: researcher, colleague, supervisor, teacher, writer, committee member, grantswriter, administrator, examiner, and, to some extent, counselor. Perhaps our novice professor brings in what we might think of as fairly sophisticated schemas about these roles and responsibilities; after all, the entry criteria to be hired would mean he would have already spent years in an academic environment, doing many of the tasks associated with these various roles.

But therein lies the rub. Most of his exposure to the university environment has been as a student; it is of necessity "student-centric" rather than "faculty-centric". Without experience, it couldn't really be otherwise. Consider our novice sitting in his first meeting about grantswriting in his department. He, quite helpfully and with enthusiasm, chirps up about what he knows to be a successful funding strategy—at least it resulted in his successful funding for his doctoral research, and he knows it is a useful and effective prototype application. Through discussion, the inappropriateness of this approach (his schema) becomes blindingly clear. Our novice has, before, sought funding only for himself, has operated within the guidelines of a single research project (and therefore a single research budget), and has justified his research only to those panels interested in single, one-off research projects. At issue here is a multiyear funding strategy involving the department, multiple colleagues, staff support, graduate assistants, and a certain overlap with similar research nationally. One way for him to learn that his schema is insufficiently elaborate is simply to receive a rejection. But, in a consciously designed apprenticeship, he would be exposed to and participate in a gradually more complex set of roles and patterns of discourse, within the realities of practice.

Perhaps, before he ever attended such a meeting, he was required to attend an orientation lecture about these matters, or taken to one side by a mentor who discussed in some depth earlier examples of successful and rejected applications. Perhaps he accompanied a more seasoned professor on interviews of the similar research, to gain a sense of how his university's project differed. Or, on the committee, he would be asked, not to head the enterprise, but to collect data or write first drafts for certain sections of the application, to be reviewed by a colleague, and then by the entire committee. No matter the actual form of the participation, all of these would reflect the principles of engaging the novice in active, social, and authentic practice. They all offer a chance for the novice to observe and model after masters, and to reflect and explore, to engage in approximating and self-directing their own learning, before attempting, with help (scaffolding, coaching), to work toward generalizing or assuming knowledge-in-practice.

It's easy to imagine this for other professorial roles as well. Before a novice professor could supervise a doctoral candidate, for instance, she might have to serve as a member of several committees, each time taking an increasingly more responsible role. Or, before another could lead a high-profile research project, he might work first on writing up the results of the last one as a junior member of the research team. Before a third counseled a student about switching from one department to another, she would have a frank and careful discussion about the implications with her department head, more seasoned colleagues, and perhaps the registrar.

In each case, the intent would be to create a forum for articulate discussion and authentic participation in the realities of practice from within the community of practice, not from just one single point of view. Only from such active involvement, and layered and cumulative experience does the novice move toward mastery; only then is there a basis for schemas to become a web of textured, indexed information that emerges effortlessly to help generalize and effectively navigate even the most bewildering situations of practice.

SUMMARY

The Apprenticeship Perspective is around us in countless examples—in families teaching tasks and social norms to their children, and in training in trades and many professions. Still, it is useful to remember that apprenticeship is not an invisible phenomenon. It has key elements: a particular way of viewing learning, specific roles and strategies for teachers and learners, and clear stages of development, whether for traditional or cognitive apprenticeships. But mostly, it's important to remember that in this perspective, one cannot learn from afar. Instead, one learns amid the engagement of participating in the authentic, dynamic, and unique swirl of genuine practice. Or, as one research subject put it:

> What do you do with knowledge? You don't stick it in a computer and leave it there; that's not knowledge, that's storage, right? You plug it out there somewhere and you use it, right? And if you teach your students that that's what we want you to do is store it, I mean it's a pointless exercise, and they know that, right? (Kathryn, personal communication, February, 1992)

REFERENCES

Berliner, D. C. (1986). In pursuit of the expert pedagogue. *Educational Researcher, 15*(7), 5–13.

Brown, J. S., Collins, A., & Duguid, P. (1989). Situated cognition and the culture of Cambridge, MA: Cambridge University Press.

Collins, A., Brown, J. S., & Holum, A. (1991). Cognitive apprenticeship: Making thinking visible. *American Educator: The Professional Journal of the American Federation of Teachers, 15*(3), 6–11, 38–46.

Coy, M. W. (1989). *Apprenticeship: From theory to method and back again.* Albany, NY: State University of New York Press.

Farmer, J. A., Jr. (1992, November). *Cognitive apprenticeship.* Paper presented at the Annual Conference of the Commission of Professors of Adult Education, Anaheim, CA.

Geertz, C. (1983). *Local knowledge.* New York: Basic Books.

Kagan, D. M. (1988). Teaching as clinical problem solving: A critical examination of the analogy and its implications. *Review of Educational Research, 58*(4), 482–505.

Lave, J., & Wenger, E. (1991). *Situated learning: Legitimate peripheral participation.* learning. *Educational Researcher, 18*(1), 32–42.

Prestine, N. A., & LeGrand, B. F. (1991). Cognitive learning theory and the preparation of educational administrators: Implications for practice and policy. *Educational Administration Quarterly, 27*(1), 61–89.

Rumelhart, D. E. (1980). Schemata: The building blocks of cognition. In R. J. Spiro, B. C. Bruce, & W. F. Brewer (Eds.), *Theoretical issues in reading comprehension* (pp. 33–58). Hillsdale, NJ: Lawrence Erlbaum.

Schon, D. A. (1983). *The reflective practitioner: How professionals think in action*. New York: Basic Books.

Sherman, T. M., Armistead, L. P., Fowler, F., Barksdale, M. A., & Reif, G. (1987). The quest for excellence in college teaching. *Journal of Higher Education, 48*(1), 66–84.

Shulman, L. S. (1986). Those who understand: Knowledge growth in teaching. *Educational Researcher, 15*(2), 4–14.

Shulman, L. S. (1987). Knowledge and teaching: Foundations of the new reform. *Harvard Educational Review, 57*(1), 1–22.

Sternberg, R. J., & Horvath, J. A. (1995). A prototype view of expert teaching. *Educational Researcher, 24*(6), 9–17.

Weinstein, C. E., & Hamman, D. (1994). Acquiring expertise in specific content areas: Implications for teaching novices. *Journal of Staff, Program and Organizational Development, 12*(1), 57–60.

CHAPTER 6

THE DEVELOPMENTAL PERSPECTIVE
Cultivating Ways of Thinking

Ric Arseneau and Dirk Rodenburg

INTRODUCTION

Ric: Before getting into medical school I took a course in comparative vertebrate anatomy. I found the course difficult to understand and overloaded with facts. In addition to my disinterest in the course, I was suffering from "mark anxiety"—from the fear of not getting into medical school. I tried to understand the material but was not rewarded for comprehension. Extra reading outside of class notes was actually detrimental to my grade. The teacher seemed to give a mixed message. Although he said he wanted us to understand and be able to compare and apply what we knew, he actually rewarded us for the reproduction of his own ideas. In fact, word for word reproduction from class notes was the most valued. As the final exam approached I realized I needed an A+ to get an overall A average. Because of time constraints and the competing demands of other exams, I decided to rehearse and memorize the lecture notes for the semester without any attention to understanding. I knew what would be rewarded: the reproduction of well-rehearsed answers. This strategy resulted in a mark of 90%—my best mark to date for the course.

Dirk: For one of my graduate level statistics exams, a question focused on calculating interval ranges for a sample of scores. The task itself was relatively mechanistic, and required some simple procedural steps and calculations. I wanted to accompany my calculations

105

with an explanation of my reasoning for each step; it seemed this would demonstrate my conceptual basis for solving the problem. To me, the ultimate accuracy of my calculations was of secondary importance, since virtually all statistical calculations are processed by computer. What was most important, I felt sure, was to demonstrate an ability to interpret an analysis. Therefore, I spent a considerable amount of time making sure that each step was accompanied by a clearly defined and written rationale linked within a coherent flow of reasoning. When I received my exam back, however, my written rationale was completely ignored. Instead, I was marked completely and exclusively, on the accuracy of my answer (which had, indeed, involved an error in calculation).

How much learning occurred in the examples above? Did the teachers believe learning had occurred? What does Ric's excellent grade and Dirk's poor grade reflect in each case? What does it mean for learning to occur? What is the role of understanding in learning? What kinds of evidence should teachers seek and accept as tangible proof of understanding? What should teachers be trying to accomplish in their teaching? What is the relationship between teaching and learning?

Seriously consider these questions rather than gloss over them. They don't have right answers, nor do we propose to provide you with any. Your answers to these questions can, however, provide you with insight into your personal theories of teaching and learning.

Our practice as teachers is informed and guided by personal theories (Rando & Menges, 1991). These theories, however, are implicit in that they are outside our usual awareness; they are assumptions that we take for granted. Insight into your personal theories will help uncover the rationale for much of your reflexive (cf., reflective) behavior as a teacher. Personal theories allow you to make sense of your teaching environment and to deal with problematic situations. Further, they are the viewpoint from which you interpret formal theories of teaching and learning. As you read this chapter (and the others in this book), you should continuously ask yourself, "Is this in keeping with what I believe?"

There is a problem, however, with trying to uncover and make explicit personal theories of teaching and learning. Often, we don't "practice what we preach"; there are discrepancies between our stated beliefs and intentions on the one hand, and the way we behave on the other. Our "espoused theories" are out of keeping with our "theories-in-practice"

(Argyris & Schon, 1978, cited in Ramsden, 1988). Espoused theories are those values and strategies we proclaim, whereas theories-in-practice represent values and strategies which inform our actions, of which we are largely unaware and over which we have little control (p. 257). Therefore, while reading this chapter, you should also consider to what extent what you say is consistent with how you behave.

Go back to the examples above. Can you infer both teachers' espoused theories? What evidence do you have of their theory-in-practice? Do you suppose they are aware of the discordance? The discordance between espoused theory and theory-in-practice is a common problem in higher education. For example, the concept of excellence, and the goals for teaching and learning usually include variations on the following themes (Ramsden, 1992):

- To teach students to analyze ideas or issues critically
- To develop students' intellectual/thinking skills
- To teach students to comprehend principles or generalizations.

Yet, our experiences in the examples above are likely more in keeping with the usual experience of learners. Several studies (Ramsden, 1992; Dahlgren, 1984) seriously question the effectiveness of higher education and conclude that:

- Many students are accomplished at complex routine skills including problem-solving algorithms.
- Many students have amassed large volumes of detailed knowledge.
- Many students are able to reproduce large quantities of factual information on demand.
- Many are able to pass examinations.
- But many are *unable* to show that they understand what they have learned, when asked simple yet searching questions that test their grasp of content. They continue to profess misconceptions of important concepts; their application of their knowledge to new problems is often weak; their skills in working jointly to solve problems are frequently inadequate.

Ramsden (1988) cites one particularly striking example in which 80–90% of U.S. college students were unable to explain concepts from ninth grade algebra despite being able to manipulate the symbols and pass behavioral objectives. They were unable to demonstrate that they understood. This example illustrates the central theme of the Developmental Perspective: *learning has occurred only when learners are able to demonstrate understanding.* Therefore, teaching from this perspective has to do with facilitating the learner's intellectual development (i.e., *development* of the intellect). The goal, then, is to close the gap between teachers' espoused theory and theory-in-practice by challenging learners to think critically, to solve problems, and to understand for themselves.

This chapter, as well as the others in this book, reflects a particular orientation toward the theory and practice of teaching adults. Not only does it provide a set of beliefs and intentions to guide specific instructional techniques, it also describes an educational philosophy consistent with our practical and theoretical understanding of cognition and learning. The Developmental Perspective parallels an emerging theoretical perspective of learning and knowing termed constructivism (e.g., Candy, 1991). The constructivist perspective is consistent with a lot of current philosophical and neurophysiological views of brain function (e.g., Anderson, 1992).

It is worth emphasizing that the Developmental Perspective represents a set of beliefs as opposed to a set of teaching behaviors. In other words, teaching is not merely the application of specific rules in specific situations. Teaching is the visible expression of an underlying set of beliefs a teacher brings to the learning environment—beliefs that help the teacher to better navigate the murky waters of practice. Therefore, the degree to which your practice reflects a particular teaching perspective in this book is a matter of the degree to which your personal theories resonate with the set of assumptions belonging to a particular perspective. Recall that most of us operate from more than one perspective. We hope to persuade you that operating from the Developmental Perspective is important in bringing about understanding. Even if your practice is primarily informed by one of the other perspectives in this book, we believe that having the Developmental Perspective operate in the background will improve your teaching.

The remainder of this chapter is divided into four main sections: key ideas, developmental principles, bridging knowledge, and examples from practice. We will begin by presenting two key ideas underlying the Developmental Perspective. The main concepts underlying the Developmental Perspective will be presented as a set of seven "Developmental Teaching Principles." This will be followed by a discussion of the "special knowledge" required to teach from this perspective. Finally, we will provide you with examples of developmental teaching from our own practices and from the literature.

KEY IDEAS

Before embarking on the main discussion of the chapter, it is important to consider two key ideas underlying the Developmental Perspective: (1) How we come to understand something, and (2) The relationship between teaching and learning.

How We Come to Understand

Have you ever wondered how a child comes to learn and understand the concept of "dog?" The child may notice, or the parents may point to a dog and say "dog." What the child sees and attends to will depend on that particular child. Does the child notice the size, the color, short ears, long ears, pointed ears, straight tail, curly tail, etc.? What is it that the child understands when the parents say "dog"? On another occasion, the child may see a cat and say "dog." The parents will correct the child and say, "No . . . Cat." The child must now take her concept of dog and change its internal representation so that it more closely matches that of her parents. With time and interaction with her parents, the child will develop a very good understanding of what a dog is (i.e., an accurate and appropriate internal representation of the concept "dog").

Obviously, the concept of dog was not transferred from the parents to the child. The child had to construct an internal representation of the concept. She used the concept to interpret (i.e., construe) and make sense of new situations (e.g., mistaking a cat for a dog). By interacting with her parents, she constructed increasingly more sophisticated and more accurate internal representations of the concept (e.g., not all small furry animals are dogs). She developed better conceptions (i.e., parents' preferred conception).

Conceptual understanding then, has to do with the dual acts of constructing and construing. Internal models are constructed and used to construe (i.e., interpret) new situations. Testing one's constructions with those of others allows us to reach a common understanding. However, given the personal manner in which internal representations are constructed, all constructions are necessarily idiosyncratic; we all have a different understanding of the same concept. Our concepts may overlap sufficiently with those of others so that we can understand and communicate with each other.

The concept of "dog" is relatively unproblematic; we can all agree on what a dog is. However, higher levels of abstraction are needed to understand concepts such as justice, beauty, and love. Each one of us understands these concepts differently based on our history with the concept. For instance, what does the word "mother" bring to mind? How might it differ in the following situations? What if you were adopted? What if you were an orphan? What if you were abused? The possibilities are endless, as are the subtle and not-so-subtle difference that each one of us carries for the concept of mother.

Although, personal constructions are idiosyncratic, there may be sufficient overlap among individual constructions within a group for agreement and understanding to occur (i.e., social constructions). For instance, the concept of "healthy looking" is a social construction. There is no such thing as healthy looking; the concept simply represents a more or less agreed-upon definition by a specific group. Considering a lean muscular woman as fit and healthy looking is a social construction of a 1990s western society. The same outward look may have a totally different meaning to a different social group or at a different time. Would this lean and muscular woman evoke the idea of healthy looking in the 1800s? Therefore, despite their idiosyncratic nature, personal constructions may overlap sufficiently for a common meaning to occur. However, common meaning may differ for different groups or at different times.

In summary, understanding comes from the personal construction of internal representations of concepts. Constructions are used to construe new situations. The iterative acts of constructing and construing allow us to refine our understanding of a concept. Further, dialogue between individuals allows the development and sharing of common meaning for some concepts (i.e., social constructions). However, social constructions are necessarily constructions and do not represent an external reality, but simply an internal representation of reality. For a given group, some constructions may be more acceptable or correct.

The Relationship Between Teaching and Learning

The relationship between teaching and learning was called into question by a cartoon in which a boy told his friend that he had taught his dog how to whistle. With his ear up to the dog's face, the friend said, "I don't hear him whistling." The boy replied, "I said I taught him. I didn't say he learned it." (Whitman, 1990)

The less than direct relationship between teaching and learning is obvious but often forgotten. It is beyond the scope of this chapter to provide a detailed discussion of this relationship. Our goal is to challenge a taken for granted assumption held by many individuals: that teaching necessarily results in learning. Given that this is a book on teaching, it is important that you not lose sight of the indirect relationship between teaching and learning. You will need to ask yourself what other forces have a positive (or negative) impact on learning. Our view of the relationship between teaching and learning will become obvious as the ideas in this chapter are developed.

DEVELOPMENTAL TEACHING PRINCIPLES

Consider the following anecdote:

> *Ric: I recently had the opportunity to supervise a junior colleague during his first clinical teaching assignment. After observing one of his clinical teaching sessions, I asked him to comment on what he thought the students learned. He was caught somewhat off guard and replied, "I think I did some good teaching, but I've actually never thought, have the students done good learning?"*

Teaching from the Developmental Perspective is Machiavellian: "the ends justify the means." Therefore teaching from this perspective has more to do with good *learning* than with good *teaching*. The focus, then, is on the development of learners' thinking, reasoning, and judgement rather than on specific teaching performances. There is no one right way to teach, only better ways depending on the content, the context, the learners, and the teacher. Therefore, this chapter will focus on the beliefs and intentions that inform teaching from a Developmental Perspective in the hopes that individual teachers will creatively interpret these into teaching actions that work for them. In another section we will provide examples from our own practices to illustrate some of the principles of developmental teaching. In reading this chapter, it might be helpful for you to consider your own teaching. Note any similarities and differences paying particular attention to your underlying beliefs and intentions as a teacher. If you have never taught, read this chapter from the learner's perspective.

We believe the best way to understand this perspective is experientially. The following seven principles and discussions will highlight the Developmental Perspective. These seven Developmental Teaching

Principles are based largely on the works of Ramsden (1988), Marton, Hounsell, & Entwistle (1984), on student learning, and on the work of Schmidt (1993) on the principles of cognitive learning.

Principle 1:   Prior knowledge is key to learning.

Principle 2:   Prior knowledge must be activated.

Principle 3:   Learners must be actively involved in constructing personal meaning (i.e., understanding) — the links are more important than the elements.

Principle 4:   Making more, and stronger, links requires time.

Principle 5:   Context provides important cues for storing and retrieving information.

Principle 6:   A. Intrinsic motivation is associated with deep approaches to learning.
B. Extrinsic motivation and anxiety are associated with surface approaches to learning.

Principle 7:   Teaching should be geared toward making the teacher increasingly unnecessary: that means, the development of learner autonomy as well as the intellect.

Principle 1

Read the following paragraph as though you were preparing for a test.

Simple Malfunctions and their Remedies: Air in the fuel system.

The fuel injection system consists of the fuel tank, fuel feed pump, fuel filter, fuel injection pump, injection line, and fuel injection valve. If air enters any part of the system, with the exception of the fuel tank, fuel will not be injected into the cylinders. Check the fuel injection "sound" in the following manner: (1) Pull out the knob for engine warp-up and place the control lever in the "half speed" position; (2) Open the delivery cock of the fuel tank; (3) Loosen the fuel strainer air-bleed bolt; (4) Move the priming lever of the fuel feed pump up and down. All the air has been bled out of the fuel line when only fuel flows out. After bleeding, retighten the bolt; (5) To "Bleed Air" from the fuel line, loosen the air venting bolt on the fuel injection pump and move the priming lever up and down until all the air bubbles out.

How well would you do on the test? Why? Unless you are a marine diesel mechanic, you probably don't understand the information. Given enough time to rehearse, you could commit the short passage to memory. But how long would you remember? What if you were asked to provide an explanation, or worse, asked to carry out the steps?

Principle 1:   Prior knowledge is key to learning.

Prior knowledge is the most important determinant of new learning. You couldn't make sense of the above information because you had no prior knowledge in this area. You couldn't understand because you couldn't connect it to something you already knew. Prior knowledge is the foundation on which new knowledge is constructed; new knowledge is built from (or onto) existing conceptions (prior knowledge).

Learners always have some relevant prior knowledge. It is your role as a teacher to access the right starting point for your learners. Make it real. Start with something they know. Stay within their "zone of proximal development" (Vygotsky, 1978): not too easy, not too abstract.

There is a direct relationship between the amount of learners' prior knowledge and the amount learners can learn. The less they know about something, the less they can take in. Paradoxically, as teachers we often try to present the most to those with little prior understanding.

Implications for teaching:

- Start with the learner.
- Teaching requires an understanding of the range of learners' prior conceptions (and misconceptions).
- It is the teacher's responsibility to adjust the content to the learners' prior understanding of it.
- For learners in an unfamiliar content area: "less is more."

Principle 2

Read the following paragraph as though you were preparing for a test.

Two is easier than three, but one is easiest. Common sense is the most important asset. Power struggles and confrontation should be kept to a minimum. Arts and crafts can provide entertainment. Don't forget snacks with TV. Keep important phone numbers handy. Money can be saved for college.

How well would you do on the test? Likely better than in the example from principle 1. Now, reread the paragraph, keeping in mind its title: Babysitting. This example shows that prior knowledge is a necessary but not sufficient condition to learning; it must be activated (Schmidt, 1993).

Principle 2:   Prior knowledge must be activated.

As a teacher, it isn't enough to only have an idea of where your learners are and to start from there. First of all, your estimation may be wrong; you may be outside their zone of proximal development (i.e., too advanced or not advanced enough). Second, even if you are right, what your learners already know may not be at the front of their mind ready for use; prior knowledge needs to be activated to be most useful.

It has been suggested that the best starting point is common sense and everyday experiences—remember, learners always have some relevant prior knowledge—and to progress to abstraction, then back again to the application of theory in practice (Ramsden, 1992). Consider the following example:

Ric: Medical students are often so caught up in "thinking medicine" that they block out their common everyday experiences.

Teacher: How long does it take for someone to excrete a free water load?

Students: Puzzled look. No response.

Teacher: Oh, come on (jokingly), you all know this . . . If you go to the movies and buy a super jumbo 10 gallon drink, what are the chances that you'll sit through the movie without having to go to the washroom?

Student 1: Not long, maybe an hour or so?

Teacher: How full does your bladder have to be before you feel you have to go?

Student 2: I see, it must start being excreted almost immediately; it just takes time for the bladder to fill before you get the sensation to go.

Teacher: If a patient is receiving too much free water IV (intravenous), what should happen?

> *Student 1*: *The patient should start excreting it almost immediately.*
>
> *Teacher*: *Exactly . . . you'd expect the same "Movie Theatre Phenomenon," unless there is something wrong. . . .*

In the case above, the medical students had useful prior knowledge but couldn't use it. A simple question from an everyday experience activated that prior knowledge and allowed them to understand. The case also illustrates the easy flow from common sense and everyday experiences to abstraction, then back again to the application of theory in practice.

An alternative strategy for activating prior knowledge is "planting." Its use and application is similar to that in literature and movies. The hero of the story should not get herself out of a tight situation with a hand grenade she just happened to be carrying in her purse. The author better have introduced the hand grenade earlier in the story for it to be believable. Similarly, you can "plant" important concepts by reactivating them from the learners' memories at the beginning of the lesson. A review and reactivation of important concepts will help with the flow, believability, and understandability of your lesson.

Finally, the reactivation of prior knowledge has a diagnostic component. It allows you to diagnose the level of your learners and to determine whether or not your lesson plan is within their zone of proximal development. For example, a teacher who begins a class by reviewing the previous class often *tells* the learners what they learned last time. Instead, the learners could tell the teacher what they actually learned. Based on this information the teacher can determine if the day's lesson plan is appropriate.

Implications for teaching:

- It is insufficient to make assumptions about your learners' prior knowledge; let them tell you (and activate it).
- A good way to activate prior knowledge is to cite common sense and everyday experience. From there, move to abstraction, then back again to the application of theory in practice.

Principle 3

Case 1
A humanities teacher is leading a small group discussion based on an assigned reading. Although the students have obviously read the pa-

*per, based on their ability to recite parts of the text, few of them seem
to have grasped the main "point" of the author.*

Case 2

*A physics teacher is correcting an exam. The students had no prob-
lems "plugging" numbers into formulas, yet few were able to satisfactorily answer questions in a second part of the exam which required them to explain concepts underlying the formulae.*

Case 3

*A disgruntled student comes in to challenge a recent low mark on an
essay. The essay assignment presented a statement and asked the students to agree or disagree, and defend their opinions. The student
complains and says "all the facts" are included. The teacher points
out that the student has simply arranged a series of facts, but hasn't
really interpreted the information or made an argument. Further, the
impression given by the essay is that the student just started writing
and stopped after fulfilling the required number of words; the essay
wasn't organized or structured. Finally, the student had not used data
as evidence, in fact, there was no indication that the difference between evidence, opinion, or example was understood.*

What do the learners in these three cases have in common? How are
they similar to the learner studying comparative vertebrate anatomy in
the anecdote in the introduction to the chapter? How are they different
when compared to the child who comes to understand the concept of
dog? From a Developmental Perspective, learning occurs only if learners
give *meaning* to knowledge and *link* it to what they already know (i.e.,
prior knowledge). The learners in the above cases focused on reproducing the content rather than understanding it. We would argue that little
(if any) useful learning occurred.

Principle 3:   Learners must be actively involved in constructing personal
meaning (i.e., understanding)—the links are more impor-
tant than the elements.

The processes of teaching and learning have many features in common with the example of how a child comes to understand the concept
of dog. The parent does not tell the child what a dog is; the child must
come to understand the concept internally. The parent has in mind the
desired conception and becomes involved in a dynamic dialogue with the
child. The child has the opportunity to test his or her conception with
that of the parent and the parent has the opportunity to correct miscon-

ceptions. Eventually the child and parent negotiate the meaning of dog, and the child's understanding comes to overlap the parent's conception.

Teachers and learners often assume that knowledge is transferred intact from teachers (and textbooks) to learners; they fail to appreciate the personal and idiosyncratic nature of learning and knowledge. According to White and Gunstone (1992),

> understanding develops as new elements are acquired and *linked* with the existing pattern of associations between elements of knowledge. Addition of new elements will often stimulate reorganization of the pattern as the person reflects on the new knowledge and sees how it puts older knowledge in a different light [italics added]. (p. 13)

Given that learners and teachers (in fact all individuals) necessarily have different patterns of associations (i.e., internal representations or maps), it is impossible for teachers to transfer a piece of knowledge to learners. Meaning and understanding have to do with the connections of a new element of knowledge to existing knowledge, rather than the new element itself. Without some way of linking the new knowledge into their current and personal maps, learners usually forget. Learners must be actively involved in constructing personal meaning from the raw materials provided by teachers if teachers are to help learners achieve understanding.

Teaching should therefore focus on helping learners construct personal meaning. Approaches to learning aimed toward this end have been termed "deep" (i.e., an emphasis on meaning) and "holistic" (i.e., an emphasis on organizing principles to understand "wholes") in contrast to those methods of learning with a focus on reproduction (i.e., "surface" approach) (Eizenberg, 1988; Marton & Saljo, 1984). According to this perspective, true learning and understanding can only occur when learners search for personal meaning by organizing information into an integrated and structured whole (i.e., use of a deep/holistic approach). The learners in the three cases above used a surface approach as evidenced by their lack of understanding and emphasis on reproduction.

Therefore, teaching from the Developmental Perspective emphasizes a *qualitative* change in learners rather than a *quantitative* one; learning has to do with knowing *differently* rather than knowing *more*. Teaching has to do with promoting a structural or morphological change in learners' thinking rather than adding to the number of facts in their knowledge base.

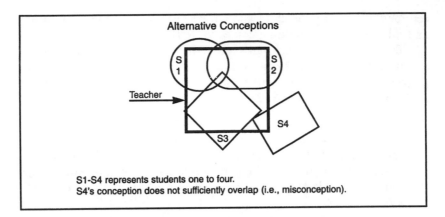

Figure 6.1 Comparison of Teacher's Conception of an Idea with That of Four Students

Given that each learner will have a different set of prior knowledge elements, each learner will necessarily have a different understanding of a concept—that is, they will construct a different sense of the information. Despite the idiosyncratic nature of each individual's understanding, it is possible for them to overlap sufficiently to come to a common understanding. This is represented in Figure 6.1. Notice the conceptions of students S1, S2, and S3 have much in common with the teacher's conception. However, S4 has a conception of the idea that is significantly different than the teacher's.

You should now have a better understanding of one of the teaching implications from principle 1: Teaching requires an understanding of the range of learners' prior conceptions (and misconceptions). Further, you should appreciate that teaching from this perspective assumes a desired endpoint (i.e., preferred conception or range of conceptions). Therefore, the teachers' role is to lead the learners from their existing conceptions to the preferred conception. For instance, learners may have a naive conception of selling price as reflecting the cost of materials and production. An economics teacher may want to move the learners to a more sophisticated understanding that includes supply and demand.

Good developmental teachers will not only have a good idea of learners' starting points and the desired endpoint, but will also know effective ways to help learners cross the bridge to new understanding. This "bridging knowledge" (Pratt, personal communication, May, 1995) has also been termed "pedagogic content knowledge" (Wilson, Shulman, & Richert, 1987) and will be discussed in the next section. It is different from simple content expertise and has to do with effective ways of representing the content for learners' understanding. Bridging knowledge is what separates an expert teacher from a content expert.

Implications for teaching:

- The developmental teacher is a guide, a coach, and a co-inquirer more than a source of knowledge and information.
- Teaching expertise has to do with ability to help learners cross from old conceptions to new ways of understanding (i.e., bridging knowledge).
- Teachers should encourage the development of a "deep" (i.e., an emphasis on meaning) and "holistic" (i.e., an emphasis on organizing principles to understand "wholes") approach to learning and discourage a "surface" approach (i.e., an emphasis on reproduction).
- Teachers should not accept verbatim reproduction as evidence of learning but should become adept at probing for understanding.
- Learners' wrong answers should be seen as evidence of misconceptions that need to be addressed.

Principle 4

An undergraduate anatomy student spends considerable time making a set of anatomy flash cards for all the major muscles including their origin, insertion, inervation, and major action. An envious (but less industrious) student convinces the first student to lend him the cards to study for the exam. Both students adopted a deep, holistic approach to learning, but one student does significantly better on the exam. What is a plausible explanation?

The first student constructed the cards according to her prior knowledge, therefore she had an advantage. But, there is another factor as well. The second student may think that the first student wasted a lot of time making up the cards, but efficiency may not be effective in the long run. This is the paradox that underlies principle 4.

Principle 4: Making more, and stronger, links requires time.

Learners need time to dwell and cognitively manipulate new ideas in order to increase the number and the strength of the links to new knowledge as it is incorporated into their personal construct system. Cementing new knowledge into the framework through meaning takes time; it cannot be short-circuited in pursuit of efficiency. Unfortunately, "the period for mulling over that is reportedly needed for learners to make interpretative sense of what is happening to them is neglected" (Brookfield, 1990, p. 140).

Learners who focus on the links between knowledge elements rather than the knowledge elements themselves are said to be elaborating their knowledge base (Coles, 1991). An elaborated knowledge base is associated with better examination scores, and also with the ability to apply knowledge to new situations and problem solving. The greater the number of links to a piece of knowledge, the greater the number of ways to access that piece of knowledge (i.e., retrieval pathways or cues). Elaboration takes time. Learners need time to link ideas both within and between subjects, and for learners in the professions, to link theory and practice. Unfortunately, in the hectic pace to cover content, teachers often leave little time for learners to reflect on what they are learning. The endpoint of learning, then, is the development of an elaborated knowledge base through the use of a deep holistic approach to learning.

Implications for teaching:

- Teachers need to build in time and opportunities for learners to elaborate their knowledge base (i.e., increase the number and strength of links).
- Teaching more (e.g., covering the syllabus) may result in learning less.
- Teachers make knowledge more accessible, more transferable, and more usable when they help students make links within and between subjects, as well as between theory and practice.

Principle 5

Case 1
Almost everyone has had the following experience. You are walking down the street and you meet someone who greets you with a familiar tone. You smile, return the greeting, and continue walking. But you just can't seem to "place" the person. Try as you might, you don't remember where you know them from. The next day at work, you come across the same person and immediately recognize them as a coworker from another department.

Case 2
Undergraduate medical education is traditionally separated into two

stages: preclinical education taught by basic scientists and clinical education taught by practicing clinicians. Many students go through growing pains as they make the transition from preclinical to clinical medicine. Although they have spent 2 years learning anatomy, physiology, and pathology, they can't seem to access the information to understand or solve clinical problems. To many students, preclinical and clinical education embody two separate and unrelated bodies of knowledge. Their understanding of glucose metabolism from the preclinical years is not very helpful for understanding diabetic emergencies when they start seeing patients. Many students , therefore, see their task as "relearning" once they enter the clinical years.

How are the two cases above similar? Can you provide an explanation? In the first case, you knew the person in a work context but were unable to access that information in a different context. Similarly, medical students are unable to retrieve information learned and stored in the context of basic scientists once they are seeing patients (i.e., clinical context). Since basic scientists and clinicians think differently, their knowledge base is linked differently and therefore accessed by different cues (i.e., retrieval pathways or cues; see principle 4); their knowledge base has a different structure or morphology (see principle 3). Some medical students recognize their task as recontextualizing the information: changing the links, the associations and the cues of their knowledge base. For other students, it becomes a matter of learning twice.

Principle 5:   Context provides important cues for storing and retrieving information.

The term *context* is used in different ways in the literature. In this discussion, context means the perspective from which the content is understood. Other contexts will be discussed later.

From a Developmental Perspective content cannot be separated from context. The information must be understood in relation to some perspective. Therefore, learning cannot be context free. Knowledge, and its organization into the student's personal construct system, is highly dependent on the context in which it was learned. Recall the anecdote from principle 1 in which the learners had prior knowledge of the "Movie Theatre Phenomenon" (i.e., large volumes of water don't take long to excrete) but couldn't explain a clinical question. Their prior knowledge was activated in order to have them understand and personally connect with a new concept. One could argue that they already understood the concept, albeit in another context. The same anecdote could therefore be used to explain principle 5. Prior knowledge does not transfer across contexts very well, just as new knowledge does not. The idea is to have learners "reach across contexts" to make links and understand new concepts in light of what they already understand (i.e., recontextualize information). Further, the more contexts from which information is learned, the more accessible and usable it is. We believe that learners can be encouraged to do such "reaching" and thus link what they are learning with what they already know. This is how we understand a deep approach to learning (see principles 4 and 5). That is, when studying new material, learners should be encouraged and assisted in relating the content to other situations.

Implications for teaching:

- Learners should be taught in the context from which they will eventually use their knowledge.
- Teaching from several contexts makes knowledge more usable, *if* learners understand the links between contextual representations of knowledge.

Principle 6

This principle involves you in a simple exercise while reading the following vignettes. Decide whether the learner is adopting a deep or surface approach to learning and comment on what you think is driving the learner to adopt that particular approach (i.e., what is the motivating force?).

Vignette 1
The first vignette is from the movie, River's Edge. *The scene depicts a classroom the day after one of its students has been found murdered at the river's edge. An animated and emotional teacher, who can best be described as a throwback to the 60s, is indulging himself in a long diatribe on the meaning of this senseless killing. One of the students in the class interrupts by lifting his hand.*
"Yes?" asks the teacher.
"Will this be on the test?" responds the student.

Deep approach/Surface approach (choose one)

*Driving force(s):*_____

Vignette 2
Two students are taking a postgraduate course in anthropology. The first student, from another department, took the course because it fit his time slot and still allowed him to play varsity soccer. Besides that, his faculty advisor strongly suggested that he take this course. The second student, from the department of education, was relieved to get into the course from the waiting list because she plans on conducting some qualitative research as part of her thesis; this course would be very helpful in understanding qualitative research methodology.

As part of the course requirements, the students have to write an essay on an assigned topic. When reading the source materials, the first student concentrates mainly on finding suitable quotes. He starts his essay by defining the concept. He makes sure to include many quotes which he groups and arranges into subheadings. He churns out his essay in time to go drinking with his buddies. The second student is concerned that the essay topic is not relevant to her needs and negotiates with the teacher to write on a topic more closely related to her thesis. She spends several days reading source materials and finds many contradictory opinions. In fact she notes that the same data is used to support opposing points of view. She interprets the information in light of her thesis proposal and adopts a particular point of view. She organizes her essay as an argument, using evidence from the literature to back her position. Further, she highlights some of the inconsistencies and possible misinterpretations from opposing camps.

Student 1
Deep approach/Surface approach (choose one)
Driving force(s): _____

Student 2
Deep approach/Surface approach (choose one)
Driving force(s): _____

Vignette 3
It's the night before the biology exam. A student sits in front of a pile of lecture notes and textbooks. How could she have left all of this to

the last minute? As she reads, she is consumed by a feeling of dread and keeps thinking, "there's so much to cover and so little time left." She has difficulty concentrating and her mind keeps drifting to thoughts of failure.

Deep approach/Surface approach (choose one)

Driving force(s): _____

Vignette 4
A final year medical student is studying for his internal medicine exam. He finds that the demands of patient care are both exciting and arduous. For the first time, he sees the relevance of much of what he is learning. Unfortunately, the end of rotation multiple choice (MCQ) exam has been hanging heavily over his head throughout the rotation. On the one hand, he wants to read topics relating to his patients to understand their illnesses and to answer questions that come up regarding their management. Unfortunately, his past experience with MCQ exams tells him that understanding is not rewarded. He knows that memorized facts are quickly forgotten but he really needs an "A" on this exam if he want to get into the residency of his choice.

Deep approach/Surface approach (choose one)

Driving force(s): _____

Vignette 5
A student attends an engineering lecture. The teacher is obviously interested in her work and concerned that her students understand many aspects of engineering. Her enthusiasm is infectious and the student listens intently, forgetting to take notes. The teacher specifically illustrates the relevance of concepts to the real world of engineering by relating vivid and humorous anecdotes. At one point during the lecture, the student has an "Aha!" experience, as a concept he has been struggling with in another course suddenly becomes clear.

Deep approach/Surface approach (choose one)

Driving force(s): _____

Vignette 6
Sam is taking part in a small group calculus tutorial. The tutorial leader poses a question to each student in order by seating arrangement. Sam's turn is next. The tutorial leader is impatient with stu-

dents who cannot provide immediate answers and ridicules them before moving on to the next student. Sam can't "think." The only thoughts that enter his mind are how stupid he will look if he can't answer his question.

Deep approach/Surface approach (choose one)

Driving force(s): _____

Now consider each vignette in terms of the driving force (i.e., learner motivation). Is the source of motivation from within the learner (i.e., *intrinsic* motivation) or is it perceived as an external pressure (i.e., *extrinsic* motivation)? Also speculate on the level of anxiety experienced by the learner. Go back and label each vignette as I. M. (intrinsic motivation) or E. M. (extrinsic motivation). Also identify those vignettes in which the learner is experiencing a high level of anxiety (H. A.). Can you detect a relationship between motivation (intrinsic vs. extrinsic) and approach to learning (deep vs. surface)? Can you detect a relationship between high anxiety and learning?

Principle 6:   A. Intrinsic motivation is associated with deep approaches to learning.

B. Extrinsic motivation and anxiety are associated with surface approaches to learning.

It is important to note that the approach to learning adopted by a particular learner does not represent a stable characteristic of that learner. Both the institutional context (i.e., departmental demands, exams, marking, teaching) and the personal context (i.e., intrinsic motivation, interest, prior experience, future goals) play an important role in determining the approach taken by a learner. Different learning materials themselves or even teaching styles or sessions may promote the adoption of different approaches to learning. Finally, high levels of learner anxiety are usually associated with a surface approach to learning.

Thus far, we have used the terms deep and surface approaches to learning without defining them to any great extent. By now, you should have a good grasp of these concepts based on the examples used. Below is a list of important characteristics of deep and surface approaches as they apply to a reading task—i.e., learning from reading (Ramsden, 1988, p. 19).

Deep Approach – the reader's intention is to understand, therefore he/she will:

- focus on what is signified (e.g., the author's argument);
- relate and distinguish new ideas and previous knowledge;
- relate concepts to everyday practice;
- relate and distinguish evidence and argument;
- organize and structure content;
- have an *internal* emphasis: driven by personal and immediate reasons for learning this content.

Surface Approach – the reader's intention is to complete the task requirements, therefore he/she will:

- focus on the signs (e.g., the text itself);
- focus on discrete elements;
- memorize information and procedures for assessments;
- unreflectively associate concepts and facts;
- fail to distinguish principles from evidence, new information from old;
- treat task as an external imposition;
- have an *external* emphasis: driven by the demands of assessments, knowledge cut off from everyday reality.

What then is your role as a teacher in encouraging learners to adopt a deep approach to learning? There is evidence in the literature that specific attempts to manipulate learning tasks in order to drive learners toward a deep approach to learning has the paradoxical effect of having them take on a surface approach (Marton & Saljo, 1984). Learners who use a deep approach when reading an assigned text have been found to interact with the text by asking themselves questions while reading (e.g., Can I summarize this section in one or two sentences? What is the relationship between sections? What are the main points?). When similar questions were used in an attempt to foster a deep approach to a reading task, the results were paradoxical: learners used a surface approach. It seems that the predictability of the "demand structure" was at fault; the questions themselves became the objective of learning rather than a means toward deep learning.

How then can you encourage your learners toward deeper approaches to learning without such a paradoxical effect? Focusing on motivation and the learning environment is key. You should nurture your learners' intrinsic motivation. You should also, as much as possible, reduce extrinsic motivation and learner anxiety.

The presence of intrinsic motivation has been associated with a deep approach to learning and spending more time on task (Ramsden, 1992). There is a synergistic and reciprocal relationship between intrinsic motivation and a deep approach. That is, the use of a deep approach while learning a concept, and the resulting understanding in itself results in increased intrinsic motivation. Intrinsic motivation may be stimulated by focusing on what is relevant to learners: specific interests, immediate real world concerns, prior experiences, future goals, etc. Highlighting positive growth and gains rather than deficiencies can have a similar effect. Even more importantly, providing learners freedom of choice in content and learning style is associated with a deep approach to learning (cf., vignette 2, student 2 writing an essay on a topic relevant to her interests and needs).

What about the engineering student attending the lecture (vignette 5)? How did you label his motivation (i.e., intrinsic or extrinsic)? What did you describe as the driving force? His motivation isn't truly intrinsic, in that it isn't from within. Yet, it isn't really perceived as an external pressure. His source of motivation can be thought of as vicarious (Hodgson, 1984). The student is experiencing interest, enthusiasm, and relevance vicariously through the teacher. There is evidence that vicarious motivation may be just as effective as intrinsic motivation in promoting a deep approach to learning. Vicarious motivation may be a bridge to intrinsic interest and motivation.

The learners in vignettes 1, 3, and 4 are preoccupied with the notion of evaluation (as was the comparative vertebrate anatomy student in the introduction to the chapter). The medical student in vignette 4 realizes that memorized facts are quickly forgotten (i.e., surface approach) but is faced with the conflict of wanting to do well on the test. Unfortunately, there is evidence that those learners who rely heavily on memorization for studying in medical school are overrepresented in the top quartile of the class and are thus being rewarded for adopting a surface approach (Regan-Smith, cited in Small et al., 1993). It would seem that the espoused theory and theory-in-practice of the medical school are at odds. Even when learners would prefer to use a deep approach, experience tells them that teachers often undervalue answers that are not close to verbatim reproduction of what they have been taught. It is argued (Ramsden, 1988) that "the most significant single influence on student learning is their *perception* of assessment" [italics added] (p. 24). Therefore, learners' perception of evaluation is the most important source of extrinsic motivation leading them to adopt a surface approach to learning. It is important to note that it is learners' *perception* of evaluation and not the evaluation itself. For instance, the medical student in vignette 4 has not taken the internal medicine exam yet. For all he knows, it may very well require and reward a deep understanding of concepts. Unfortunately, this student's past experience with multiple choice type exams has left him with a perception of what is required (i.e., rote memorization). Therefore, teachers need not only change exam requirements, but also, they must alter the learners' perception of what is required of them.

A factor that may further aggravate the problem of perceived evaluation requirements is that of curriculum overload. Principle 4 informs us that a deep approach to learning takes time; the concept of "efficient" learning is not compatible with the Developmental Perspective. What happens when learners are given too much to learn in a given amount of time? By predicting and attending to the perceived demands of evaluation, learners can save effort and energy. Therefore, curriculum overload compounds the problem by providing another source of extrinsic motivation leading learners to adopt a surface approach to learning. Unfortunately the strategy is "penny wise and pound foolish"; learners are successful on exams but understand and retain little.

Now, consider Sam in vignette 6, anxiously waiting his turn to be questioned. How did you describe his approach to learning? You may argue that he was so anxious that no learning occurred at all; he was preoccupied with preserving his self-esteem. Interactive teaching and learning occurs in an ego-intensive environment where learners and teachers hate to say "I don't know" (Whitman, 1990). In an effort to preserve self-esteem, learners may try to hide areas of deficiency in understanding. It has been our experience that learners' prior experience with inquisition style questioning under the guise of the Socratic method leaves them uneasy with not knowing. Learners often mistake questioning as a method of teaching with questioning as a means of evaluation. Other sources of anxiety may come from past failure and lack of self-confidence. Anxiety may also be related to evaluation (cf., vignette 3, student studying for biology exam). It becomes easy to see how anxiety may inhibit learners from taking a deep approach to learning.

This brings us to an important question: Can you teach from the Developmental Perspective without also operating from the Nurturing Perspective? (See Chapter 7.) Conversely, can you teach from the Nurturing Perspective without also operating from the Developmental Perspective? We argue that both perspectives are closely linked and that one needs to operate from both to be successful in either. That is, one perspective becomes foreground while the other becomes background. The Nurturing Perspective is concerned with facilitating personal agency. There is a high regard for the learner's self-concept and a concern in developing the relationship between learner and teacher. One could argue that the goal is to help change learners' conception of themselves. This is accomplished in part by fostering a climate of trust and respect. Therefore, both perspectives focus on changing conceptions (i.e., understanding) in an atmosphere of trust and respect. To teach from the Nurturing Perspective requires helping learners change their self-concept. Similarly, to teach from the Developmental Perspective requires an ability to have learners want to take risks in an ego-intensive environment. As seen in vignette 6, learners may not engage in deep approaches to learning if the environment is not supportive of their self-concept. Therefore, successful teaching from the Developmental Perspective requires reducing learner anxiety by operating from the Nurturing Perspective in the background. Learners are more likely to engage in a deep approach to learning in a climate of mutual trust and respect. Learners know when teachers are genuinely interested in them; they can recognize a fake in 2 seconds flat. Further, by enhancing learners' self-esteem through encouragement and support, intrinsic motivation may be *nurtured* and therefore facilitate a deep approach to learning.

Finally, let's consider the student (vignette 2) who demonstrated no real interest in anthropology, and took the course because of the time slot and persuasion from his advisor. Extrinsic motivation is manifested by the way he approached the essay assignment. He can be distinguished, however, from the other extrinsically motivated learners in the other vignettes. The source of extrinsic motivation in the other learners can be ascribed to the "institutional context" (i.e., departmental demands, exams, marking, teaching). His extrinsic motivation is a result of "personal" context (Gibbs, Morgan, & Taylor, 1984). Learners undertake schooling or take courses for various reasons. Some may simply attend to be part of collegiate culture (i.e., sports and fun). Others may be focused towards gaining qualifications and employment or self-improvement. Finally, some may be stimulated by academic interest (i.e., intellectual interest). Given that teachers are driven by academic interests, they may be at odds with learners' personal contexts. It is unlikely that most, or even many, learners will be academically oriented; and teachers are unlikely to have a significant influence on learners' personal context. Therefore, teachers need to understand that there are some sources of extrinsic motivation over which they have little control. Be careful of labeling a learner as lazy; reasons for taking different courses may vary. This person may in fact be academically oriented and intrinsically motivated in other areas.

Implications for teaching:

(A) Intrinsic motivation is associated with deep approaches to learning.
(B) Extrinsic motivation and anxiety are associated with surface approaches to learning.

Teachers should focus on nurturing intrinsic motivation, and diminishing extrinsic motivation and anxiety by:

• attending to what is relevant to learners;
• giving learners some control in learning;
• showing enthusiasm for their content area (i.e., vicarious motivation).

Teachers need to change learners' perceptions of evaluation demands as well as the evaluations themselves by:

• demonstrating how understanding and evaluation requirements overlap;
• avoiding curriculum overload (i.e., teaching too much content);
• Creating a safe place where learners can risk not knowing (c.f., Nurturing Perspective).

Attempting to manipulate approaches to learning should be undertaken with caution, as the predictability of the demand structure may have the paradoxical effect of encouraging a surface approach.

Principle 7: The Guiding Principle

Unlike the first six developmental teaching principles, principle 7 does not directly concern cognitive development and therefore does not build on the others; instead principle 7 "oversees" and guides the other principles by providing an ideal (cf., General Model of Teaching in Chapter 1). It is therefore not possible to provide you with a cognitive exercise to illustrate principle 7. Instead, a quote will introduce the ideal that guides the first six principles.

Thomas C. King . . . believes that the overriding purpose of education is to make the learner independent of any need for a teacher (1983). Dr. King contends that anything you do to build dependency is bad, and anything you do as a teacher to build independence is good. Thus, he concludes that the teacher as an information giver is performing an immoral act! (Whitman, 1990, p. 85)

Although thought provoking, this comment is impractical and overly simplistic. Learner dependence-independence in learning does not exist as a dichotomy but rather as a continuum. Teaching from the developmental perspective, then, focuses not only on the development of the intellect, but also on movement along the continuum toward greater independence.

Teachers often burden themselves with the impossible task of teaching everything (or as much as they can) about their area of expertise. This is not only unrealistic but can be counterproductive in the long run (cf., principle 4). Instead, teachers should see themselves as occupying a brief but important role in the student's development, not unlike a pair of training wheels on a child's first bicycle. Anything we do that fosters learner dependence in learning counters our espoused theory of helping learners become independent self-directed learners. If we are working toward this end, we should feel increasingly unnecessary as our learners take charge of their own learning. Unfortunately, teachers may mistake the feeling of being needed with that of being helpful.

Principle 7:   Teaching should be geared toward making the teacher increasingly unnecessary: that means, the development of learner autonomy as well as the intellect.

How then can we help learners become more effective and independent learners? Addressing this important and controversial question requires more space than can be provided in this section (see Candy, 1991, for an in-depth treatment). We will only provide you with food for thought and some general guidelines for practice.

It is often assumed that providing learners with opportunities to exert control over learning will ultimately result in greater learner autonomy. Learner control is an important and necessary condition, but not a sufficient condition for promoting independence. Providing learners with opportunities to exert control over learning is only the first step in fostering personal autonomy in learning. Other means are needed to complement and reinforce learners' independent efforts. One often neglected, but effective, way to foster learner independence is to make learning an object of reflection (Candy, 1991). Learners are usually so caught up in trying to learn the content of courses that they seldom consider the process of learning itself. Teachers need to help make learners aware of the strategies and approaches used in learning (e.g., surface vs. deep). Further, they need to help learners recognize the relationship between the strategies used and learning outcomes. As mentioned earlier, context is all important in learning—the same applies to learning about learning. Therefore, the techniques for helping learners acquire such awareness should not be taught as a self-contained set of learning skills. Instead, they should be built into all subject matter being taught.

Perhaps the most important factor in promoting learner autonomy is helping learners believe they can. This aspect of developing learner autonomy is more likely the domain of the Nurturing Perspective. Either way, teachers need to encourage learners to believe in their own abilities. An important corollary is helping learners identify the sources of their successes and failures. Success should be attributed to hard work rather than luck or favoritism. Conversely, failure should be understood as resulting from lack of effort rather than lack of ability. It is now possible to appreciate that shifting control to learners is not sufficient for promoting autonomy in learning. Teachers holding to this misconception can unwittingly have an adverse effect on autonomy. For instance, learners thrown into the "deep-end" and required to fend for themselves may only end up learning that they are incapable of taking control of their own learning. The ideal of fostering learner autonomy in learning is not a call for "bootstrapism."

From a practical perspective, teachers have three main ways of influencing personal autonomy in learning (Candy, 1991): (1) helping learners develop a sense of personal control (cf., Nurturing Perspective); (2) providing access to learning resources; and (3) helping learners develop the competence to take control of their learning. Some of the competencies that might be built into all subject matter being taught include:

- locating and retrieving information
- setting goals
- time management skills
- question-asking behavior
- critical thinking
- self-monitoring and self-evaluation

In reading principle 7—Teaching is geared toward making the teacher *increasingly* unnecessary: that means, the development of learner autonomy as well as the intellect—pay particular attention to the word "increasingly." Above, we discussed the concept of the student's "zone of proximal development" in terms of the complexity of content in learning (principles 1 & 2). Similarly, each learner has a zone of proximal development in exerting independence in learning. The outer limit of this zone should be out far enough to challenge the learner but not so far as to cause frustration and self-doubt. Likewise it should not be too close as to bore the learner. Further, each learner will necessarily occupy a different place on the dependence-independence continuum. It is important to recognize that the dependence-independence continuum is represented as linear and unidimensional for the sake of conceptual clarity. It is actually better understood as multiple continuums each representing a different capacity or skill (e.g., goal setting; locating and retrieving information). Each learner will necessarily differ in amount and kind of autonomy in learning. As mentioned, throwing all learners into the deep-end may be detrimental in the long run in that it undermines the goal of helping learners develop a sense of personal control. Teachers should start by providing adequate *support* and *direction* in learning with the intention of slowly phasing these out as learners take greater control and responsibility for their learning (Pratt, 1988). The teaching skills of providing adequate support and phasing out are similar to the skills of scaffolding and fading discussed in the Apprenticeship Perspective of teaching. Different learners will necessarily start at different points on the continuum, move at different rates, and need different kinds of help on their journey toward greater independence in learning. Further, autonomy in learning is a situational attribute rather than a personal one. That is, learners may display varying amounts of self-direction depending on the specific content area and situation (Pratt, 1988).

Implications for teaching:

- Teachers should start by providing learners with opportunities to exert control over their own learning.

Teachers need to go further in promoting learner autonomy by:

- making learning an object of reflection.
- encouraging learners to believe in their own abilities.
- helping learners identify sources of successes and failures.
- helping learners develop the competencies needed to learn independently (e.g., goal setting).
- helping learners identify learning resources.

Teachers should provide the necessary *support* and *direction* to move learners along the dependence-independence continuum by:

- becoming aware of the types and range of independence in your learners.
- providing learning tasks that accommodate this range and allow for
  different rates of progression and different endpoints.

Now that you are familiar with the seven Developmental Teaching
Principles, we will consider the special knowledge needed to be a good
developmental teacher.

BRIDGING KNOWLEDGE:
TEACHERS' SPECIAL KNOWLEDGE

Consider the following examples:

> *A student is attending a seminar as part of her course work. The
> seminar leader is enthusiastic. He tries to engage her. He asks ques-
> tions. She just doesn't seem to understand. The harder he tries, the
> more confused and frustrated she becomes. He obviously knows his
> stuff; he just can't get her to understand. She leaves feeling that she
> understands less than when she came in.*

What characterizes gifted and inspired teachers? Do they have a better
understanding of their subject area? Do they use more effective teaching
behaviors? If not, what specialized knowledge and skills distinguishes
them?

To view and assess the quality of teaching in terms of methods and
techniques is simplistic and narrow; unfortunately this has been the focus of much research in adult teaching. Moreover, this instrumental view
provides insight into the assumptions that underlie the teaching and
learning relationship. These assumptions include the beliefs that effective
teaching or specific methods are necessarily related to (and responsible
for) learning, and that a focus on improving teaching behaviors (i.e.,
skills) will therefore result in better learning. If learning does not improve, blame is usually placed on the learner. This limited view of teaching denies the complexity of learning and its emphasis over teaching. It
also reduces teaching to a decontextualized set of effective teaching behaviors.

The idea of generic and transferable teaching skills is of limited use-
fulness; the separation of content and process is artificial. You can't just
teach; you have to teach something. Unfortunately, much research has

been preoccupied with what teachers need to do rather than what they need to know. From this perspective, the teacher's role is that of installing or implementing the curriculum. A more useful idea is that of teachers occupying an important place between the curriculum-as-plan and the curriculum-as-lived experience (Aoki, 1991). The teacher's role, then, becomes one of interpreting the curriculum plan into meaningful experiences from the student's viewpoint. It is this ability to serve as bridge or translator, we argue, that separates gifted and inspired teachers from merely adequate teachers.

Consider the similarities between a teacher as interpreter and a language translator as interpreter. The ability to translate from English to Japanese requires more than a knowledge of translation. It requires a special ability to translate *that specific language*. You cannot separate the skills of translation from the language itself. You cannot simply translate; you must translate something. Otherwise, the special translation skills would be transferable to another language. Further, translation has to do with understanding and getting a message across. The focus is on meaning rather than the elements of speech or text. For instance, "Boys' night out" has nothing to do with male children playing outside in the evening.

Therefore, to teach from the Developmental Perspective is to act as a bridge from the curriculum-as-plan to the curriculum-as-lived by the learners. It requires more than subject matter expertise (i.e., content expertise); special skills in translation are required. However, translation skills are content-specific; they cannot be usefully separated from the subject area. Finally, the primary focus of translation is to get the message across—i.e., focus on learners' understanding.

The special "bridging knowledge" (Pratt, personal communication, May, 1995) required for translation of subject matter into learner understanding is also known as "pedagogical content knowledge" (Wilson, Shulman, & Richert, 1987) or "content-specific pedagogy" (Reynolds, 1992). It occupies an important place among the other types of knowledge used by teachers: knowledge of content area, knowledge of other content, knowledge of curriculum, knowledge of learners, knowledge of teaching and learning process. Unfortunately, bridging knowledge has been neglected until recently. More emphasis has been placed on content expertise (i.e., subject matter expertise) and process expertise (i.e., expertise in the general principles of teaching).

Content expertise is necessary but not sufficient for becoming a good teacher. The seminar teacher in the example above "knew his stuff" but

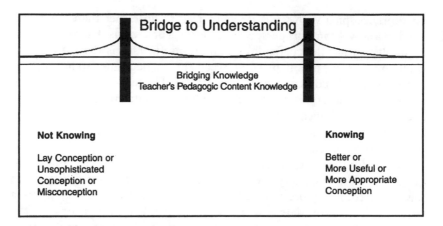

Figure 6.2 Bridging Knowledge: Moving Students from "Not Knowing" to "Knowing"

was unable to communicate it to others. On the other hand, a process expert, unfamiliar with the content area, is just as unlikely to promote learner understanding. Bridging knowledge is the knowledge needed to transform the content for the purposes of teaching: "We use the general term 'transformation' to designate the set of activities engaged by the teacher to move from her own comprehension of a matter, and the representations most useful for that understanding, to the variations of representation, narrative, examples, or association likely to initiate understanding on the part of the student" (Wilson, Shulman, & Richert, 1987, p. 113). It is no longer useful to think of effective teaching as a two-sided coin comprised of content expertise and process expertise. A place must be created for bridging expertise.

Teaching from the Developmental Perspective has to do with helping learners cross the bridge to understanding: the bridge from "not knowing" to "knowing." More importantly, teachers help learners cross the bridge to knowing differently: the bridge from "lay conceptions/unsophisticated conceptions/misconceptions" to "better/more useful/more appropriate conceptions." Teaching from the Developmental Perspective assumes a knowledge of learners' starting points (existing conceptions—less sophisticated or misconceptions), a knowledge of where you want to take them (better or preferred conception(s)), and a knowledge of effective routes for the transition (i.e., bridging knowledge). (See Figure 6.2.)

The seminar teacher in the first example was lacking in bridging knowledge and is not unlike many experts who have difficulty teaching. Content experts or other people with subject matter expertise sometimes have difficulty with the unthinking of an idea or concept which has become commonplace or reflexive for them (Marton, Hounsell, & Entwistle, 1984). These teachers can't remember not knowing and therefore make assumptions about what learners know and don't know. These assumptions are usually not conscious in that they are usually taken for granted. A similar phenomenon can occur when lecturers don't interact with their learners. As their content expertise increases over the years, they become increasingly less able to communicate their understanding to learners; they no longer speak the same language.

Our discussion about bridging knowledge so far has been somewhat vague and theoretical. Unfortunately, there is no way around this. Bridging knowledge is very specific—not only to a content area, but also to specific learners. The knowledge needed to make nuclear physics understandable to first-year university students is necessarily different from that needed to make anthropology understandable. Further, the knowledge needed to transform the content of respiratory diseases into learning will be different for medical students, nursing students, and respiratory therapy students. Even the same learners will require different representations of knowledge at different levels of training. First-year medical students will have different needs than medical interns and residents.

Although we cannot be more explicit in our discussion of bridging knowledge, we can make some general comments to help guide you in the development of bridging knowledge for your specific subject area and your specific learners. When reading each of the points below, search for examples from your experience as a teacher in a specific content area.

- Become familiar with:
  - the usual range of learners' conceptions and misconceptions;
  - the teaching strategies, methods, and activities that make your content more understandable;
  - the progression and changes in learners' conceptions over time;
  - the "sticky points" and conceptual stumbling blocks that slow learners' understanding and require special attention and extra time;
  - the appropriate pace for introducing new and more complex concepts. Watch for cues from learners that your pace is too slow or too quick.

- Learn to choose, adapt, and use curricular materials that facilitate understanding in your content area.
- Develop, collect, and use analogies, anecdotes, metaphors, and examples that are striking and provide insight.
- Develop the capacity to introduce variations on a theme: alternative representations of your subject matter. That is, develop a representational repertoire for the subject matter you teach (Wilson, Shulman, & Richert, 1987).
- Learn to juxtapose elements in order to provide your learners with an "Aha!" or "Eureka!" experience.
- Speak the same language as your learners; don't make assumptions about what they know and don't know.
- Sequence your teaching to promote understanding. A good starting point is common sense and everyday experiences moving to abstraction, then back again to the application of theory in practice.
- Maintain a balance between the "big picture" and the "elements" in your presentations. Bring the focus back to the big picture before introducing the next element.
- Don't burden yourself with providing a complete understanding of concepts all at once. Sometimes "white lies" are OK. Simplified or incomplete representations may be appropriate depending on learners' level of understanding and sophistication. Think of these as "transitional" representations. Increasing levels of complexity can be added in layers, as learners master each level. For instance, having first-year medical students think of the heart as two pumps in series is a good first approximation of a difficult and complex concept. A common mistake made by many content experts who teach is to deny the importance of transitional representations. They confuse transitional representations with misrepresentations and misinformation. They err on the side of comprehensive coverage of concepts and usually confuse learners.

Those of you with considerable teaching experience can probably think of examples for each of the points above. Those of you with less experience may need to rely on your experience as learners for insight. Our goal has been to provide you with a framework for interpreting and understanding the special knowledge that enables you to transform your content for the purposes of teaching.

Experience will play an important role in the development of your bridging knowledge. Experience is necessary but not sufficient in developing bridging knowledge expertise. Ten years of experience without reflection is just 1 year's experience repeated nine times. Teaching should be a reflective, thinking activity (Calderhead, 1987). Unfortunately, many teachers are "surprisingly unreflective about their work" (Ashton, 1984, p. 31). Reflection will enable you to learn from your experience as a teacher. Recall that teaching from the Developmental Perspective has to do with helping learners cross the bridge to understanding. Reflection on your experience will help you in refining the routes and creating alternative routes (i.e., expand your representational repertoire). Make reflection a routine part of your work as a teacher. Questions to ask yourself after a teaching session might include the following:

- What worked? Why?
- What didn't work? Why?
- Was the sequencing of material appropriate and helpful?
- Was the pace appropriate?
- What would you do the same next time?
- What would you do differently next time?

TEACHING FROM THE DEVELOPMENTAL PERSPECTIVE: EXAMPLES FROM PRACTICE

The developmental teaching principles and bridging knowledge can be interpreted in an infinite number of ways. We would like to present a few examples of how these might be played out in the teaching moment.

The first example comes from Eleanor Duckworth's work with children, while doing research with Piaget in the 1950s, and presents a key idea underlying the Developmental Perspective (Eleanor Duckworth, 1987).

> With a friend, I reviewed some classic Piagetian interviews with a few children. One involved the ordering of lengths. I had cut 10 cellophane drinking straws into different lengths and asked the children to put them in order, from smallest to biggest. The first two 7-year-olds did it with no difficulty and little interest. Then came Kevin. Before I said a word about the straws, he picked them up and said to me, "I know what I'm going to do," and proceeded, on his own, to order them by length. He didn't mean, "I know what

you're going to ask me to do." He meant, "I have a wonderful idea about what to do with these straws. You'll be surprised by my wonderful idea."

It wasn't easy for him. He needed a good deal of trial and error as he set about developing his system. But he was so pleased with himself when he accomplished his self-set task that when I decided to offer them to him to keep (10 whole drinking straws!), he glowed with joy, showed them to one or two select friends, and stored them away with other treasures in a shoe box. (p. 1)

Compare Kevin's experience with that in the example below.

Ric: I recently took a Coastal Navigation course to improve my sailing skills. The sessions consisted mainly of noninteractive lecturing followed by the application of concepts as chartwork: plotting a position on a chart, a course (i.e., direction), speed, etc. The teacher was explaining the procedure to sort out how far off course the boat drifted after sailing for a while. I then had a thought, "Hey, once you have this information, you could actually correct ahead of time and end up on course." More than pleased with my insight, I lifted my hand, and proposed this idea to the teacher. "Uh huh," he said, annoyed by the interruption, "we'll get to that in a few minutes." I learned to keep my special insights to myself.

According to Duckworth, the "having of wonderful ideas" is the essence of intellectual development. The essence of good teaching then, is to provide occasions for having wonderful ideas and to let learners feel good about having them. There are two important concepts here: first, the notion of providing opportunities; second, the notion of allowing learners to feel good. The thing about wonderful ideas is that they may not seem all that wonderful to others—including teachers. You need to be aware of and vigilant for unexpected insights in your learners. Share in your learners' joy of discovery. Again, notice the important overlap of the Nurturing Perspective.

Before moving on to some specific examples, we want to drive home one more message: specific techniques (i.e., actions) don't belong to a particular perspective of teaching. Behaviors that appear superficially similar may in fact be informed by contradictory intentions and beliefs, and therefore have totally different learner outcomes. For instance, lecturing per se does not equate to transmission. It is possible to lecture from the Developmental Perspective (as well as the other perspectives), and we provide some tips on how to do so in a section below. Questioning (also discussed below) can be approached from different perspectives (or with disregard to some). For example, questions may be asked to assess factual recall (i.e., if a piece of information was transmitted and received). Questions can be posed to activate prior knowledge and promote linking between elements. Also note that bad experiences with inquisition style questioning under the guise of the Socratic method can leave learners uneasy with not knowing and less likely to engage in future discussions (i.e., this approach violates the Nurturing Perspective). Therefore, don't confuse a teaching technique with a particular perspective.

We will now provide some examples of the Developmental Perspective at work. The sections below are not meant to provide an exhaustive analysis and discussion; they are simply meant as illustrations and suggestions for implementing the Developmental Perspective in your work as a teacher.

The "10–2" and Its Variants:
The Developmental Perspective and Large Group Teaching

One of the criticisms lodged against the Developmental Perspective of teaching is that it is difficult to implement with large groups; we disagree. If you review the seven Developmental Teaching Principles and the summary points of "teachers' special knowledge" (i.e., bridging knowledge) we are sure that you can come up with endless possibilities for your specific context.

At the risk of overstating the obvious, we suggest that the Developmental Teaching Principles and the main points summarizing pedagogic teaching knowledge be used in precisely this way: review them while asking yourself the question, "How does this apply to a *specific context*?"

Other ways of implementing the Developmental Perspective for large group teaching that we have found successful are the "10–2 lecture" (Rowe, 1983, cited in Small, 1993) and its variants. Of note, the idea of the 10–2 lecture is informed by the Transmission Perspective of teaching. We have simply slanted the technique toward the Developmental Perspective. The technique is simple. Approximately every 10 minutes the audience is invited to discuss a question in groups of two or three for 2 minutes. The purpose, from a Transmission Perspective, "is to clear short-term memory so that *incoming information* can again enter and be *transmitted* from short-term to long term memory" [italics added]

(Small, et al., 1993, p. S89). The intentions for using the variants of the 10–2, from a Developmental Perspective, include the following: actively involving learners in constructing personal meaning, elaboration (i.e., time = links), and activation of prior knowledge. Here are some variations of the 10–2.

- Have groups of two to three learners explain to each other what they have understood from the key concepts presented in the prior 10 minutes.
- Throw out an "understanding" question and have the learners explain their answers to each other.
- Throw out a question relating to what will be presented in the next 10 minutes in order to activate prior knowledge or unmask common misconceptions.

A related technique can be used to connect a subsequent lecture.

- Leave 10 minutes at the end of a lecture. Invite learners to write a question requiring evidence of having understood the lecture content.
- Have the learners pose their questions to each other in groups of three.
- Have them select and submit the best of the three questions.
- You can collect/evaluate/collate the questions and provide a copy for the learners to use as a learning tool. Perhaps you could include a comment on misconceptions that become evident as you review the questions.
- Alternatively, you could use these questions for evaluation. Informing learners of your intention to do so could have interesting (and useful) results. Imagine learners collating and sharing the questions, as well as discussing and debating "right answers" in preparation for the exam. This should encourage a deep approach to learning by changing both the demands of evaluation and the students' perception of the demands (see principle 6).

Perhaps now you are starting to get a better appreciation of one of our earlier statements: teaching from the Developmental Perspective is Machiavellian: "the ends justify the means." You can also see why we are skeptical of prescriptive how-to manuals for teaching. The idea that effective teaching behaviors can be listed and learned is limiting. The possibilities (the means) for promoting learners' understanding (the ends) are limitless! Allow your creative imagination and your specific context to collide and you will come up with an explosion of ideas for implementing the Developmental Perspective in your practice.

Don't Tell Them: Let Them Figure It Out.

"Remember: Don't tell them, let them discover. What we discover for ourselves lasts a long time; what we are told vanishes into our notes. One carries *meaning;* the other does not" [italics added] (Bateman, 1990).

Walter Bateman (1990), in his book, *Open to Question*, suggests simply starting with data. He provides an example used to help students discover assumptions about race. He starts with the data first. He asks one student to read the metaphorical meanings for the word "white" from the dictionary, while another writes them on the board.

> White: free from spot or blemish; free from mortal impurity; innocent; marked by upright fairness; not intended to cause harm; favorable; fortunate; conservative or reactionary.
>
> He then switches to the metaphorical meanings of the word "black."
>
> Black: thoroughly evil; wicked; soiled; dirty; invoking the devil; gloomy; calamitous; sullen; hostile.
>
> " . . . you need ask no questions. Wait. Listen. The comments will begin long before the list is finished. The class will teach themselves . . ."(p. 97)

Bateman's technique is simple but effective in providing an opportunity for your learners to have "wonderful ideas."

- Start with data.
- Stand aside.
- Let them discover.

When you feel they are taking too long and feel you should intervene—don't. Give them even more time.

> *Ric: I use this technique a lot when teaching on the hospital wards in small groups. Medical teachers often quote the literature while reviewing patient cases. They fail to appreciate the difference between quoting the literature and interpreting it (as do their students). For instance, a team of six physicians-in-training (i.e., learners) and I were reviewing a patient with AIDS. One of the students asked me what the recommendations were for using AZT (a medication) in these patients. Rather than providing them with a cook-book list of recommendations, I presented them with a synopsis of the results*

*from a couple of landmark studies and asked them to make recom-
mendations for treatment based on them. Two students came up with
conflicting recommendations. They were each asked to defend their
point of view. The others joined in the debate on how to apply these
study results to clinical practice. Interestingly, the two conflicting recommendations proposed by the students were in keeping with an existing dilemma being debated in the medical literature.*

Asking Questions from a Developmental Perspective

The outcome of using questioning as a teaching technique will depend on the intentions for asking questions and the types of questions
asked. Intentions for asking questions from a Developmental Perspective
include the following:

- assessing prior knowledge
- activating prior knowledge
- helping learners structure knowledge—i.e., make links within and between subjects
- probing for understanding
- providing opportunities for the "having of wonderful ideas"

We see two main errors when teachers use questioning as a teaching
strategy. The first is obvious and requires no explanation: asking learners
questions that demand simple recall. The second error is the way teachers
handle learners' right and wrong answers. Learners' wrong answers provide a window to learners' misconceptions. It becomes more important
to discover the faulty reasoning behind a student's wrong answer than to
replace it with the correct one. By investigating wrong answers, teachers
can map out learner deficiencies, inconsistencies, and misconceptions.
Similarly, it is important for teachers to probe for supporting evidence of
learners' correct answers. Teachers may be surprised how often learners
get "the right answer for the wrong reason" or how often learners are
simply parroting answers with no clear understanding. White and Gunstone (1992) indicate that questions beginning with "Why," "How," and
"What if" are more likely to probe understanding, whereas, questions
beginning with "What," "Who," "Where," and "When" are more likely
to test recall. How often do you ask "Why," "How," and "What if" in
your teaching?

You should send a clear message to learners that *all* of them are required to think, not only the learner to whom a question is posed. Fur-

ther, you shouldn't turn off learners' thinking by accepting or critiquing the first answer given by a learner. Not all learners think at the same pace. Some may require a little more time to come up to speed. We have found the following follow-up questions useful to both these ends. Redirect the focus of discussion to another learner (or the group as a whole) by asking one of the following questions in follow up to a learner's response:

- What do you think of that answer?
- Do you agree?
- Why is it right?
- Why did I ask that question?
- You're nodding your head (in agreement to another student's answer). Explain the answer for us.

It's important that you not use these follow-up questions only when the first learner is wrong. Otherwise learners will pick up on this cue and not commit to their answers.

We often think of good teaching in terms of the presence of facilitating teaching behaviors (i.e., doing it well). We fail to appreciate the equally important concept of the absence of "non-facilitating teaching behaviors" (i.e., not doing it badly) (Napell, 1976). Below we list 6 behaviors that you should avoid while asking questions. For each of these behaviors, use the concepts presented above and the Developmental Teaching Principles to explain how they might inhibit learning. Also, suggest more appropriate ways of dealing with each situation.

1. Insufficient wait time—i.e., not waiting long enough after asking a question.
   - This behavior inhibits learning because. . . .
   - A more appropriate way of dealing with this situation is. . . .

2. Teachers answering their own questions.
   - This behavior inhibits learning because. . . .
   - A more appropriate way of dealing with this situation is. . . .

3. Rapid Reward—i.e., accepting and rewarding the first answer given (e.g., right or good, etc.).
   - This behavior inhibits learning because. . . .
   - A more appropriate way of dealing with this situation is. . . .

4. Nonspecific feedback questions—e.g., "Does everybody understand?" or "Are there any questions?"

- This behavior inhibits learning because. . . .
  HINT: What the learner hears: "Is there anybody stupid enough to admit they don't understand?" (compare Nurturing Perspective).
- A more appropriate way of dealing with this situation is. . . .

5. Teacher "ego-stroking" questions—i.e., questions to which only the teacher could possibly know the answer asked to show how much the teacher knows (and how little the learners do).
   - This behavior inhibits learning because. . . .
     HINT: compare Nurturing Perspective
   - A more appropriate way of dealing with this situation is. . . .

6. Fixation at a low level of questioning—i.e., asking questions that only demand factual recall.
   - This behavior inhibits learning because. . . .
   - A more appropriate way of dealing with this situation is. . . .

SUMMARY

We won't bore you by repeating and summarizing the main points in this chapter. If you're interested in doing so, just go back and read all the bullets. Instead, we want to present you with an argument: all learning (not just that associated with teaching) follows the key points outlined in this chapter. Reflect on your experience as a reader of this chapter (i.e., learning from reading). If we have done a good job of presenting the material in this chapter, several examples of the seven Developmental Teaching Principles will come to mind. For instance, we often introduced new concepts with examples from everyday experiences (e.g., activation of prior knowledge). We required active engagement with the text to promote the construction of personal meaning. We also spent a lot of time (cf., more links = more time) approaching concepts from several angles rather than simply stating things once.

We don't take credit for the concepts presented in this chapter as they are not our original thoughts but the work of many researchers and practitioners. We do, however, take credit for its representation. We can now cite a specific example of bridging knowledge (i.e., pedagogic content knowledge). We could have simply listed the seven Developmental Teaching Principles and provided brief explanations. We chose instead to represent the ideas using examples, anecdotes, analogies, and metaphors that we thought would be helpful in promoting understanding. We assumed (perhaps wrongly) that you would not have an extensive understanding of these concepts before starting and we sequenced the material in such a way that demanded an increasingly sophisticated understanding. Only you can determine how successful we have been in transforming the words and ideas of others for your learning. Finally, we hope to have provided you with opportunities for the "having of wonderful ideas." We tried to let you figure it out as often as we could. Our main goal was to have you *understand*, which is the main focus of the Developmental Perspective. We hope to have convinced you of the strengths of this perspective by having you experience it. Hopefully, you will try to apply some of our ideas to your own context.

REFERENCES

Anderson, O. R. (1992). Some interrelationships between constructivist models of learning and current neurobiological theory, with implications for science education. *Journal of Research in Science Education*, 29(10), 1037–1058.

Aoki, T. (1991). *Inspiring curriculum and pedagogy: Talks to teachers*. Calgary, AB: University of Alberta.

Ashton, P. (1984). Teacher efficacy: a motivational paradigm for effective teacher education. *Journal of Teacher Education*, 35(5), 28–32.

Bateman, W. L. (1990). *Open to question: The art of teaching and learning by inquiry*. San Francisco: Jossey-Bass.

Brookfield, S. (1990). *The skillful teacher*. San Francisco: Jossey-Bass.

Calderhead, J. (1987). *Exploring teachers' thinking*. London: Cassell Education.

Candy, P. C. (1991). *Self-direction for lifelong learning* (1st ed.). San Francisco: Jossey-Bass.

Coles, C. (1991). Is problem-based learning the only way? In D. Boud & G. Feletti (Eds.), *The challenge of problem based learning* (pp. 295–307). London: Kogan Page, Ltd.

Dahlgren, L. (1984). Outcomes of learning. In F. Marton, D. Hounsell, & N. Entwistle (Eds.), *The experience of learning* (pp. 19–35). Edinburgh: Scottish Academic Press.

Duckworth, E. (1987). *'The having of wonderful ideas' and other essays on teaching and learning*. New York: Teachers College Press.

Eizenberg, N. (1988). Approaches to learning anatomy: developing a programme for preclinical medical students. In P. Ramsden (Ed.), *Improving learning: New perspectives* (pp. 178–198). London: Kogan Page, Ltd.

Entwistle, N., & Marton, F. (1984). Changing conceptions of learning and research. In F. Marton, D. Hounsell, & N. Entwistle (Eds.), *The experience of learning* (pp. 211–228). Edinburgh: Scottish Academic Press.

Gibbs, G., Morgan, A., & Taylor, E. (1984). The world of the learner. In F. Marton, D. Hounsell, & N. Entwistle (Eds.), *The experience of learning* (pp. 165–188). Edinburgh: Scottish Academic Press.

Hodgson, V. (1984). Learning from lectures. In F. Marton, D. Hounsell, & N. Entwistle (Eds.), *The experience of learning* (pp. 90–102). Edinburgh: Scottish Academic Press.

Marton, F., Hounsell, D., & Entwistle, N. (1984). *The experience of learning*. Edinburgh: Scottish Academic Press.

Marton, F., & Saljo, R. (1984). Approaches to learning. In F. Marton, D. Hounsell, & N. Entwistle (Eds.), *The experience of learning* (pp. 36–55). Edinburgh: Scottish Academic Press.

Napell, S. M. (1976). Six common non-facilitating teaching behaviors. *Contemporary Education, 47*(2), 79–82.

Pratt, D. D. (1988). Andragogy as a relational construct. *Adult Education Quarterly, 38*(3), 160–181.

Ramsden, P. (1988). Studying learning: Improving teaching. In P. Ramsden (Ed.), *Improving learning: New perspectives* (pp. 13–31). London: Kogan Page, Ltd.

Ramsden, P. (1992). *Learning to teach in higher education*. New York: Routiledge.

Rando, W. C., & Menges, R. J. (1991). How practice is shaped by personal theories. In R. J. Menges & M. D. Svinicki (Eds.), *College teaching: From practice to theory* (pp. 7–14). San Francisco: Jossey-Bass.

Reynolds, A. (1992). What is competent beginning teaching? A review of the literature. *Review of Educational Research, 62*(1), 1–35.

Schmidt, H. G. (1993). Foundations of problem-based learning: Some explanatory notes. *Medical Education, 27*, 422–432.

Scientific American, 267(3), September, 1992

Small, P. A., Jr., Stevens, C. B., & Duerson, M. (1993). Issues in medical education: Basic problems and potential solutions. *Academic Medicine, 68*(10 October Supplement), S89-S98.

Vygotsky, L. S. (1978). *Mind in society: The development of higher psychological processes.* Cambridge, MA: Harvard University Press.

White, R., & Gunstone, R. (1992). *Probing understanding.* London: The Falmer Press.

Whitman, N. (1990). *Creative medical teaching.* Salt Lake City: University of Utah School of Medicine.

Wilson, S. M., Shulman, L. S., & Richert, A. E. (1987). '150 different ways' of knowing: Representation of knowledge in teaching. In J. Calderhead (Ed.), *Exploring teachers' thinking* (pp. 104–124). London: Cassell Education.

CHAPTER 7

THE NURTURING PERSPECTIVE
Facilitating Self-efficacy

Caddie T'Kenye

Teaching is a vastly over-rated function. (Rogers 1983, p. 119)

I agree. At best, good teaching can facilitate a meaningful engagement between a learner and content. At worst, teaching can be a source of diminished self-efficacy, convincing learners that they are not cut out to succeed, or not inclined to learn. Thus, this perspective recognizes the potential for either wounding or nurturing that comes with the role of teacher.

But how is it possible that any adult could think of themselves as wounding a learner? This would be the antithesis of an educator's central purpose, and I doubt very much that many teachers would like to hold themselves accountable for it. I do think, however, we must all shoulder some responsibility for such an outcome. Let me illustrate, with a story about myself:

Once, when I was a little girl, I was given a grade of 100% for my composition notebook. That meant, of course, a gold star on my chart posted at the front of the room. But 50% of that mark was taken away to teach me a lesson: I had ruined my book by drawing in the margins. I did learn a lesson: I learned to hide an important part of myself from teachers. I learned that my desire to speak in pictures as well as words was wrong. And, since I can no more stop drawing than I can stop breathing, I learned to be ashamed of my

151

*weakness as yet another scribbled drawing would appear almost
without my volition in the margins of my notebooks.*

I know that my teacher wanted the best for me—in her opinion. She
wanted to teach me tidiness, penmanship, and self-discipline. However,
what I learned was shame, fear, and a distrust of my own instincts. I am
sure that my teacher did not spend a great deal of time wondering what
this learning experience might look like from my point of view; if she
had, perhaps she would have tried to find another method of helping me
confine my drawing to a venue she felt appropriate. I am sure she never
intended to teach me that it was the act of drawing itself that was wrong
but, nonetheless, she caused me harm.

Now, when I facilitate workshops for adults who see themselves as
"artistically challenged," I continually meet people who are timidly attempting to reclaim a similar part of their identity, and almost every one
has vivid memories similar to mine. They learned somewhere along the
line that they were not good at—and thus not entitled to do—art. Other
people I've known are convinced they cannot dance, cannot play sports,
cannot learn science, or cannot learn math; nearly every field of endeavor
suffers from this inadvertent by-product of teaching: "That's not for
me—I know I can't do it." There are substantial numbers of adult learners who are both attracted to and repelled by particular content areas or
particular types of educational interactions because of similar beliefs.

I know this situation is not rare. I also know that such learners do
not belong to a low-achievement or low-potential stereotype. In fact, I
believe that many—perhaps most—adults have one or two areas in their
educational matrix that were adversely affected when relationships between teacher, learner, and content became unbalanced; when they were
not provided the nurturing and support that would encourage their sense
of efficacy. This damage could be limited, related only to a specific content area, or it could be global, related to the learner's concept of their
capacity to learn. When a belief that one is incapable of learning is
global, it tends to be visible and may be labeled a learning disorder; however, a proscribed belief related to a specific content area can be quite
well hidden.

DEVELOPING BELIEFS ABOUT SELF

*A few years ago, I was required to take a statistics course, a prereq-
uisite for graduate students in the social sciences and the arts. Out of*

a class of 25, not a single individual had less than 7 years of post-secondary education; these learners were the crème de la crème: if any group could be imagined to know how to learn, this was it. But on the first day of class, an observer would have been forgiven for imagining she was in a remedial learning group; the language around me, as I listened, was almost exclusively that of failure, fear, and anxiety.

One woman I knew to be the recipient of a scholarship based on academic merit was deeply worried that she would fail the course, as she had "never passed a math course" in her life. Given where she was placed academically, that claim seemed unlikely and I said so; but she insisted. She dated her claim back to the seventh grade, when her math teacher had used sarcastic humor to keep control of his class' behavior. Because she was very careful not to misbehave and never asked any questions, she hadn't been singled out for particular scorn, but she had taken other children's humiliations onto herself. When others asked questions and the teacher ridiculed them, she understood that she must be at least as stupid as those who did speak up, because she didn't know the answers, either. The teacher's oft-repeated phrase, that they weren't in "baby math" anymore, she had internalized into a belief that she had reached the highest level of her capacity to learn math.

She had her belief confirmed by getting much lower marks in math that year than in any other subject, and much lower marks in math than she ever had before. She went on to the next level of math feeling ill-prepared and stupid, but afraid to reveal the extent of her feelings of inadequacy. Through the rest of her academic career, she avoided math as much as possible, rarely risking questions that would reveal the depths of her "stupidity". As her fear grew, math became more and more difficult for her to understand.

By the time I met her, while there was no objective reason why she could not be successful in a statistics course, there were powerful subjective beliefs; enough to prevent engagement with and mastery of such content. Before any possibility of effective learning could be entertained, no matter how skillful content presentation might be, her teacher would have to work with her to help her deconstruct her convictions and replace them with more sustaining ones.

This woman, along with the rest of the grad students, also viewed the course as a kind of university-imposed academic boot camp, where we would "pay our dues" by being pushed through drills, humiliated by our failures, and close-marched over well-rutted tracks through the rigors of statistical methodology until we emerged with a minimum of a "pass" grade stamped on our transcripts. After that, we would be free to forget everything we'd supposedly learned and would never have to deal with statistics again for the rest of our lives—if we were lucky.

We hoped to be able to accomplish our goal on our first attempt; but we were more than willing to take onto ourselves any blame for our failure to, literally, make the grade should we not measure up. Those who proved unworthy—that is, "stupid at math"—would drop by the wayside this term, and have to face a second run through the morass of statistical methodology next term. We all accepted this as the norm; that is, just "how things are" in the worlds of university education and of math.

But in the language of transactional analysis, those who are repeatedly scripted away from certain behaviors will eventually lose the ability to think rationally about those behaviors (Walters & Marks, 1981) and will thus have recourse only to hunches or impulses to guide their actions. They will be more comfortable with acting out a dysfunctional script than they will be in trying to guess their way through to "another way of being". According to Cochran, one seeks situations or seeks to alter situations so that they will be in accord with the position one has taken vis-à-vis how the world works (Cochran, 1985).

Since we already knew that we were terrible at math, and this course was math, we knew that we were more than likely doomed to fail at it—just like we always had before. We were hoping our professor might be in possession of some kind of "magic bullet" that could take over where we were lacking; or that he might know of a technique that could, by some violent means of injection, stuff enough math "tricks" into our heads to get us through the required quizzes, midterms, and finals. We suspected this was unlikely, but hoped that at least some math would cling to us long enough to get us through the course.

A few of us were certain that no technique existed that would prove powerful enough to counteract our math idiocy. There were two such victims in our class; one was the woman discussed previously, the other was a man terrified that he wouldn't pass this, his second, run through the territory and would face a third and final chance at the

*same material. He didn't want to even think about what would hap-
pen if he failed three times.*

*Personally, I don't suffer math phobia but I don't like the stuff, either.
I saw the course mainly as a prolonged exercise in frustration, of trying to match pointless formulae with baffling numerals to make my
answers match those in the back of the book—without looking up
the answers first and working backward. The university could make
me take this course, but they couldn't make me anything more than
the most tepid of participants. I knew I could do stats, but I didn't
want to—when it comes to math, my defenses are usually up.*

Defensiveness, *in this sense, means resistance to events and experiences that don't fit in with how we view ourselves or the place we
have assigned ourselves in the world. Because congruity is essential
to the maintenance of identity, people will go so far as to misperceive
interactions with threatening events in such a way they will be able
to align those perceptions with their own reality, regardless of
whether that sense of reality is ultimately beneficial or harmful to
them. "Thus, people construct defenses to keep the world a stable
place that makes sense, not necessarily good sense, just predictable
sense.*

*The professor assigned to our section had a class full of beliefs and
expectations that were potent blocks to learning. Although these beliefs had little to do with the expressed content area of the course,
they had everything to do with our ability to engage with it. These
beliefs about self and efficacy would be vital factors in determining
how we interacted with the professor and the content; and it would
be up to the professor how, or even whether, these factors would be
addressed.*

WHAT CAN AN EDUCATOR DO?

Because many teachers—and learners—believe that content areas
like math and science lend themselves only to particular types of instruction methodology, nurturing education is not often considered when
teachers are contemplating approaches to practice. As a result, many
who teach in these areas are unfamiliar with the critical need on the part
of the learner to be in a position from which learning can be possible.
Furthermore, because of a lack of exposure to the nurturing philosophy

and perspective, many teachers are uncomfortable with addressing issues that seem to be off the topic, not realizing that grappling with these issues will enhance the likelihood that content will become more accessible to learners.

Drawing on my own previous math course experience, I thought it more than likely that our math instructor would have a history of consistent personal success at math, and would be entirely unable to relate to my merely tepid interest in the subject. It was equally likely, if not more so, that our professor would not even be able to recognize the existence of wounded learners in the class, let alone be able to empathize with their feelings of being "stupid at math." The chances that our professor might have some insight as to how to work with such attitudes were, in my opinion, quite small.

Our professor turned out to be a doctoral candidate in math and physics, named Jackson. He spent a good deal of time guiding us through content, providing us with the familiar chalkboard drills, homework, and mimeographed handouts. He gave the required, standardized quizzes and weekly assignments, midterm, and final examinations, but it became clear early on that Jackson had something beyond the course outline on his agenda.

In a subtle manner, he seemed to be challenging us: he didn't doubt in the least our capacity to grasp the material—his faith in our math capabilities far outstripped our own. He readily admitted that the university had us all up against the wall as far as a set curriculum and evaluation criteria were concerned, him as much as us, and he ruefully admitted we'd just have to work around that.

But he spent a lot of time, especially in the early days, reminding us of our successes, not just in this class but outside, in our real lives. During our first class, he asked who we were academically and personally; but unlike most polite professors, he remembered what we'd told him and referred to it, often reminding us that we were his peers. He deferred to our knowledge base and looked to us for examples from our fields of expertise when clarifying points. He worked hard to make us "knowers" as well as "learners," and to place himself beside us rather than above us, blurring the demarcation between our roles and our relative status positions.

He asked us about our math myths, and recounted some math horror stories of his own, stories we were surprised to find that he had, and we could understand where his empathy was coming from. We soon began to feel very close to him, to feel that he understood us. Jackson seemed to really care whether or not we did well, according to our own terms, not the university's. He was patient with our frustrated annoyance at being "forced" to take statistics.

Over time, we began to accept that Jackson had a wider vision that encompassed us. Jackson believed, in some way that we didn't quite understand, that statistics could enhance our lives. He wanted us to be able to make decisions about statistics in our professional lives from a position of strength and efficacy, rather than one of looking on stats, like all math, as a mystery inherently beyond our grasp.

As we began to trust Jackson's perceptions, we slowly began to place ourselves in a more positive position toward the course content, and to permit in ourselves the development of a vision of ourselves as, if not math-lovers, at least now willing to address his ideas about statistics and about our potential to learn this foreign "language."

Jackson seemed to return our trust in an unusual way: he assumed that we appreciated the implications and limitations of the situation we were all in. He never "went over the rules" with us, but presumed we had convened in his class for a particular purpose whose successful outcome was as important to us as our presence in his class was to him. We felt he appreciated our being there, appreciated our trying hard and our "stupid" questions; and he indicated his appreciation through his supportive language and his open attitude. He behaved toward us as though we were all participants in a silent contract of mutual respect; he had his role and we had ours, but neither of us was set above the other. In order to help us toward our goal—that of successfully passing the course according to university protocol— Jackson did everything conceivable to get at the underlying problem: he worked hard to take the fear out of stats.

He poked fun at studies whose findings flattered the funding bodies. He brought in studies that featured laughably poor interpretations, and brought in exceptionally good ones. He solicited examples from each of our disciplines, and we found ourselves in familiar territory searching "our" professional journals for statistical studies. He demonstrated how conclusions extracted from the same data could prove two different things at once; then challenged us to use our social sciences rhetoric to determine which conclusion might be more legiti-

mate—then he challenged us to think up circumstances that would reverse our conclusions.

Sessions with Jackson were stimulating, exciting and seemingly had absolutely nothing to do with math, though he often illustrated important points with some numbers or used a set of data as a take-off point for discussion. However, when my study group (one of several formed at Jackson's suggestion) met to do assignments from the text, we were usually astonished to realize that data the textbook presented as intimidating symbol- laden formulae and complex word problems was the same sort of material that Jackson had translated into "our" language during class. We found that Jackson was right about us, we were able to understand stats.

Jackson had guided us toward a belief that we could learn stats, if we were given a context that would not prove humiliating or harmful to us. However, unlike many teachers before him, Jackson had not only done no harm, he had helped to undo harm: he had helped us heal. I am certain that those teachers responsible for our math anxieties, be they parents or grandparents or school system employees, did not intend to hurt us, but hurt us they did.

TO WOUND OR TO AWAKEN?

To be a teacher is to wield a double-edged sword; one can wound as well as awaken. We can't always have good days. We can't always take the ideal approach for each learner. We can't always comprehend what effect our actions might have. But unless we are mindful of the possibility that our actions can injure, not only can we do a great deal of damage, we may not even be aware of it. It is unsettling to our sense of ourselves as professional educators to entertain the idea that someone, somewhere may be thinking of us as the "bad teacher" that damaged them. It is easier to focus on content or on skillful presentation and assume that a high percentage of passing grades indicates teaching success.

However, the skillful nurturing educator needs to pay attention to this aspect of the teacher-learner relationship before, during, and after educational interactions. We must be mindful of the potential dual nature of educational encounters. "Do no harm" is the cornerstone of our belief system. Because it is essential to monitor the possibility of causing harm, we need to educate ourselves, we need to learn to be sensitive to indicators of emotional reaction.

Many educators gain personal experience of the emotive states associated with learning, resistance, and positioning by entering into personal counseling, group therapy, or encounter therapies. Others use meditation or seek out experienced peer educators of similar intentions and beliefs with whom to discuss practice, its challenges, and its rewards. Most participate in a combination of techniques. Each path aids the educator to become and to remain emotionally receptive to learners in the midst of highly charged relationships that develop when issues of damaged self-esteem and related pain are raised within a learning context.

To nurture is to sustain and to aid in growth; the educator of adults must have faith that learners can grown, can learn. We must work toward helping the learner share this conviction, against the massed evidence learners have accrued from previous experience that has told them they cannot. If, to paraphrase Rogers (1983), we do have faith that individuals are competent to develop to their maximal potential, we can focus on facilitating opportunities for them to engage meaningfully in the relationships within the learning experience. We can permit the learner to choose their own method and direction of approach to content. This does not imply that content is irrelevant; indeed, there are many settings in which content is of the essence.

For example, a man I know teaches wilderness survival skills with juvenile offenders. He is not at liberty to allow those in his care to "just wing it." A minimum acceptable standard of content mastery is necessary to ensure that nobody drowns! Therefore, assessment of individualized mastery levels is very much a part of his role, and has to be incorporated within firm boundaries appropriate to each individual in his care, with a delicate balance struck between expectations of competence and expectations of performance.

EVALUATING COMPETENCE VS. PERFORMANCE

In early childhood education, the relationship between competence and performance is maintained at a healthy distance; but by late grade school, the majority of educational endeavors have been tied to measures that are believed to evaluate how much learning has been accomplished.

Most of these measures appraise performance, as though performance and competence are synonymous; this is, however, not the case. Performance is an externally based evaluation strategy with an implied or overt comparison outside of the self, either with competitors or standards. Competence, on the other hand, is an internal measure.

Using Elliot Eisner's example from the *Art of Evaluation*, if I run 10 miles and survive the experience, it could be said that I am competent (I have the ability) to run 10 miles. If I practice running, I may be able to enhance my performance. However, though I practice diligently, it may be that my personal best will never allow me to run more than 15 miles. If you compare me to marathon runners, my paltry 15 miles will certainly not measure up, and my performance will never be considered exceptional; even though my performance and my competence are congruent and optimal for me.

To compare me to a marathon runner and qualify my performance as mediocre is to imply that I can do what I cannot. If such requests are made of me frequently, it is likely that I will come to agree with this impartial evaluation, denigrate my own performance, and perhaps even begin to expect the impossible from myself. My sense of legitimate mastery of the 15 miles that I have accomplished will suffer, although I have actually accomplished as much for myself as the marathon runner has done for himself—we are both "100%" but we are in different races.

Nurturing educators keep themselves mindful, therefore, that evaluation must be concerned with competency levels rather than performance levels; competency is not standardized and must inevitably be idiosyncratic. Expecting performance to outstrip competence is a formula for diminished self-esteem. Comparison between oneself and externally based standards that may or may not be congruent with one's capacity is seen to be an inherently damaging mode of evaluation and is little used, unless it is imposed by outside forces, such as the university-imposed criteria for passing statistics courses.

However, if one does not have recourse to standard measures to assess learning success, then how can one determine if learning has occurred? First, we must be willing to invest time and energy in getting to know learners well enough to anticipate their potential competence, and therefore gain a sense of that learner's individual capacity. We must then assess the relationship between the learner's potential and their performance at present.

Jackson was fortunate in that he was able to assume that the learners in his group were likely to be capable of high levels of competence, because they were in graduate school. He could assume that their difficulties were performance-related; that is, related to self-esteem and self-doubt rather than capability.

But what about people who are judged by performance criteria to be not competent? It is an accepted truism that even though children are not equally competent to address learning tasks at the same performance levels, all children are competent to learn at some level or another. Early childhood educators are willing to trust children to learn up to their personal competence levels in incremental stages. Educators and parents have faith that children will seek to learn in conjunction with expanding competencies.

We don't, as a rule, want young children challenged with content in the same manner that we are willing to tolerate in older individuals. We seem instinctively to understand that their self-image as successful interactors with learning is of crucial concern, possibly because we realize that it is upon this foundation that all future learning successes will rest. Nurturing educators of adults share this faith.

We make the assumption that a learner has the potential for competence at a level appropriate for himself or herself. This may or may not have a direct relationship to performance levels; it will have a direct relationship with beliefs about personal efficacy and self-esteem. A guiding principle, then, of nurturing education is that mastery of content is considered secondary to the way in which mastery is achieved.

Socially, we uphold these principles when we seek out educators for our young children. We look for early childhood educators with warm, nurturing interpersonal skills in addition to professional training and qualifications. We see no incongruity between expecting that these educators will be able to coordinate effective learning interactions between members of a demanding learning group, with many diverse levels of competence, and content areas that would appear uninspiring at best. At the same time, we expect that no child will suffer diminished self-esteem during these learning encounters. Yet as soon as the learner has passed out of the early childhood phase, we assume that this style of educational encounter is now either inappropriate to the age group or impossible to establish with content areas such as math, science, or other basic skills.

However, regardless of the age of the learner or the type of content, the nurturing educator's major role is to facilitate healthy intrapersonal development in conjunction with learning encounters; if this mandate is carried out successfully, a sense of the self as an efficacious learner will result.

The nurturing educator of adults has the advantage that the majority of adult learners have entered the learning situation purposefully; they may not necessarily be volunteers to it, but they do have a mandate for their presence in a learning context. Even though a learning situation may be externally imposed, an adult has an inherent capacity to extract life-enriching influences from any learning situation, if the situation is constructed so as to provide them.

Although learners may have come accompanied by resistances and impediments to learning, the quality of the relationship established between the learner and the content, as influenced through the interactive relationship we call teaching, can facilitate a learning experience of great moment. The nurturing educator believes strongly in others' predilection to seek growth through learning, and believes in the inherent honesty of purpose underlying that search.

This belief, that the learner has an internalized drive toward self- realization, allows freeing of the educator's focus from strict attention to content, and permits attention to turn toward the relationships established within an "educational triangle" of learner, content, and teacher. The establishment of a fluid and potent dynamic in these relationships will determine whether or not a nurturing learning encounter is ultimately successful. Demonstrated caring for the learner as an individual, with concerned attention paid to the learner's experience through sensitivity and empathy, will establish a nurturing environment in any locale and with any body of content. It is here that most educators run into difficulty with nurturing practice. How does one demonstrate the caring attitude appropriately?

WHAT IS NUTURING EDUCATION?

Regardless of whether they practice from the nurturing perspective or not, many educators believe they know exactly what nurturing education is: it is andragogy which in North America is almost synonymous with Malcolm Knowles' work. It is important to note, however, that Knowles' most popular volume, *The Modern Practice of Adult Education*, devotes only 35 pages to clarifying the assumptions and beliefs underlying the prescriptives advanced in the remaining chapters. Although many of Knowles' recommendations do "fit the framework" as to how nurturing encounters might look in an ideal world, there is little discussion of the nurturing educator in practice, and almost no elaboration of the "hows and whys."

For example, it is recommended that adult education take place in settings that do not resemble traditional grade schools or high schools. Why? Apparently to reduce unpleasant associations with schooling. But how can one determine if unpleasant associations exist? Will changing the venue be effective in changing those associations? What if learners bring their associations with them not because of school settings, but those associations are related to learning per se? How should an educator who has only a limited choice of settings deal with that, if they still wish to address the problem of unpleasant associations surrounding early learning?

Unfortunately, in a handbook format, issues are presented as if acknowledgment of them is sufficient grounding: it is as though these complex issues are self-explanatory. One is almost invited to take the tenets of andragogy on faith, as if one is either born to educate in this manner (and thus understands the perspective intuitively) or one can diligently follow the practices outlined and expect that an internal shift in perspective will just happen.

I think this assumption implies an exclusivity that is both inaccurate and essentially unjust to caring and motivated educators. I may not incorporate any andragogical practices into my teaching, but will still be teaching from the Nurturing Perspective. Because the beliefs and commitments shared by nurturing educators can be learned, any motivated educator can cultivate a nurturing perspective in their practice. Indeed, aspects of the Nurturing Perspective can enhance any caring educator's practice. Sensitivity toward, and empathy with, learners' subjective experience of content and context can enrich any learning environment.

Interestingly, many qualities associated with nurturing educators are traditionally thought of as "feminine": empathy, sensitivity to others' emotional needs, practice of "intuitive" (in reality, keen and practiced) understanding of others' emotional states, and an ability to offer support during emotional crisis, and so forth. Indeed, it is the case that many nurturing educators are women, particularly those involved in early childhood education. Perhaps because of this association nurturing education suffers a slightly discredited reputation, as is often the case with stereotypical "female" roles in society, particularly those associated with children and childcare. It is quite common that, when seminars on teaching practice and philosophy are held, the nurturing educational perspective is conspicuous by its absence. It is just as often missing from scholarly examinations of teaching. It is assumed that absolutely anybody can successfully nurture. The stereotype would have us believe that it need not be taught—one must be to the manner born!

For most of us, the most common nurturing relationship—parenting—is taken for granted. We may acknowledge that there are different philosophies that underly good and effective parenting, and we may acknowledge that there exists successful practitioners and those who are less so. Most parents believe that it is possible to learn how to nurture and, in fact, many are willing to be taught ways and means of "filling the gaps" in their own childhood experience of nurturing.

We expect "successful" parents to understand and empathize with their child; and that they will provide kind, compassionate, and loving guidance through content areas of utmost difficulty—content of every sort from the mundane frustration of matching buttons with button holes to the understanding of complex moral dilemmas such as violence, racism, sickness, and death. Clearly, nurturing is an accepted, albeit taken for granted, part of our lives.

The nurturing educator works with other issues, perhaps, in different contexts and different age groups, but the underlying attributes and concerns remain the same. Learners' efficacy and self-esteem issues become the ultimate criteria against which learning success is measured, rather performance-related mastery of a content body. Ironically, although content is apparently neglected, children taught by nurturing educators do continue to master it at much the same rate as children taught by curriculum-driven teaching methodologies. I believe there is no significant difference between adults and children in this respect.

A belief that there is more to learning than there is to schooling has encouraged many teachers to expand their repertoire of educative interactions into nurturing behaviors. Usually, acquisition of these behaviors has followed, rather than preceded a shift in perspective about what it means to teach. I believe, then, that it is the perspective on teaching, focused on the importance of a healthy and integrated sense of the self as learner, that underlies an educator's desire to acquire the skills necessary to develop a nurturing practice. The first step along the road to becoming a nurturing educator is to ask, "How is a nurturing educator different from what I am now? What do they do? Why do they do it?"

WHAT DO THEY DO? WHY DO THEY DO IT?

First they practice empathy. Empathy in this sense is not the commonly understood idea of being able to "see from another's point of view" which is a cognitive image, but an ability to experience the emotive relationship between that point of view and the experience, as though one were, in a sense, the experiencer. As a result, they are able to perceive the emotive and reactive states of the learner with an understanding that includes both the intellectual (to know why someone does what they do), and the emotional (to have a feel for the emotions that provoke the behavior and the emotions caused by the behavior).

Empathy is most easily achieved with others who have had personal experiences similar to one's own. In Jackson's case, and in my own, we became nurturing educators likely because we had experienced the pain of dysfunctional relationships within prior learning contexts: Jackson had his math horror stories; I had my gold star episode. However, empathy based entirely on similarity of experience is limiting—Jackson was not teaching art; and I was not teaching math.

The range of our empathy can be expanded, however, through practicing empathic skills—attentive listening, mirroring of speech, engagement with nonverbal cues rather than ignoring or "cutting off" tears, sighs, and physical agitation. Through practice, nurturing educators can learn to extend empathy into learning areas in which they do not have direct empathic experience. Like most skills, repeated performance of empathic identification does enlarge one's capacity as well as one's range.

Practice must, however, rest on a base of informed belief; listening and mirroring a learner without a genuine interest or caring concern is simply going through the motions. Very few people can be fooled for long by the appearance of concern, regardless of how well it is done. As a nurturing educator I listen attentively because I really want to know how the learner feels within this learning situation. It is only with understanding that I will be able to establish a meaningful relationship with that individual and understand his or her learning difficulties.

We must envision learning as arising from within the possible for each individual. If we come, as most teachers do, from a background of traditional grade school and university education, we must diligently practice viewing evaluation as internally focused. This is difficult to achieve and will require much introspection and reflection. It is very difficult to divorce our sense of personal achievement and the justification of our activities from a performance-based system, especially when, as is the case in many settings and with some types of content, there are externally based regulations with which we must comply.

However, as nurturing educators, we have to respond to more pertinent questions: has a sense of competence been established in the learner, with a concurrent sense of the possibility of enhancement of performance? Has movement toward that goal been undertaken? Is there a perception within the learner that a personal best is possible? And, in rare cases, has that place been reached?

We must be centered in approach to evaluation, because this is where we are most vulnerable to criticism by proponents of other teaching perspectives, who may object to the apparent lack of focus in the nurturing learning encounter. If we come from a background where proof of our competency as professionals is based on the measured performance levels attained by our learners, letting go of this can be very challenging. If we are not firmly grounded in the nurturing belief system, it will be difficult for us to have the confidence that learners will choose to encompass internal, competency-related mastery, and that these levels will be entirely appropriate.

In order to establish ourselves within the belief system underlying the Nurturing Perspective, we may have to develop new ways of interpreting cues given by learners, and replace the externally based markers that delineate success in alternate perspectives. These new ways of understanding and perceiving will, ultimately, become cognitive schemas and significant belief structures (see Chapter 9) which will expand our repertoir of responses to situations both new and old.

Schemas are built, first, by recognizing the existence of a phenomenon. This may be the most problematical phase; we are all taught culturally, socially, and individually to "see" certain things and to "ignore" others. Generally speaking, the more fundamental an aspect is to our belief structures, the more "invisible" it will be. As nurturing educators, we need to cultivate a questioning attitude about our world and its culture, in order to be able to note phenomena that occur and take a stance of inquiry toward them. Observation is followed by examination and tentative comprehension of the phenomenon on a superficial or introductory level. Repeated observation and/or experience will ultimately develop our understanding into a deeper comprehension of the phenomenon and its subtleties.

Perhaps we notice that every time learners apparently "get it"; they smile broadly and say, "Hey, look at this!" to peers in adjacent seats. In traditional evaluation strategies, this reaction would either go unnoticed or be seen as a discipline problem and be cut off immediately.

However, we simply note the phenomenon, wonder about it and then begin purposefully to watch for its recurrence. The next time we see it, we ask the learner what has occurred. The learner responds, "I don't know, I was just excited and wanted to tell somebody." We then take this information, excitement and a drive to share it, and reflect on what it might mean. Perhaps we read a journal or discuss it with a colleague. Is this an evaluation by the learner?

Based on our discussions, we seek out related readings and find that, in counseling psychology, this phenomenon is known as "consensual validation of experience." According to the theory, the learner is seeking to inform peers of, and thus confirm to herself, that a learning shift has indeed taken place. She is claiming to have learned and is confident enough in her claim to go public with it.

We now have a named schema to take back into practice. With an enhanced vision, we are more sensitive to the next occurance of this phenomenon. It may occur couched in other behavior or in another learner, but because we now have a wider vision, we may be able to see and compare different occurances of the same phenomenon.

Because we are more experienced, more subtle aspects of the phenomenon previously overlooked are also easier for us to see. We note that when the learning announcement is made, the learner's peers both acknowledge and test the claim. They ask that the learner to teach what has been learned, by asking the learner to show or demonstrate the claimed mastery. If the learner is well-grounded in a sense of efficacy, she will demonstrate what she has learned. If the learner's claim is somewhat hesitant, she may demur; perhaps refusing to demonstrate it, or issuing advance disclaimers before making an attempt. We take these observations, again, back to reflection.

Thus, we expand and elaborate our repertoire of schemas in ways that provide us with several gradations of self-evaluation. First, there is the statement of belief by the learner; the challenge of that by peers; followed by the learner's commitment to her self- evaluation. Both learner and peers are willing to accept that learning has occurred, and the learner is entitled to try to confirm her belief. To challenge someone to teach us is, indeed, a potent evaluation strategy, because we do not seek to be taught by those we feel do not know.

Through observation, reflection, discussion, and reading, the educator has learned to hear and see new and valuable cues. However, to begin this cycle of observation and learning, we had to trust that what we saw was important. To do so, we had to put aside our personal preconceptions about teaching, about learning, and about learners, and be willing to examine "irrelevant" phenomena.

We also had to put aside status concerns and be willing to trust that we would be accurately informed by the learner. Although learners may not have the language of education, nor the language of nurturing, they do have a language of self, that only they can know. As educators, we must believe that this is the case, and believe that learners will share their perceptions as accurately as they are able with us. Authentic nurturing interaction are spontaneous, arising within context, and may be subtle and fleeting. Understanding the dynamics of interpersonal relationships is at the best of times difficult. When teaching, it is perhaps much easier and certainly much safer to confine ourselves strictly to content and traditional methods of evaluation. Nurturing education is difficult and energy-consuming and requires a certain degree of faith and trust in the inherent goodness and value of learners.

PARAGONS OF VIRTUE?

So where do these nurturing educators come from? So far, we've determined that they are kind, sensitive, intuitive, trusting, honest, sincere, and compassionate—how did they get like that? Certainly, none of us are entirely like that, at least not consistently when we're teaching. Does this mean that we're just not cut out to be nurturing educators?

I think the key to becoming (or being) a practicing nurturing educator is to be both self-reflective and forgiving. We need to examine our own relationships within the learning triangle, and to ponder our own reactions to learning, to learners, and to teaching. We need to be humble enough to question our practice and admit to colleagues our puzzlement and insecurity about the nature and quality of the events occurring within our classes or workshops.

Then, we must forgive ourselves for those many times that we fell short of our goals. We have to remind ourselves frequently that learning is, in essence, a private and individual event. The nurturing educator can choreograph flawlessly, work intensely to enter an empathetic state, observe with acumen, and maintain a delicate balance between support and intrusion, but until the learner is positioned emotionally and cognitively and is prepared to make an internal shift, learning will not take place.

We must be equally ready to forgive ourselves for overreaching in those situations where we do think we have succeeded. It is a human foible to want to take on a learner's accomplishments. We'd like to tell ourselves that it was our talent, our compassion, our skill, and our empathy that has made a difference. It is so tempting to bask in our glory! Even more perilous to us as practitioners is the tendency on the part of the learner to want to give us credit. Because of the warmth and closeness of the relationship established with the educator, often a novel experience for the learner, learners often do want to transfer credit for their successes to us. It is tempting to accept what seems like fair acknowledgment of our hard work; nurturing educators do work hard. We assist in dismantling old blockages, we remove impediments from the path; we do our best to make sure that no new blockage is put in its place. We listen carefully; we make suggestions and countersuggestions, while trying to remain nonintrusive; we guide if we can, and try to find a path when we cannot guide. Sometimes we just work hard at keeping our temper when resistance is strong. However, regardless of how hard we work, no educator, nurturing or otherwise, is able to force movement or make learning happen.

Yet, success in learning may be unfamiliar and even frightening to some learners. Although that may not seem sensible to those outside this perspective, it is true, especially when something threatens the person's self-concept. The result is resistance—sometimes fight; sometimes flight. We have a strong urge to protect our self-concept, even when learning is required but not comfortable. When learning rocks our image of ourselves and our established place in the world it can have a domino effect in our lives that we are not prepared to deal with. Ironically, if we suddenly see ourselves succeeding in arenas in which we knew ourselves to be failures, we may not want to acknowledge that or be forced to integrate it into our self-image. Even that threat to self can be resisted.

Instead, learners may reconstruct the situation and interpret the success as a "gift" from a benevolent teacher, or given because she or he likes me. When this happens, the teacher is given credit for the success, not the learner. This may be an emotionally gratifying position for the teacher. However, it cannot be stated too strongly that the learner must always own the success of learning. That means, of course, no matter how flattering it may be to believe otherwise, successful achievement must never be attributed to the educator. To do so undermines the very soul of the Nurturing Perspective—the development of self-esteem and self-efficacy.

Thus, we must practice being able to forgive both ourselves—for not being able to achieve the impossible: the perfect, always efficacious, learning situation; and the learner—for not always being able to accept what we can offer. We need also to forgive ourselves for being too human, for wanting to be the instrument of another's healing. It is possible that this desire to intervene and take onto oneself that which rightfully belongs to others may be the biggest hazard to the educator's peace of mind in the Nurturing Perspective.

It is true that many who work in nurturing education find that they suffer severe burnout after a relatively short period of practice. They find it difficult to maintain appropriate boundaries between themselves and learners. Because the relationship between learners and educator tends to be more intense and more personal than is the case in other perspectives, a common difficulty is that of learners' transfer of inappropriate emotional bonds to the educator, as well as the educator's seeking inappropriate emotional rewards from the learning situation.

For example, many students in Jackson's statistics class believed that the secret to their successful learning rested in Jackson himself, and their behavior was little short of adoration. It was an important aspect of his relationship to students to dismantle this misperception, and to "cut himself down to size." He could only do this by remaining aware of his role and by paying close attention to the dynamics of the relationships in his teaching context.

Such reflection on our own needs and our beliefs about content, learners, and our role as educators is a crucial part of our formation as professional nurturing educators. It is flattering to be thought exceptional; the special teacher that could do what others could not. It is equally flattering to be treated with affection and respect; to be honored as the "very best teacher I ever had." We would love to claim this distinction as an accurate reflection of our merit; sad to say, we cannot in good conscience, do this.

We must remain on a par with the learner in essential ways. An enhanced command of a content area must not be allowed to be translated into a disparate power relationship between seekers and guru. Learners need to be guided toward owning their successes, to be able to build from that a sense of efficacy that will ultimately enhance their lives. It is only through successful acknowledgment of one's achievements, based on an internalized belief in one's competence, that self-esteem is gained.

As nurturing educators, we want learners to be empowered, not to empower ourselves at their expense. It is only when we can look at ourselves, as Rogers so aptly described, as imperfect human beings with many feelings and many potentialities that we will be able to extend our vision to include those who may be in a learning relationship with us, and see them as teachers of themselves, and potential educators for us.

WHAT'S IN IT FOR ME?

What do I derive from the difficult and often exhausting experience of attempting to break down resistance and aid healing? Simply stated, I achieve spiritual and emotional growth through nurturing educational practice. Each individual with whom I make contact is vitally important to me:

> They help me remain inspirited, turned on to my life. And when they need help . . . I use my time and resources to help them live more fully, joyously and meaningfully. They give to me and, just as important, they accept from me . . . and acceptance of my giving validates me [when] my existence enhances that of another. (Jourard, 1971, p. 54)

To have made contact between my heart and soul and a hurting person's heart and soul, to have effected at least a tiny measure of relief, is a reminder to me to live beyond myself, to challenge my own limitations. To make intimate contact with another, I must accept the mandate to see not what they see, but how they see, and this is to be enabled in a unique way. When I "look" into a learner looking back at me,

> I see them as the embodiment of incredible possibilities. I see imaginatively what they might become if they choose. I may [by teaching] invite them to activate possibilities they may not have envisioned. (Jourard, 1971, p. 55)

Therefore, if to teach is to participate in wounding by upholding and perpetuating out-of-balance and inharmonious educative relationships, then I am no teacher and refuse to be one. If to teach is to aid in the awakening of an inner quest for knowing oneself without externally imposed limitations, then I can accept the designation. I am an idealist and a visionary, I suppose, and I'm hooked on the joy I see when I'm lucky enough to be there when healing happens.

REFERENCES

Cochran, L. (1985). *Position and the nature of personhood: An approach to the understanding of persons.* London: Greenwood Press.

Eisner, E. W. (1985). *The art of educational evaluation: A personal view.* London: The Falmer Press.

Eisner, E. W. (1985). *The educational imagination: On the design and evaluation of school programs* (2nd ed.). New York: Macmillan.

Jourard, S. M. (1971). *The transparent self* (2nd ed.). New York: Van Nostrand Reinhold Co.

Knowles, M. (1980). *The modern practice of adult education: From pedagogy to andragogy.* Edgewood Cliff, NJ: Prentice Hall Regents.

Rogers, C. R. (1983). *Freedom to learn for the 80s.* Columbus, OH: Merrill Publishing.

Walters, G. A., & Marks, S. E. (1981). *Experiential learning and change: Theory, design, and practice.* Toronto, ON: John Wiley & Sons, Inc.

CHAPTER 8

THE SOCIAL REFORM PERSPECTIVE
Seeking a Better Society

Tom Nesbit

> Knowledge of basic mathematics and statistics is an important
> point of gaining real popular, democratic control over the
> economic, political, and social structures of our society. Liberatory
> social change requires an understanding of the technical
> knowledge that is too often used to obscure economic and social
> realities. When we develop specific strategies for an emancipatory
> education it is vital that we include mathematics. (Marilyn
> Frankenstein, 1987, p. 180)

This chapter concerns the fifth perspective on teaching: social reform. Teachers holding a Social Reform Perspective are most interested
in creating a better society and view their teaching as contributing toward that end. Their perspective is unique in that it is based upon "an
explicitly stated ideal or set of principles linked to a vision of a better
social order" (Pratt, 1992). Social reformers do not teach in one single
way, nor do they hold distinctive views about knowledge in general, the
specific content they teach, their learners, or their own role as teachers;
these factors all depend on the particular ideal that inspires their actions.
In this chapter, I examine a "radical" approach to teaching mathematics
as an example of the Social Reform Perspective. After providing a brief
introduction to the ideas of radical education in general, I discuss reasons
for using this approach with mathematics. First, I describe and analyze

some features of traditional mathematics education, then consider how a radical approach challenges some of the common assumptions about mathematics and mathematics education. The work of several radical mathematics teachers provides examples of how the curricula changes with this approach and is illustrative of the Social Reform Perspective.

RADICAL EDUCATION

A radical approach to education is based on the view that education is not ideologically neutral; every educational system incorporates biases which reflect the views and interests of those in possession of social, economic, and political power (Apple, 1979; Shor & Freire, 1987; Williams, 1976). The notion that all knowledge is socially constructed is central to this view (cf., the developmental perspective). This means that knowledge is created through interaction with others in specific social, historical, cultural, and political contexts, and therefore, necessarily structured in particular ways.

However, radical educators regard the notion that knowledge is socially constructed as limited. Specifically, for them, it does not explain how certain social and cultural meanings are promoted to the exclusion of others, or how "a reality comes to be constructed in particular ways, and how and why particular constructions of reality seem to have the power to resist subversion" (Whitty, cited in Apple, 1979, p. 27). Hence, one task for radical educators is to question how and why knowledge is constructed in the way that it is, how and why some constructions are supported while others are not, whose interests are served by these constructions, and whose interests are excluded or marginalized. For radical educators, simply comprehending power differences is insufficient; they seek to extend this comprehension by arousing people to take social action to address the problems and issues that beset them.

Radical educators regard the world and its constituent societies as full of contradictions and marked by imbalances of power and privilege. Hence, they regard such problems as poverty or illiteracy neither as isolated incidents nor as manifestations of individual inadequacy, but as results of larger social issues. Furthermore, individuals, as social actors, both create and are created by their social worlds. As Karl Marx put it: "Men make their own history . . . not under circumstances chosen by themselves, but under circumstances directly encountered, given and transmitted from the past" (1852/1950, p. 225). Radical educators believe that social phenomena exist in the objective world as well as in the mind, and that relationships and regularities between phenomena can be discovered and examined.[1] Radical education, therefore, involves people in exploring and analyzing their social reality as the context for the subjects they study. Indeed, in radical education, learners' lives become the curriculum.

To do this, radical adult educators often use a "problem-posing" approach to learning. Problem-posing recognizes that knowledge begins with the asking of questions and is produced through a constant mediation between the learner and what is to be known. Problem-posing requires learners not only to describe and personalize their problems but also to analyze and socialize them in the search for solutions. Central to this process is praxis: an ongoing, cyclical, and transformative process of active investigation, reflection, and further investigation. Through problem-posing, learners come to ask their own questions and find their own answers rather than accept the questions and answers that others provide. They experience education as an active process rather than as something that just happens to them.

WHY MATHEMATICS?

There are several reasons why mathematics is a particularly appropriate subject area to illustrate a radical approach to education. In significant ways, mathematics, as an area of knowledge, is unique. Numbers and number systems are, like language, a fundamental feature of human activity, and most scientific and technological development is based on the ability to perform mathematical calculations. For many people, mathematical knowledge represents a certain and value-free objective reality, and its pursuit becomes the search for timeless truths. Numeracy—mathematical ability—is regarded as key to being economically productive and successful in modern, industrial society. Consequently, mathematics functions as a "social filter" for economic success, and is probably the one subject that is taught in every school in the world. Despite this, mathematics often engenders attitudes of antipathy or outright hostility in many people who subsequently try their best to avoid it whenever possible.

Math As Objective Reality

Mathematics is largely regarded as the ultimate body of absolute, timeless, and objective truth far removed from the concerns and values of humanity. It represents the most certain part of human knowledge, a basis on which most scientific and technological advances have been built. Because of this, mathematics also serves a central function as a tool of those with power in society.

Radical educators are concerned with how mathematics is used to justify all sorts of policies and decisions, including those which may be considered inhumane (such as increasing defense spending while cutting social security payments, or closing local industries). Of course, one may argue that the policies are the result of political decisions, and mathematics merely serves to provide the evidence or prove the point. However, radical educators would argue that the supposedly abstract world of mathematics cannot be divorced from the real world of politics; one cannot focus on mathematics without also considering its uses.

Numerical data is often used to support or promote a certain position because numbers (and mathematics) are largely seen as objective, and, therefore, beyond criticism. Indeed, in this context, numbers are often described as "hard" data. Consider the presentation of governmental policy documents; endless charts and tables of statistics. They look right, don't they? So the conclusions that the chart-writers draw from such data must also be right, mustn't they? In these situations, mathematics is as often used to obscure and confuse as it is to provide evidence or prove points. How many of us feel skilled enough to look beyond the numbers to interpret what the charts mean? How often are we prepared to take statistical information and their stated conclusions at face value?[2]

In addition, how many of us question, or even think about, why anyone wants to collect such statistics in the first place, and for what purposes? Further, do we question the production of such information, and how the research process that produces the data is shaped by context? For example, decisions about whether to use a particular research design, or particular methods, often depend on available resources or the availability of particular sources of data. Similarly, data collection, analysis, interpretation, and presentation are often heavily influenced by a rational and objective view of reality, esoteric statistical methods, and the arcane language of mathematicians.

The public's unconsidered perceptions that mathematics represents truth or reality intrigues radical educators. They question why peoples' abilities to discern opinion and bias in other types of information often disappear in the face of graphs and statistics. They also draw attention to how an overemphasis on numerical data obscures the daily reality of peoples' lives, and diverts attention away from changing that reality (Frankenstein, 1989).

Math As a Social Filter

Numeracy is commonly recognized as a major determinant for job and career choices within industrialized societies (Handler, 1990; National Research Council, 1989). Hence, numeracy levels in society are regularly monitored by educators, government, and business leaders in both North America and Europe. However, mathematical ability is also more than simply a pre-requisite for a good job. Those who do not feel confused or threatened by numbers and data can expand their ways of understanding and perceiving reality, critically examine the assumptions that others take for granted, and act as informed participants within society.

To understand the role of mathematics as a social filter, it is instructive to consider an analogy. Formerly, access to higher education (and hence to becoming part of a social elite) was partly controlled through studies in rhetoric or Latin. Only those who passed examinations in these subjects were allowed to attend university. Nowadays, rhetoric and Latin have been replaced by mathematics. In most countries, passing examinations in mathematics is necessary for access to higher education (and hence to higher-paying work) regardless of the area of future study. Possession of mathematical knowledge is seen as governing learners' future occupational and economic roles. In this way, mathematics becomes "cultural capital" indicative of future economic success.

Radical educators are also interested in how mathematics education reinforces social position. For example, Jean Anyon (1981) studied the teaching of mathematics (among other subjects) in five schools and found that although all the schools used the same textbooks, the teaching differed dramatically. Teachers in the two working-class schools focused on procedure without explanation or attempts at helping students understand (cf. the surface approach in the Developmental Perspective). Teachers in the middle-class school offered more flexibility and made some efforts toward developing student understanding (cf. the deep approach).

The professional school teachers emphasized discovery and experience as a basis for the construction of mathematical knowledge. Finally, teachers in the executive-class school extended this discovery approach through further instruction on problem-solving and encouraging students to justify their answers. Given mathematics' role as a social filter, it is not surprising to discover that people have strong attitudes about mathematics.

Attitudes toward Math

Many studies indicate that mathematics arouses strong feelings of hostility or antipathy. The one subject that is supposedly so free of values and emotional content produces the strongest negative emotional reaction of any curriculum area. The discussion of peoples' negative attitudes toward mathematics often centers around the concept of "math anxiety", described most rigorously as "a psychological state engendered when a person experiences (or expects to experience) a loss of self-esteem in confronting a situation involving mathematics" (Michael, 1981, p. 58). Mathematics anxiety is regarded as one result of the deficiencies in school mathematics education with its concentration on the technical acquisition of a predetermined set of basic skills and knowledge, an abstract and decontextualized approach, rote memorization of theories and formulae, relentless calculations, the primacy of the correct solution, and regular testing.

Remember, however, that radical educators do not locate problems within individuals, but look to broader social influences and causes. To them, therefore, math anxiety—an individual characteristic—does not suffice as an explanation for widespread adult innumeracy. How then is innumeracy viewed in larger social contexts?

First, innumeracy is not considered as socially unacceptable as its counterpart illiteracy. One often hears statements about people's mathematical inadequacies, spoken without any apparent embarrassment: "I've never been able to work out how much to tip"; "I never check my change from the store"; or "I'm a people person, not a numbers person." One mathematician, John Allen Paulos, claims that part of people's lack of concern about their mathematical ignorance comes because the consequences of innumeracy are not as "obvious as other weaknesses" (1988, p. 4). Radical educators are interested in the discrepancy between mathematics' social necessity, and its lack of perceived need. How relevant is mathematics (as it is taught in school) to our daily lives?

Despite the links between mathematics, scientific and technological advances, and economic mobility, many people still regard mathematics as tangential to their lives and avoid it whenever they can. Although mathematical ability can be found in most human activity, it is seen as doing so in an abstract and depersonalized way which reinforces a social view of mathematics as belonging only

> to a closed club of people who subscribe to the same rules and speak the same language. Arguing that mathematics is abstract, objective and independent of social, cultural, and political conditions has left the members of the club in an elitist and privileged position. (Burton, 1989, p. 17)

Mathematics exists, therefore, as a fundamental subject, necessary for access to power and privilege in most societies, which also can arouse powerful negative emotions. The paradox between the way mathematics is regarded in society and how deeply people are disempowered by it marks it as an especially appropriate subject for radical education.

TRADITIONAL MATHEMATICS EDUCATION

Radical educators are particularly critical of traditional education. This, they argue, is designed to reproduce the existing economic, status, and power hierarchies, and socialize learners into accepting the status quo. Because traditional mathematics education cannot be excluded from this analysis, radical educators would consider the curricula and teaching methods most common in traditional mathematics education, common experiences of that education, and the uses of mathematics in peoples' daily lives.

Curricula and Methods

The traditional mathematics curriculum consists of an abstract and hierarchical series of objective and decontextualized facts, rules, and answers. Much of this curriculum covers a fixed body of knowledge and core skills largely unchanged for centuries. It is based on the assumption that learners absorb what has been covered by repetition and practice, and then become able to apply this knowledge and these skills to a variety of problems and contexts.

Teaching methods in traditional mathematics education use largely authoritarian and individualizing techniques that depend on memorization, rote calculation, and frequent testing (Bishop, 1988). These methods convince learners that they are stupid and inferior if they can't do simple calculations, that they have no knowledge worth sharing, and that they are cheating if they work with others. When education is so presented as a one-way transfer of knowledge from teachers, mathematics can be regarded merely as collections of facts and answers. Knowledge is seen as largely separate from learners' thought processes, and education is experienced as a static, rather than a dynamic, process. In many ways, this approach typifies the Transmission Perspective on teaching described earlier.

Consequently, many learners of mathematics find themselves in classes in which little effort has been made to place the subject matter in any meaningful context. For many, mathematics remains a mystery unrelated to other subjects or problems in the real world; they often come to regard mathematics as a subject largely irrelevant to their own lives. The prevailing curricula in mathematics education are also considerably influenced by two factors: the aims of mathematics education, and the use of set textbooks.

Aims of Mathematics Education

In general, two rationales are given for why mathematics should be taught: (1) Mathematics is necessary for personal life and a prerequisite for many careers; and (2) Mathematics improves thinking, because it trains people to be analytical, logical, and precise, and it provides mental exercise. Of course, these rationales do not specify *what* mathematics should be taught, merely that *some* mathematics should be. One could expect, therefore, that mathematics education could differ substantially from place to place. It is surprising, then, to see how little diversity exists in mathematics classrooms the world over.

Radical educators, noting that the aims of mathematics education are often discussed in isolation from any social and political content, identify several professional groups who have distinct aims for mathematics education: mathematicians, representatives of business and industry, and those in higher education. They argue that these groups do not decide the aims of mathematics education on rational or educational grounds, but based on their own particular group interests. Hence, the aims for mathematics education are decided by those who already have authority and privilege within society. Little wonder that they do not advocate approaches that challenge that authority.

In addition, radical educators argue that it is as much the form as the content of mathematics education which conveys its social aims. The manner in which mathematics is traditionally taught tends to promote competition, individualism, and authoritarianism; successful learners are those who best absorb these values. Indeed, one study found that teachers regarded mathematical ability as a "behavioral badge of eligibility for employment," and mathematics as a way of inculcating work ethic values seen as important in society (Cooper, 1989).

Textbooks

The content and structure of most mathematics courses are also determined by the content and structure of the set textbooks. In many ways, the textbooks are the curriculum, codified. A comprehensive survey of research on teaching and learning mathematics found that "the textbook was seen as the authority on knowledge and the guide to learning" (Romberg & Carpenter, 1986, p. 867) in all of the studies they surveyed. It concluded that many teachers "see their job as covering the text," and that mathematics was "seldom taught as scientific inquiry [but] presented as what the experts had found to be true" (p. 867). These conclusions are supported by a study of adult mathematics classes in Sweden which found that teaching practices "were organized on a 'cramming' basis [where] the teachers play the part of 'living textbooks' " (Höghielm, 1985, p. 207). It is not unrealistic to expect teachers to use some textbook or other; it is common practice in most classrooms. However, as radical educators ask: Whose books are these? Who writes them? For whom? and Why?

Basing teaching largely on a textbook has several consequences. Mathematics textbooks embody and objectify a top-down curriculum. They are written by experts who presume not only what learners need to know but also how they need to learn it. Second, they make no distinction between what different learners bring with them to the classroom. By depersonalizing and generalizing learners, textbooks privilege content over process. They encourage the teaching of subject matter, rather than the teaching of people. Further, learning mathematics is seen as impersonal: learners are discouraged from making their own meanings, or finding significance for themselves. Finally, textbooks present mathematics in a supposedly value-free and decontextualized way. Usually, textbook problems, as written, have only one answer and one method of solution. But the world is not like that: many problems coexist, have multiple methods of solution, and often have several answers.

Experiences of Math Education

The traditional mathematics education described above is certainly common. As noted earlier, mathematics is probably taught in every school in the world. So, mathematics is commonly provided, but is it commonly experienced? What are some common experiences of mathematics education and innumeracy? Does traditional mathematics education subtly exclude certain "disadvantaged" groups?

Can you remember your own mathematics education? Did it include reciting the times tables? A concern with getting the right answer, as quickly as possible? Trying not to look foolish in the process? Endless calculations and problems that seemed to have little to do with your own life? An obsession with word problems that asked you, for example, to find the rate at which two trains hurtled toward each other from opposite directions, how long it took three men to dig a ditch that would take each one so many hours, and how much you could repay each year if you borrowed a certain sum at such a percentage?

Would it surprise you to learn that nothing has really changed very much today? People still find mathematics education threatening and bewildering. Perhaps the times tables aren't chanted quite so frequently, but people are still asked to routinely make meaningless calculations and solve irrelevant problems. Commonly used mathematics textbooks for adults usually include pages of drills and such problems as:

1. You are now twice the age you were 16 years ago. How old are you?

2. A movie theater had a certain number of tickets to give away. Five people got the tickets. The first got 1/3 of the tickets, the second got 1/4 of the tickets, and the third got 1/5 of the tickets. The fourth person got eight tickets, and there were five tickets left for the fifth person. Find the total number of tickets given away.

In any case, the problems that you were asked (and that are still being asked of mathematics learners today) often seem devoid of any social or political content. But, why should they? After all, mathematics is universal and context-free, isn't it? Isn't addition the same everywhere?

Doesn't 2 + 2 = 4 regardless of context or culture? "2 + 2" and "1 = 1" may have universal "meanings" in the abstract world of mathematics but do they make any sense in the real world? Radical educator Munir Fasheh argues that:

> "One equals one" is mathematical fact, but its description and interpretation and application differ from one situation to another and from one culture to another . . . one dollar in 1970 is not equal to one dollar in 1980. [Further,] different opinions emerge when we say for example, that "women are equal to men." Strictly speaking, "one equals one" does not have true instances or applications. (1982, p. 6)

It certainly seems that politics has little to do with mathematics in the real world. But, consider these problems:[3]

> Twenty-three peasants are working in a field. At midday, six guerrilla fighters arrive to help them from a military base near their field. How many people are working in the field? (Mozambique)

> Once upon a time a ship was caught in a storm. In order to save it and its crew the captain decided that half the passengers would have to be thrown overboard. There were 15 Christians and 15 Turks aboard the ship and the captain was a Christian. He announced that he would count the passengers and that every ninth one would be thrown overboard. How could the passengers be placed in a circle so that all the Turks would be thrown overboard and all the Christians saved? (USA)

> When worker Tung was 6 years old his family was poverty-stricken and starving. They were compelled to borrow five *dou* of maize from a landlord. The wolfish landlord used this chance to demand the usurious compound interest of 50% for 3 years. Please calculate how much grain the landlord demanded from the Tung family at the end of the third year. (China)

It is obvious that all of these problems contain assumptions about the society from which they come. Don't they seem more political than the ones you were asked to solve as a child? Perhaps you never noticed the political quality of your mathematical problems. But radical educators would argue that problems about borrowing money or men digging ditches have a political and cultural content too. They question teaching that does not draw attention to the values and opinions inherent in all mathematical problems. In contrast, traditional mathematics education largely ignores questions about the nature of mathematics and its relationship to the society in which it is produced.

Perhaps a radical approach to mathematics education would merit less attention if the traditional approach succeeded in educating more people. Most societies already value mathematical ability. Yet, without exception, the education systems of industrialized countries teach, test, and reinforce a fixed curricula using individualizing methods that leave the majority of their people unable to perform all but the simplest calculations. Radical educators, who eschew individualized educational remedies (such as treating each innumerate learner as math anxious), therefore question the effect of traditional mathematics education on societal levels of innumeracy. Does traditional mathematics education work?

Mathematics in Daily Life

Over the last decade there has been an increasing realization that innumeracy is a growing problem affecting many adults. As explained above, innumeracy restricts achievement and economic mobility, and can also be psychologically disabling, undermining people's self-esteem and confidence in their own thinking skills. Furthermore, their unease with numbers can cause adults to be susceptible to the "mystique" of mathematics, and often, therefore, overly dependent on the views of professionals or experts (Evans, 1989). And yet, most people do appear to function perfectly well without ever needing to use much of the mathematics that they remember from school. What happens?

In recent years there have been a number of studies of the uses of mathematics in adults' work and everyday life. These studies document the distinctive character of the mathematical skills and procedures used in work and everyday life as compared with those taught in school mathematics. For example, in one study, street vendors who successfully performed many calculations daily in their heads, found similar calculations (to be performed with pencil and paper, outside the context of the street market) exceedingly difficult, and made many more errors (Carraher et al., 1985).

Another study found that there were many adults who were unable to cope confidently and competently with any everyday situation that required the use of school mathematics (Sewell, 1981). Further, the need to use mathematics could induce feelings of anxiety, helplessness, fear, and guilt. Is this simply math anxiety? Interestingly, these uncomfortable feelings were especially common among those with high academic qualifications, who felt that they ought to have a confident understanding of mathematics. Further findings included a widespread sense of inadequacy amongst those who felt they either had not used the proper method, obtained the exact answer, or performed with sufficient speed when solving mathematical problems. Is this symptomatic of a problem located solely within the learner, or, potentially, in greater areas?

Other studies have found that traditional mathematics education particularly discourages women, members of certain ethnic minorities, and the working class from learning mathematics. Marilyn Frankenstein identifies a social function in this pattern: failure in mathematics will restrict access for these groups to academic, economic, and civic achievement. The discouragement may work at an individual level, but it has societal implications:

> Sexual stereotyping leads many women to believe that learning mathematics undermines their femininity; intellectual stereotyping leads many people to believe that learning mathematics is too hard for them; meaningless, boring school work serves to prepare people for meaningless, boring jobs. (1981, p. 11)

She highlights how traditional mathematics education can discourage students: "Too many teachers baby-sit instead of helping students learn; too many teachers convey their own hatred or fear of mathematics to their students; the mathematics curriculum is irrelevant to students' lives; the math curriculum is boring" (1981, p. 11).

So, in spite of near universal provision of mathematics courses, the existing curricula and classroom practices in traditional mathematics education clearly don't work for everybody, and are seen as contributing to the growth of innumeracy. Traditional methods seem to reinforce notions that mathematics is value-free, devoid of social context, and can best be learned by following textbooks and copying what the teacher says. Traditional methods also result in worriedly high levels of adult innumeracy and disparate levels of access and participation in academic, economic, and public affairs.[4] Radical educators find this unacceptable, and propose a qualitatively different approach.

RADICAL MATHEMATICS

The overarching ideal for radical mathematics educators is best described by the quote from Frankenstein that introduced this chapter.

Thus, a radical approach to mathematics education analyzes how mathematics functions in society at both an individual and societal level. The Danish educator Mogens Niss (1983) proposes that mathematics education should "enable students to realize, understand, judge, utilize, and perform the application of math *in society*, in particular to solutions which are of significance to their private, social, and professional lives" (p. 248). Radical mathematics educators challenge the hegemonic[5] and supposedly neutral role of mathematics in society by raising key questions: What is mathematical knowledge and whose interests does it serve? What are the effects of culture, ideology, and language on mathematical knowledge and use? How is mathematical knowledge used to understand or obscure political, economic, and social issues? Can mathematical knowledge be emancipatory, and, if so, what would such a curriculum look like?

Radical educators replace traditional hegemonic practices with specific curricula and methods to develop adults' mathematical abilities as well as their capacities for critical awareness and action. For example, the curricula could be drawn from the students' experiences of work. In many workplaces, discrepancies exist between the wages earned by male and female workers doing similar jobs, or between the jobs performed by those from differing racial backgrounds. Mathematical activities, based upon experiences from learners' own workplaces, can be developed which lead to the compilation and analysis of statistics of class, race, and gender inequalities in workplaces. Radical educators would also extend this by providing opportunities for learners to investigate examples of inequity in larger systems. In this way they encourage learners to understand that individual experiences of discrimination are neither unique, nor the result of personal inadequacy, but rather, indicate a societal failure to ensure equality.

Quintessentially, a radical approach must also offer a vision of a better society. For example, two radical statisticians describe how, in a society dedicated to justice and human liberation:

> We would replace accountancy in terms of money and profit by accountancy in terms of social trends. We would replace the definition of social goals by those at the top of the bureaucratic pyramids, by democratic self-control over all collective activities. We would then require new means of measuring our needs and goals which expressed their great variety rather than reduced them to money values or standards imposed from above. (Shaw & Miles, 1979, p. 36)

This approach toward mathematics (and toward mathematics education) requires reconceptualizing what we regard as mathematics.

Reconceptualizing Mathematics

Radical educators regard mathematics (like all knowledge) not as a body of objective truth, but as a personal and social construct (D'Ambrosio, 1985; Ernest, 1989). Learning mathematics is not the gradual revelation of absolute truths, but, as with all knowledge, a product of peoples' ideas, interests, and conflicts. For example, there is no universal concept of "right-angled triangles" awaiting discovery and explication. Consequently, there is nothing logical or natural about our current knowledge of mathematics; it is more a collection of accumulated experience rather than a system of universal truths.

This suggests that there can be alternative views of mathematics. As all cultural groups generate their own mathematical ideas, Western mathematics can be seen as only one among many. Two aspects of interest to radical educators are (1) the notion that mathematics is more than simply arithmetic, and (2) the concept of "ethnomathematics."

Mathematics Is More Than Arithmetic

In Western culture, mathematics is commonly regarded either as a fixed set of abstract and unchallengeable scientific truths, or as the supreme example of a scientific and rational mode of thought. In each case there is "a general disinclination to locate mathematics in a materialistic base and thus link its development with economic, political, and cultural changes" (Joseph, 1987, p. 22). However, mathematics can be viewed—as it was within ancient Greek, Chinese, Indian, and Arabic cultures—as a dynamic body of knowledge relating to many areas of human understanding, capable of, and subject to, interpretation. David Henderson claims modern mathematics is not only a series of techniques for solving analytic problems, but also a way of perceiving beauty, order, and unity. He compares mathematics with music: "the techniques and theory of mathematics are analogous to the techniques and theories of music. And, like music, there is beauty and meaning behind the techniques and theory" (1981, p. 13). However, recognizing that "most people derive meaningful pleasure from art and music, but very few people derive meaningful pleasure from mathematics" he suggests that we alter our approach to mathematics so that it becomes a subject that everyone can, to some degree, manipulate and enjoy.

Although different forms of mathematics are generated by different cultural groups, they are the result of broadly similar activities. Alan Bishop (1988, pp. 182–183) identifies six fundamental mathematical activities which he regards as universal, necessary, and sufficient for the development of mathematical knowledge. Contrast a more conventional definition of "arithmetic" with these six activities:

Counting: using a systematic way to compare and order discrete objects [involving] body- or finger-counting, tallying, using objects . . . to record, or [using] special number words or names.

Locating: exploring one's spatial environment and conceptualizing and symbolizing that environment with models, diagrams, drawings, words, or other means.

Measuring: quantifying amounts for the purposes of comparison and ordering, using objects or tokens as measuring devices.

Designing: creating a shape for an object or for any part of one's spatial environment.

Playing: devising and engaging in games and pastimes, with more or less formal rules.

Explaining: finding ways to represent relationships between phenomena.

Reconceptualizing mathematics goes further than consideration of mathematical processes; it is also important to recognize our unquestioned assumptions about mathematics. The common Western view of mathematics reflects the views of "the people in charge of mathematics . . . [who] have been mostly Western (white), upper/middle class males" (Henderson, 1981, p. 13). For example, Henderson cites one mathematical idea—the Saccheri quadrilateral—which instead of being named after the person (a Persian) who first introduced the ideas to the world (in Arabic), is instead named after the person (an Italian Christian) who first translated the idea into a Western language. In this way the development of mathematics becomes seen as a uniquely Western phenomenon, and the contribution of non-Western mathematicians is ignored or treated with contempt. Such ethnocentrism often masks or marginalizes the mathematical activities of indigenous people. Radical mathematical educators, by contrast, intentionally explore the mathematical traditions present in different cultures.

Ethnomathematics

Ubiratan D'Ambrosio uses the term "ethnomathematics" to describe "the art or technique of understanding, explaining, learning about, coping with, and managing the natural, social, and political environment by relying on processes like counting, measuring, sorting, ordering, and inferring" (1985, p. 45). Ethnomathematics, which links cultural anthropology, cognitive psychology, and mathematics, can challenge the dichotomy between "practical" and "abstract" mathematical knowledge. Frankenstein and Powell (1994) after reviewing hundreds of related articles claim that its study encourages learners to consider others' thinking patterns, to reexamine what has been labeled "nonmathematical," and to reconceptualize what counts as mathematical knowledge.

The work of several distinguished mathematics educators can illuminate these different understandings of mathematics. Marcia Ascher (1991) looks at the mathematical ideas in the spatial ordering and number system used by the Inca people in South America. Paulus Gerdes (1988) focuses on the mathematics "frozen" in the historical and current everyday practices of traditional Mozambican craftsmen, whose baskets, weavings, houses, and fish traps often demonstrate complex mathematical thinking, as well as the most efficient solutions to construction problems. Rik Pinxten et al. (1983) examine spatial concepts in the cultural traditions of the Navajo people. Unlike Western people who tend to regard the world statically and atomistically, the Navajo have a more dynamic and holistic worldview which fundamentally influences their notions of such geometrical concepts as points, distance, and space.

Turning to the dominant culture within North America, Jean Lave (1988) considers the mathematical experiences inherent in common workplace and domestic activities. In one example, she compares adults' abilities to solve arithmetic problems arising while grocery shopping in a supermarket, with their performance on similar problems in a pencil-and-paper test. The participants' scores on the arithmetic test averaged 59%; in the supermarket they managed to make 98%—virtually error free. Lave argues that test taking and grocery shopping are very different activities and people use different methods in different situations to solve what can be seen as similar arithmetic problems. In fact, learners use mathematical procedures depending on context and environment, rather than, as is commonly thought, on the mathematical nature of the problems they wish to solve (Boaler, 1993).

By drawing upon the mathematical traditions present in different cultures and basing mathematical activities on adults' day-to-day experiences of their social and physical environments, radical educators broaden the traditional and often narrow approach of mathematics education. Furthermore, they bring the learning of mathematics "into contact with a wide variety of disciplines, including art and design, history, and social studies, which it conventionally ignores. Such a holistic approach serve[s] to augment rather than fragment [learners'] understanding and imagination" (Joseph, 1987, p. 27).

Adults exposed to these broader definitions and practices of mathematics can examine both their own concepts of mathematics and their own mathematical knowledge. Hence, they can realize that they already know more mathematics than either they think or that standard tests indicate (Frankenstein, 1989). Similarly, adult learners asked to explore the mathematics in other cultures learn that mathematical concepts and methods can differ, and that exploring the mathematics of others can provide rich illustrations of mathematics in use. These two factors alone contribute greatly to adults' confidence in learning from their own experience and in trusting their own learning abilities.

Radical educators thus change the content and curricula of classes. However, they also consider it essential to change the teaching methods used.

Changing Teaching

In general, mathematics education has traditionally been based on the assumption that learners absorb what has been covered by repetition and practice, and that they then become able to apply this knowledge and these skills to a variety of problems and in a variety of contexts. Such an approach is based on a widely held preconception about mathematics: that it represents a particular form of intelligence. Many people believe "in the primacy of mathematical thinking and of the assumption that ability or training in mathematics will transfer to other areas" (Smith, 1994, p. 61). Often, this belief is translated into standardized tests (for example, the Scholastic Aptitude Test), which use mathematical ability as a primary instrument to judge admissions to college programs. Those who design and use this test believe that skill in mathematical reasoning transfers to other areas that require logical reasoning. However, according to Smith, "no empirical evidence exists to support such a claim . . . especially the proposition that the learning of mathematics will facilitate . . . the learning of the logic of physics or . . . of economics" (p. 62).

A radical approach to mathematics education is based on different assumptions. Fundamentally, "what is to be learned" and "how it is to be learned" are both regarded as equally significant. Conventionally, the content is seen as most important; the methods are simply the means of getting there. However, as one seminal radical educator, Paulo Freire, argues: "methods cannot be dichotomized from its content, as if methods were neutral and equally appropriate for liberation or domination" (1972, p. 44). Hence, new methods, as well as new content, are important in a radical education approach. Extending Freire's ideas to mathematics, Frankenstein criticizes much mathematics teaching in schools as:

> based on "banking" methods: "expert" teachers deposit knowledge in the blank minds of students; students memorize the required rules and expect future dividends. At best, such courses make people minimally proficient in basic math and able to get somewhat better paying jobs than those who can't pass math skills competence tests. But they do not help people learn to think critically or to use numbers in their daily lives. At worst, they train people to follow rules obediently, without understanding, and to take their proper place in society, without questioning. (1981, p. 12)

Traditional approaches to mathematics education often result in feelings of helplessness and low interest in mathematics. However, if learning mathematics is changed from the cognitive acquisition of infallible, objective knowledge to a more process-oriented inquiry—a "coming to know"—it becomes a catalyst for critical thinking and social empowerment. Precisely because students so often enter these classes with a sense of personal deficiency, this reorientation of content and methods has an extraordinary impact. It also produces another effect.

An understanding built on life experiences and exploration of the learners' own interests can increase an awareness of how mathematics affects people, and yield concrete examples of mathematics in everyday life. In such a process, it is likely that learners will raise questions that the teacher cannot answer. This provides adult learners with the important experience of realizing that the teacher is not always an expert with all of the answers (Frankenstein, 1984). As Freire (1972) claims, liberating education does not dichotomize the activity of teacher and learner, and teachers thus become "co- investigators" in the process of teaching/learning. Radical educators seek to act not so much as experts, but more as facilitators, encouraging, probing, and guiding learners to search for information to answer their own questions and to develop the skills of critical thinking and research. Learners, of course, gain confidence and become more willing and able to challenge others' assumptions, in mathematics as well as in other areas.

A radical approach to mathematics education also includes collective and collaborative learning. By working with others, learners begin to break the pattern of competition which traditional schooling tends to encourage. By participating without competing, sharing approaches and solutions, evaluating different problem-solving techniques, and analyzing and learning from each other's mistakes, learners shed the assumptions that they know nothing and have little to contribute. Also, by explaining a mathematics concept to someone else, learners can increase their own understanding. Small group and class discussions which use mathematics to analyze complex issues can increase adult learners' intellectual self-image and challenge "the dominant society's view that the intellectual activity of those without power is always characterized as non-intellectual" (Freire & Macedo, 1987, p. 127).

Practicing Radical Mathematics

Radical mathematics courses have been run with uneducated adults and with schoolteachers in the Israeli-occupied West Bank (Fasheh, 1982). In one activity designed to stress the importance of considering different interpretations of the mathematics present in learners' everyday lives, women learners were each asked to keep and analyze a record of the time they spent cooking, cleaning, washing, and taking care of children. In a second course focusing on spatial relationships, workers were each asked to draw maps of their neighborhood (a battle zone) for a visiting friend and describe their preferred routes to get from one site to another. In each case, what had been seen as a routine and nonproblematic task produced widely differing results and began a series of class discussions about using mathematics in everyday situations and activities.

Frankenstein's work also provides a good example of radical mathematics in practice. She questions why mathematics is taught as a separate subject when it is so closely linked to many spheres of human activity. She suggests that teachers can link mathematics with all subjects and gives examples of her own work linking math with art, anthropology, politics, and economics. For example, in her adult literacy text (1989), Frankenstein asks students to read and write about artwork, short stories, and poems concerning mathematics, or to consider and discuss such mathematical problems as:

> The United States has about 9,000 strategic nuclear warheads pointed at the Soviet Union. The Soviet Union has about 6,000 strategic nuclear warheads pointed at the United States. The combined population of the United States and the Soviet Union is about 500 million. Each warhead could kill about 2 million people. If all these warheads were released, how many people would be killed?[6]

Frankenstein claims that the second problem can illustrate how there can be several correct ways to solve a problem, how correct calculation can still lead to wrong answers, and offer classroom opportunities to discuss ideas about solving problems in general. She suggests that talking about problems such as this not only helps with mathematical problem solving, but also releases some of the confusion, anger, and upset that such problems often generate. As she puts it: "Critically analyzing the distressing facts about our world is an important step in changing those facts" (1989, p. 63).

Finally, Frankenstein's work presents convincing arguments for the notion that all mathematics knowledge is political:

> Most schooling and daily life bombard us with messages supporting the status quo. Even trvial mathematics applications, like finding the total from a grocery bill, carry the non-neutral message that it's natural to distribute food according to individual payment. Even traditional math courses which provide no real-life data carry the non-neutral hidden message that learning math is separate from helping people understand and control the world. (1989, p. 5)

Some Objections

Despite the success of these courses, radical approaches to teaching mathematics are not common. Several reasons for the lack of a radical approach can be found: the pluralist nature of many Western societies (which resist the adoption of unitary or utopian philosophies), the conservative ideology of educational institutions, and their prevailing focus (at least in North America) on personal and individual change, rather than on social or political change. Questioning or trying to change dominant attitudes and assumptions can be seen as threatening by those in authority who can exert their influence in a variety of subtle and less than subtle ways.

Other factors prevent teachers from developing radical mathematics education. Although most teachers of mathematics to adults have received some formal training in mathematics, often to degree level, few of these teachers have been exposed to any radical or even liberal adult educational approaches. This tends to increase their tendency to rely on traditional, school-based teaching methods. In addition, most teachers of mathematics to adults have little influence over the curriculum they are expected to teach, and little time to develop or implement different approaches. In many ways, mathematics teachers are enmeshed within a tightly woven network of "articulated" courses and curricula and an education system that holds them accountable for covering the mathematics terrain (Nesbit, 1995).

Finally, learners may view radical approaches to education as too threatening or irrelevant to their immediate needs. Often, adult learners, whose only educational experience has been traditional schooling, may have internalized others' views that they lack ability, general knowledge, or critical thinking skills. Becoming aware of those attitudes can be initially challenging and painful, and resistance to them an understandable reaction. Learners may also question the incorporation of economic, political, social, and cultural issues into a mathematics curriculum. They might feel that learning mathematics is "confused" by discussion of different interpretations. Even though they have been unsuccessful in learning or remembering much school mathematics, adult learners can adopt the same negative ideas about learning mathematics that their previous teachers and texts presented. For example, Frankenstein (1989) cites several common misconceptions about learning mathematics: there are people who can do math (and there are those who can't); people good at math can work out the right answers straight-away, and in their heads; asking questions or making mistakes is a sign of stupidity; there is only one correct answer to, and one correct way of solving, each math problem; and the teacher is the only one who has the answers. Of course, a radical approach to mathematics education would attempt to dispel these misconceptions by raising and discussing them in public, but adult learners are often initially reluctant to discuss their failings.

SUMMARY

In this chapter, I have discussed an approach to mathematics education that reflects a radical education philosophy. Traditional approaches, which largely replicate the perception of mathematics as a body of decontextualized facts, procedures, and principles, have resulted in widespread adult innumeracy, disparate access to societal benefits and achievements, a prevalence of math anxiety, and an enshrinement of statistics, graphs, and "expert" opinions, regardless of social implications.

By contrast, a radical approach views mathematics education as a vehicle for empowering individuals and reshaping society—teaching mathematics while simultaneously raising political consciousness and creating a more informed citizenry. Its methods challenge existing authoritarian teacher/student relationships by increasing adult learners' involvement in developing the curriculum. The aim is to concurrently develop the mathematical tools necessary to question and challenge dominant ideas, while also providing cooperative learning experiences to serve as models for creating and living in a more equitable society. Teaching adults to question and to doubt, to argue and to experiment, and to think critically about existing beliefs and ideologies aids the process of changing society (Fasheh, 1982). A radical approach to mathematics education not only helps adults feel less confused or manipulated by numbers, but it also can equip them to be more effective citizens.[7]

Because of the nature of the intertwined relationships between how radical educators see their role, design their curricula, envision their educational goals, select their methods, and respond to the unique experiences of each learner, they embody the Social Reform Perspective. They share, with other perspectives, respect, care, and concern for the individual student, but reject the notion of locating educational deficiencies or achievements solely within individuals. Because of this, radical educators invoke the broad social context of learners' collective lives, and design their actions to empower students to, above all, become socially active, critically thoughtful, and educated, responsible, and cooperative citizens. In this way, they reflect the key elements of the social reform perspective.

ENDNOTES

1. See Bhaskar, R. (1989). *Reclaiming reality: A critical introduction to contemporary philosophy*. London: Verso.

2. For a wealth of examples of the use (and abuse) of statistics in academia and the public opinion, medical, and advertising industries see Crossen, C. (1994). *Tainted truth: The manipulation of fact in America*. New York: Simon & Schuster, and Paulos, J. A. (1995). *A mathematician reads the newspaper*. New York: Basic Books.

3. From Maxwell, J. (1991). Hidden messages. In M. Harris (Ed.), *Schools, mathematics, and work* (pp. 67–70). London: Falmer Press. Note: the problems are undated.

4. See, for example, Cockcroft, W. H. (1982). *Mathematics counts*. London: HMSO. Kirsch, I. S., Jungeblut, A., Jenkins, L., & Kolstad, A. (1993). *Adult literacy in America*. Pittsburgh: Government Printing Office. Statistics Canada. (1991). *Adult literacy in Canada: Results of a national study*. Ottawa: Author.

5. Hegemony as used here refers to the process by which dominant groups within society exercise their domination over less-privileged groups by defining conventional social practices (rather than imposing them by physical force). In other words, dominant groups promote their ways of seeing and valuing the world so that they seem normal and natural, and obscure any unequal relations of power and privelege. See Gramsci, A. (1971). *Selection from the prison notebooks*. New York: International Publishers. Williams, op. cit.

6. Taken from *The Nation*, 25 August, 1981.

7. To this end, several of the authors cited in this chapter have created the Critical Mathematics Educators Group. For more information and a copy of their newsletter contact Marilyn Frankenstein, College of Public & Community Service, University of Massachusetts, Boston, MA 02125, USA.

REFERENCES

Anyon, J. (1981). Social class and school knowledge. *Curriculum Inquiry, 11*(1), 3–42.

Apple, M. W. (1979). *Ideology and curriculum*. Boston: Routledge.

Ascher, M. (1991). *Ethnomathematics: A multicultural view of mathematical ideas*. Belmont, CA: Brooks/Cole.

Bishop, A. (1988). Mathematics education in its cultural context. *Educational Studies in Mathematics, 19*, 179–191.

Boaler, J. (1993). The role of contexts in the mathematics classroom: Do they make mathematics more "real"? *For the Learning of Mathematics, 13*(2), 12-17.

Burton, L. (1989). Mathematics as cultural experience: Whose experience? In C. Keitel, P. Damerow, A. Bishop, & P. Gerdes (Eds.), *Mathematics, education, and society* (pp. 16–19). Paris: UNESCO, Division of Science, Technical, and Environmental Education.

Carraher, D., Carraher, T., & Schliemann, A. (1985). Mathematics in the streets and in the schools. *British Journal of Developmental Psychology, 3*, 21–29.

Cooper, T. (1989). Negative power, hegemony, and the primary mathematics classroom: A summary. In C. Keitel, P. Damerow, A. Bishop, & P. Gerdes (Eds.), *Mathematics, education, and society* (pp. 150–154). Paris: UNESCO, Division of Science, Technical, and Environmental Education.

D'Ambrosio, U. (1985). Ethnomathematics and its place in the history and pedagogy of mathematics. *For the Learning of Mathematics, 5*(1), 44–48.

Ernest, P. (1991). *The philosophy of mathematics education*. London: The Falmer Press.

Ernest, P. (Ed.). (1989). *Mathematics teaching: The state of the art*. London: The Falmer Press.

Evans, J. (1989). The politics of numeracy. In P. Ernest (Ed.), *Mathematics teaching: The state of the art* (pp. 203–220). New York: The Falmer Press.

Fasheh, M. (1982). Mathematics, culture and authority. *For the Learning of Mathematics, 3*(2), 2–8.

Frankenstein, M. (1981). A different third "R." Boston: *Radical Teacher, 20*, 10–14.

Frankenstein, M. (1984). Overcoming math anxiety by learning about learning. *Mathematics and Computer Education, 18*(3), 169–180.

Frankenstein, M. (1987). Critical mathematics education: An application of Paulo Freire's epistemology. In I. Shor (Ed.), *Freire for the classroom: A sourcebook for liberatory teaching* (pp. 180–210). Portsmouth, NH: Boynton/Cook.

Frankenstein, M. (1989). *Relearning mathematics: A different third R - radical math*. London: Free Association Books.

Frankenstein, M., & Powell, A. B. (1994). Toward liberatory mathematics: Paulo Freire's epistemology and ethnomathematics. In P. L. McLaren & C. Lankshear (Eds.), *Politics of liberation: Paths from Freire* (pp. 74–99). New York: Routledge.

Freire, P. (1972). *Cultural action for freedom*. London: Penguin.

Freire, P. (1985). *The politics of education: Culture, power, and liberation*. South Hadley, MA: Bergin & Garvey.

Freire, P., and Macedo, D. (1987). *Literacy: Reading the word and the world.* South Hadley, MA: Bergin & Garvey.

Gerdes, P. (1988). On culture, geometrical thinking, and mathematics education. *Educational Studies in Mathematics, 19,* 137–162.

Handler, J. (1990). Math anxiety in adult learning. *Adult Learning, 1* (7), 20–23.

Henderson, D. (1981). Three papers. *For the Learning of Mathematics, 1* (3), 12–15.

Höghielm, R. (1985). *Undervisning i komvux: Ideal och verklighet i grundskolekurser* [Teaching processes in municipal adult education: Ideals and reality in ABE courses]. Malmö, Sweden: CWK/Gleerup.

Joseph, G. G. (1987). Foundations of Eurocentrism in mathematics. *Race & Class, 28* (3), 13–28.

Koblitz, N. (1981). Mathematics as propaganda. In L. A. Steen (Ed.), *Mathematics tomorrow* (pp. 111–120). New York: Springer-Verlag.

Lave, J. (1988). *Cognition in practice: Mind, mathematics, and culture in everyday life.* Cambridge, England: Cambridge University Press.

Marx, K. (1852/1950). The eighteenth brumaire of Louis Bonaparte. In K. Marx & F. Engels (Eds.), *Selected Works* (Vol. 1). London: Lawrence & Wishart.

Michael, B. (1981). Math anxiety and avoidance. In G. Akst (Ed.). *New directions for college learning assistance: Improving mathematics skills* (pp. 57–63). San Francisco: Jossey-Bass.

National Research Council. (1989). *Everybody counts: A report to the nation on the future of mathematics education.* Washington, DC: National Academy Press.

Nesbit, T. (1995). *An analysis of teaching processes in mathematics education for adults.* Unpublished doctoral dissertation. University of British Columbia, Vancouver, Canada.

Niss, M. (1983). Considerations and experiences concerning integrated courses in mathematics and other subjects. In M. Zweng, T. Green, J. Kilpatrick, H. Pollack, and M. Suydam (Eds.), *Proceedings of the Fourth International Conference on Mathematical Education* (pp. 247–249). Boston: Birkhaüser.

Paulos, J. A. (1988). *Innumeracy.* New York: Hill & Wang.

Pinxten, R., Van Dooren, I., & Harvey, F. (1983). *The anthropology of space.* Philadelphia: University of Pennsylvania Press.

Pratt, D. D. (1992). Conceptions of teaching. *Adult Education Quarterly, 42* (4), 203–220.

Romberg, T. A., & Carpenter, T. P. (1986). Research on teaching and learning mathematics: Two disciplines of scientific inquiry. In M. C. Whittrock (Ed.), *Handbook of research on teaching* (3rd ed., pp. 850–873). New York: Macmillan.

Sewell, B. (1981). *The mathematical needs of daily life*. London: Advisory Council for Adult and Continuing Education.

Shaw, M., & Miles, I. (1979). The social roots of statistical knowledge. In J. Irvine, I. Miles, & J. Evans (Eds.), *Demystifying social statistics* (pp. 27–38). London: Pluto.

Shor, I., & Freire, P. (1987). *A pedagogy for liberation: Dialogues on transforming education*. South Hadley, MA: Bergin & Garvey.

Smith, M. K. (1994). *Humble pi: The role mathematics should play in American education*. Amherst, NY: Prometheus Books.

Williams, R. (1976). Base and superstructure in Marxist cultural theory. In R. Dale (Ed.), *Schooling and capitalism* (pp. 202–210). London: Routledge & Kegan Paul.

SECTION III

Whereas Section II was descriptive of five perspectives on teaching, Section III provides an analysis of those perspectives and the means for evaluating teaching within, and, across perspectives. Chapter 9 introduces three sets of "key belief structures" that can be used as analytical tools to compare and contrast perspectives. Chapter 10 applies those tools, analyzing and revealing the essential structures and commitments that differentiate between perspectives. If you have not been convinced before, I would hope Chapter 10 persuades you that we cannot choose among perspectives any more than we can choose among world views or personalities. Finally, Chapter 11 explains how teaching can be evaluated in ways that are equitable, yet rigorous, by examining both technical and substantive aspects of teaching.

CHAPTER 9

ANALYTICAL TOOLS
Epistemic, Normative, and Procedural Beliefs

Daniel D. Pratt

The chapters in Section II, each in a unique way, answered the question, "What does it mean to teach from this perspective?" Presented as they are, in different voices and using different types of descriptions, the chapters may have sparked a variety of reactions to these perspectives. Did you see an image of yourself in the "mirror" of these chapters? Or, did you find yourself strongly reacting to parts of each? Section II was designed to give you a more visceral sense of each perspective in actual contexts; this chapter will give you a more systematic way to compare their elements. To do that, we first have to clear up some possible confusions, and then consider more fully the role of a few tools in determining perspectives.

As you read Chapters 4 through 8 you may have felt there was some overlap between perspectives. Indeed, there is, due to the fact that similar (even identical) actions, intentions, and beliefs can be found in more than one perspective. We may, for example, have similar intentions about using questions to help people reflect or think deeply about something. Thus, we may have similar beliefs about the importance of higher level questions in promoting effective learning. However, the kinds of questions we ask, the way in which we ask those questions, and the way we listen and respond when people consider our questions is directly related to our beliefs about learning, knowledge, and the appropriate role of an instructor.

Similarly, every perspective shares a regard for the dignity of learners and the need to respect that dignity in all aspects of teaching. Yet, the way in which it manifests may vary across perspectives, depending on

other beliefs that interact with this view of personal dignity and its relationship to learning. Any belief, in isolation from other beliefs, is not a
reliable indicator of one's perspective on teaching.

Two points are important to emphasize here: First, perspectives are
not defined by a single belief; nor are beliefs the exclusive property of one
perspective. Perspectives share individual beliefs but are characterized by
a unique belief structure, that is, a cluster of interrelated beliefs. The
cluster of beliefs, in turn, interact in such a way as to not only define the
perspective but to influence the nuance of meaning for each of the beliefs.
Thus, an affiliation with two or three perspectives, is to be expected. Although perspectives are philosophical orientations to teaching, they are
not mutually exclusive orientations.

This overlap of perspectives leads to two common misunderstandings. First, because many instructional actions (e.g., techniques) are common across perspectives, many people mistakenly confuse perspectives
with approaches to the process of teaching. I have had people say to me,
"I use all five of these, depending on who I'm teaching and what we're
trying to accomplish." To these people, the perspectives seem more like
teaching methods or techniques that they can choose among as teaching
conditions change. Because actions are the most visible aspect of perspectives it is quite understandable that perspectives can be mistakenly confused with approaches to teaching. But, as discussed in detail in Section
I, techniques are the visible "tip" of teaching; beliefs and intentions, the
core of the perspectives, are invisible.

The second misunderstanding also relates to common aspects. People
often say, "More than one of these perspectives 'fits' who I am and what
I do as an instructor." These people have, quite correctly, identified over-
lapping beliefs shared by two or three perspectives. As a result, they resist
any hint of being adequately described by just a single perspective and
want to claim two or three as their orientation to teaching. This is entirely in keeping with my understanding of perspectives on teaching. As
I said in the original research article (Pratt, 1992), most instructors hold
not just one, but two or three perspectives. However, one perspective is
usually more dominant while the others act as auxiliary or backup perspectives. That is, there is usually something about one perspective that
is more central to people's values and personal philosophies than other
perspectives. No teacher we studied held all five perspectives.

Undoubtedly, critical readers will have more questions arising from
the overlap of perspectives. This chapter will provide some analytical
tools for answering questions about the perspectives. Such tools need to

address two factors which manifest in teaching: belief clusters, and types of power. The belief clusters refer to epistemic, normative, and strategic beliefs. The types of power resolve into four categories, and show how teachers' epistemic and normative beliefs translate into issues of control and authority within each perspective.

DEFINING KEY BELIEF STRUCTURES

Fundamental to the research behind this book is the assumption that one's perspective on teaching is directly linked to underlying belief structures, that is, complex and interrelated clusters of beliefs that give meaning to each other and to the nature of one's commitment in teaching. These are the most distinctive and defining features of each perspective and yet are usually "invisible." In order to make them more visible by reflecting upon them (remember those first moments in a foreign culture?), it is helpful to understand what types of belief are so fundamental to perspectives, and also some ways to make your own belief structures visible. There are three types of beliefs, each of which is discussed in turn.

Epistemic Beliefs: Knowledge, Learning, and Evaluation (of Learning)

Everyone has a view of knowledge, that is, a way of deciding when something (or someone) is believable. Some base their views on what they can see, hear, touch, or otherwise empirically observe in the world about them. Others may find truth in the experience of living and interpreting the world. Still others may find that the only true knowledge is that which is divine; their struggle is one of seeking that divine truth.

The key to identifying and understanding someone's epistemic beliefs lies not in the first questions we ask (what?, when?, or how?) but in the subsequent question of "why?" For example, if you were inquiring into a colleague's epistemic beliefs about the content they teach (knowledge), it would be reasonable to start by asking: "What do you want people to learn?" In response, you might hear a listing of topics, basic skills, appreciations, attitudes or values, or even a facility at critical thinking or problem solving, and so forth. Nevertheless, the question of "why?" is likely to be more revealing. Teachers must dig deep to give cause or justification for what they do. It is in the elaboration of that justification that a person's epistemic beliefs about knowledge begin to come forth. The answer to "why" opens a path leading to an individual's commitment(s), and the focal point of his or her perspective.

Our views of knowledge, or personal epistemologies, have an important impact on how we represent the content, what we require people to learn, and how we assess that learning. These epistemic beliefs form the heart of each perspective on teaching.

As a way of explaining epistemic beliefs, think of a course or topic you taught and ask yourself the following questions:

Knowledge   1. What do you want people to learn?
             2. Why is that important?

Learning   3. How do people go about learning your content?
             4. How do people differ in approach to learning that content?
             5. What problems do they have learning it?
             6. Why do you think they have those problems?

Assessment   7. How do you know when they are successful at learning?
             8. What is a good indicator that people have learned the essential aspects of your content?
             9. What distinguishes between levels of achievement (for example, A, B, C, D, or failure)?

These are questions related to your personal epistemology. Epistemic beliefs indicate what you think is important within your content and how you would know when someone else has learned it sufficiently.

We don't usually talk about this using the term *epistemology*, but it is appropriate in this case because I am trying to emphasize that perspectives on teaching are philosophical orientations. Your epistemology (philosophy of knowledge) is essentially your judgment of truth. How do you know when something is true? What kinds of evidence or sources of authority are most convincing to you in judging something as true?

This becomes particularly important when confronted with evidence or opinion that is contrary to what you believe. Who or what is so convincing a source of authority that it might cause you to question your present beliefs or knowledge? For some, it might be their experience. Others might say it depends on the question and that they listen to the person's reasoning, or logic. Still others might ask someone they consider to be an authority, like a physician, or accountant, or scientist, and so forth. We each have an epistemology or basis for knowing and way of justifying what we think is true. Thus, our personal epistemologies lead us to notions of truth, sources of authority, and forms of evidence which we do not easily surrender.

When our notions of truth, authority, and evidence come into conflict with others, especially in matters where we hold strong conviction or values, the clash can have serious consequences. As an example, consider the story of a friend of mine and his experience with conflicting sources of authority and forms of evidence.

Several years back my 9-year-old daughter was recommended for a special class for youngsters who were emotionally or mentally handicapped. When I first learned of the school's decision I was shocked and asked to meet with her principal and teacher to discuss the matter. Sometime in late October I was invited to attend a meeting to discuss their recommendation. When I arrived at the school the staff was already meeting and I was asked to wait outside the conference room for 15 minutes before joining the meeting. When invited in I was introduced to eight people, many of whom I knew from previous events at the school—the principal, vice-principal, area counselor, nurse, learning assistance teacher, district psychologist, special needs teacher, and, of course, my daughter's fourth-grade teacher.

The principal began by expressing his confidence in the wisdom of the group to come to the best decision for my daughter. They had, of course, carefully considered the matter and reached a consensus that she should be transferred immediately to the special needs class. When I asked the basis for their decision all eyes turned to the district psychologist. It seems she had "evidence" which was irrefutable. She had administered an intelligence test and was quite confident that it was a "true" indicator of my daughter's ability. Even though others in the room had challenged the assessment, based on classroom observations, their evidence was considered less valid than standardized intelligence test scores.

Again I was shocked, and raised objections, looking to the classroom teacher for support, commenting on the social and academic achievements I had witnessed at home and in her classroom. While I talked about my observations at home, and tried in vain to enlist the classroom teacher's support, my evidence was not convincing. It was, as someone in the room said, necessary to be as objective as possible in this matter, and not let our personal wishes interfere with our good judgment. Besides, there was more reliable evidence: intelligence test scores.

While I argued with personal anecdotes the psychologist countered with reliable indicators that were more objective. It was, the psychologist said, a matter of trying not to be subjective in this matter but, rather, to trust the best evidence available—the intelligence test scores. Most in the room agreed, they were the most trustworthy evidence. Nothing I could say or offer carried sufficient weight to counter standardized intelligence tests. Their evidence was simply irrefutable; my daughter should be placed in the special needs class.

What my friend experienced was a clash of epistemologies, that is, beliefs about what kinds of evidence and authority are the best indicators of some "truth." In this case, his own evidence was not sufficient to argue against the more scientific evidence of intelligence tests. As a result, he withdrew his daughter from the school and enrolled her in a small, private school where they discovered she had a learning disability which interfered with her reading and concentration.

In teaching, you are constantly making decisions based on your personal epistemology, decisions about what to teach, how to teach it, and how to assess people's learning. In essence, you are judging whether or not people have learned. You have implicit or explicit understandings of what it means "to learn" and "to know" something. From that you trust some kind of evidence (tests, performance, intuition, writing, learners' testimony, experience, etc.) as the basis for judging the effects of your teaching and the extent of people's learning. It is the nature of that evidence and your confidence in it that points toward the epistemic dimensions of your perspective. No other aspect of teaching is more indicative of someone's perspective than his or her chosen (not forced) means of evaluating learning.

Normative Beliefs: Role, Responsibility, and Relationship

The second set of beliefs that indicate someone's perspective on teaching is related to one's roles, responsibilities, and relationships. These are the social norms of a teacher's perspective, much like the social norms that govern the interactions within other social groups, for example, a family, work unit, congregation, or club.

Every social group develops a set of norms related to roles, responsibilities, and relationships. In families, the roles of mother, father, children, grandparents, cousins, etc. revolve around individual responsibilities and acceptable (and unacceptable) ways of relating to each other. Although they vary from culture to culture, and across historical periods, it is usually clear to the members of a family or other group what roles, responsibilities, and relationships define appropriate ways of relating to each other.

Teachers also take on particular roles and from those roles define more specific responsibilities and relationships with their learners. For example, several of the teachers I studied saw their primary role to be that of "content expert," responsible for accurately representing and delivering the content to the learners. These teachers, most often, characterized their relationship with learners as friendly, but impersonal (at arms length or business-like); it was not to influence evaluation or assessment of learning. Others described their role in terms of being a combination of friend and counselor, primarily concerned with building self-esteem in their learners. Their primary responsibilities were the provision of support and challenge; they set high standards but provided sufficient support and encouragement to ensure people's success. As you can imagine, their relationship with learners was personal, often developing into a friendship that extended beyond the boundaries of teacher and learner. The literature on teaching adults also suggests a number of different roles for teachers. They include:

1. content specialist and facilitator of adult learning (Knowles 1984);

2. artist, facilitator, and critical analyst (Brookfield 1990);

3. developer of an active and supportive learning environment (Knox 1986);

4. one who helps people see things deeply, more critically (Apps 1991);

5. authority and motivator, guide, facilitator, and consultant (Grow 1991);

6. one who fosters critical reflection (Mezirow 1994).

Whatever your role as instructor, tutor, facilitator, or teacher, your normative beliefs define patterns of authority, communication, and relationship. It may be easiest to explain this through a series of questions about your experience teaching. If you haven't had any teaching experience, think of what you would like to teach, whom you would teach, and a possible setting or context for your hypothetical teaching. Then, consider the following:

1. What is your primary role as a teacher? For some of you this will be easy to answer; others might want to check the list of possible roles below and select the name(s) that best describes their role. It is not unusual to think of more than one role, so don't limit yourself. However, if you choose several, try to look for the underlying or central meaning that links the roles you identified. What is the essence of those roles for you as teacher?

Instructor	Guide	Expert
Co-traveler	Facilitator	Role model
Presenter	Planner	Coach
Interrogator	Co-inquirer	Provocateur
Change-agent	Mentor	Resource
Explorer	Co-learner	Friend

2. Each role suggests both a set of responsibilities and relationship to learners. Given the role(s) you have selected, what does that entail? What responsibilities are associated with the role or roles you identified? What does it suggest about the relationship you have (or try to have) with learners? Try to go beyond the name of the role and specify what it means in terms of responsibility and relationship.

   What distinguishes your role(s) from the others in terms of your responsibility and/or relationship with learners? Some suggest responsibilities that are tied to content (e.g., clear presentation, ability to clarify, organizing, and pacing of content). Other roles such as friend, co-traveler, and co-learner suggest more about the relationship you want to have with your learners, as well as a posture you might take with regards to the content. Collectively, these speak to a kind of "psychological contract" between the learners and you.

   Take it one step further. Can you see any relationship between roles and views about knowledge, learning, and/or the evaluation of learning?

   As you may have already guessed, the roles we assume as instructor are a product of the beliefs we hold about knowledge, learning, and evaluation. What we believe about knowledge affects our role; and what we believe to be our responsibilities affects how we evaluate people's learning. Objectivist beliefs about knowledge result in quite different roles and responsibilities for instructors than do subjectivist views. In turn, beliefs about one's role and authority, in relation to content, have a powerful influence on what might be considered believable evidence that learners have mastered any content. The issues of *how* evaluation can be done are discussed more fully in Chapter 11; at this point, it is sufficient for you to understand there is no separating normative and epistemic beliefs; they are reciprocally determinate of each other.

Procedural Beliefs: Tactical Knowledge and Strategic Beliefs

Most texts and short courses on teaching within adult and higher education focus on a set of techniques and routines that are presumed to be related to helping people learn. Teaching is, implicitly, defined as the matching of means (actions) to ends (intentions), with an emphasis on the means, i.e., the actions of teaching. Similarly, Smith's (1987) review of the general literature on teaching identified three of the most common definitions of teaching as a process of (1) imparting information, (2) enhancing learning, or (3) intentionally creating change.

What is glaringly absent (with the exception of such books as Apps, 1991 and Brookfield, 1990) from the literature reviewed by Smith, as well as most texts that line adult educators' shelves, is any mention of the underlying belief structures that give meaning, direction, and justification to both the means (actions) and ends (intentions) of teaching. Even activities that are assumed to be neutral techniques, such as lectures and discussions, are infused with intentions and justified by beliefs related to knowledge, learning, and the teacher's role. Thus, we assume that even the most routine of activities, once it leaves the page of a book and enters a teacher's repertoire, becomes an expression of underlying belief structures of two kinds: i.e., tactical knowledge (knowing *how* and *when* to adjust intentions and actions to evolving circumstances) and strategic beliefs (understanding *why* adjustments in intent and action may be necessary).

Tactical Knowledge (and Skill)

Certainly, all teachers develop routines—actions they engage in with some regularity—that represent their style of teaching. It may be the way in which an instructor begins a lecture, reviews an assigned reading, asks questions, bridges from one session to another, leads discussions, or responds to people's questions. Whatever the routine, it becomes a relatively stable and predictable way in which the person enacts his or her role, responsibility, and relationship while teaching.

Effective teachers use a variety of routines, procedures, and techniques (tactics) to achieve desired intentions. More experienced teachers tend to have a well-developed repertoire of activities and adjust their tactical knowledge to evolving circumstances. They move easily between activities such as those listed below:

- planning one or more sessions
- developing goals and objectives for learning
- beginning and ending instructional sessions
- providing overviews and reviews of past lessons
- giving clear directions, explanations, or lectures
- guiding discussions
- making transitions within and between lessons
- asking different kinds of questions
- clarifying misunderstandings
- providing feedback to learners

Routines, procedures, and instructional techniques are not difficult to learn; they are essentially actions that can be performed in various ways, serving a host of different purposes or intentions. They are necessary, but not sufficient, for effective teaching. Indeed, one of the features that distinguishes novices from veteran teachers is the ability to be flexible and adaptive, even creative, with routines, procedures, and techniques: deciding when to involve quiet members, how to encourage someone, how to move a discussion to a new level of analysis, what to do when attention is waning during a lecture, how to deal with resistance to learning, knowing when people are ready for a change in direction, and so forth. This we call tactical knowledge, because it goes beyond enacting scripts and cookbook recipes of technique or routine, to incorporate decision making and judgment gained from experience.

Strategic Beliefs

However, even tactical knowledge must have ground upon which to justify itself if challenged. Whether under the press of evaluation or the quiet of reflection, a teacher's ability to know *why* provides justification for both teaching actions and intentions. To know *how* and *when* to adjust routines, procedures, and/or techniques may separate beginners from experienced teachers, but tactical knowledge must ultimately be answerable to "Why?" for one to move beyond accumulated experience to reflective expertise. This is the role of strategic beliefs.

Strategic beliefs are either causal or legitimating and provide the basis for predicting or justifying one's teaching. Causal beliefs are of means-end relationship, or if I do this, then that will happen. They give silent voice to our decision making as we adjust to changing circumstances, as in "If I reinforce John he's only going to interrupt people again. I'll try ignoring his comment." The belief that ignoring a behavior will extinguish that behavior is the foundation for deciding what to do. Without causal beliefs there would be no basis for predicting that one action is more likely to succeed than another.

When teachers are asked to justify or explain their actions and intentions, they rely on another form of strategic beliefs—legitimating beliefs. They are statements about what ought to be, what is proper, right, or appropriate, as in "I believe that shy participants are entitled to participate in class discussions on their own terms, without being interrupted by more aggressive participants." Legitimating beliefs are statements of conviction or commitment that justify actions or intentions. They are most obvious and necessary when teachers are challenged about their choice of teaching content or process (Pratt, in press).

Strategic beliefs are clarified and reinforced through reflection on experience, that is, through applying tactical knowledge and reflecting on its affect, both intended and unintended. They are rooted in personal epistemologies and commitments, and, like other beliefs, are held with different degrees of clarity, confidence, and centrality. Most teachers eventually develop a set of beliefs that explain and legitimate what they do. However, in the end, strategic beliefs are just one part of the interconnected web of key belief structures. Epistemic beliefs give support and meaning to normative and strategic beliefs. In turn, normative and strategic beliefs help define and clarify epistemic beliefs. These complex webs of belief structures provide the foundation for perspectives on teaching; they also provide the basis for four types of power evident within perspectives.

TYPES OF POWER

Beliefs are not benign; they are substantial precursors to privilege and power in every teaching perspective. Just as beliefs and ideals are present, though not necessarily acknowledged, in each perspective, power is also present in every teaching session, and in every perspective on teaching. For some, it is hidden, kept out of the conversation, assumed not to be an issue. For others, it is a part of the agenda of teaching, though not necessarily dominant. And, for still others, it is the dominant theme and directly related to the goals of teaching.

Within the five perspectives we found four types of power related to belief structures. Each type of power is a slightly different reflection of epistemic, normative, and strategic beliefs. A description of the four types of power follows:

1. *Social or institutional title and role*: Some teachers establish patterns of communication and relationships with learners by calling attention to their official titles or role designations. This intensifies their power and authority in relation to learners and to the discourse of learning. While it might be convention in some situations, for example the military, it is usually justified on the basis of normative beliefs about the nature of professional roles and relationships to learners.

2. *Language or symbol system of content*: There are teachers who do nothing, or very little, to translate their expertise and knowledge into language that is accessible to learners. This slows the process of learning and perpetuates an imbalance of power and dependency in relation to the content. This is often justified on the basis of the need to uphold standards regarding accurate and appropriate representation of knowledge.

3. *Gatekeeper to practice*: Teachers are expected to make judgments about learners' readiness to move ahead in their careers. For example, when they write letters of reference for students, teachers hold a form of covert power over the students' future. This type of power comes from a combination of epistemic and normative beliefs related to the teacher's status and authority within a community of practice, an acknowledged expertise related to that status, and an officially recognized responsibility for judging when (and if) learners are ready to enter practice.

4. *Evaluation of learning*: When teachers have authority over the evaluation of learning, in fact they shape and direct peoples' learning and establish what counts as legitimate knowledge. This is the most taken for granted yet prevalent form of power held by teachers. It accrues from authority over decisions related to what will be learned and judgments as to when people have learned it. The combination of epistemic beliefs about the role of teacher in relation to knowledge (e.g., whether the teacher dispenses knowledge or encourages the con-

struction of knowledge) is significantly related to the exercise of power over the evaluation of learning.

I am not suggesting these are the only types of power manifest in teaching; clearly, there exist issues of power based on class, race, and/or gender. However, among the 253 teachers studied, these forms of power were most readily observed and associated with epistemic, normative, and strategic beliefs. In our interviews, for example, we found that teachers who were predominantly in the Transmission or Apprenticeship Perspective made no mention of power; nor was it openly addressed by them in the teaching we observed. Although most certainly present, it was not a part of their focus or agenda. Thus, although not necessarily by intent, power was disregarded and concealed *beneath the table*.

On the other hand, power was an important issue with many whose dominant perspective was Developmental or Nurturing. Indeed, those teachers often talked of empowering learners, or of trying to reduce the effects of the power differential between themselves and learners. For these teachers, power was put *on the table* and became, for many, an important aspect of their teaching.

Those within the Social Reform Perspective took a variety of positions regarding power, but the most vocal and visible position regarding power was similar to that shown by the radical educators described in Chapter 8. For social reform teachers, power was an important part of their ideals and central to all aspects of their work. For these teachers, power was not just on the table, it *was the table*.

Thus, while power is a fact of life in every teaching situation, it is acknowledged and represented quite differently across perspectives.

SUMMARY

Perspectives are not defined by, nor can they be recognized by, isolated actions, intentions, or beliefs. They are a complex web of interdependent beliefs and commitments. Like a spider's web, each belief and commitment is a necessary and integral part of the whole structure; tug on one belief and the entire web responds. Each belief is dependent on other beliefs for its meaning and place within the structure of the perspective.

As I said at the opening of this chapter, there may be many questions still unanswered about the nature of each perspective and the relationship between them. Because they do overlap, it is necessary to be as specific as possible about their essential and unique characters. Yet, it would be wrong to suggest that each perspective can be definitively drawn by listing beliefs, intentions, and actions. That would miss the central point thus far: that perspectives are based on complex, interrelated belief structures. Therefore, the next chapter will provide a portrait of each perspective, and identify the most essential attributes and relationships among its defining belief structures.

REFERENCES

Apps, G. W. (1991). *Mastering the teaching of adults.* Malabar, FL: Krieger Publishing Co.

Brookfield, S. D. (1990). *The skillful teacher.* San Francisco: Jossey-Bass.

Grow, G. O. (1991). Teaching learners to be self-directed. *Adult Education Quarterly, 41*(3), 125–149.

Knowles, M. S. (1980). *The modern practice of adult education: Andragogy versus pedagogy.* New York: Association Press.

Knowles, M. S., & Associates. (1984). *Andragogy in action.* San Francisco: Jossey-Bass.

Knox, A. (1986). *Helping adults learn.* San Francisco: Jossey-Bass.

Mezirow, J. (1994). Understanding transformation theory. *Adult Education Quarterly, 44*(4), 222–232.

Pratt, D. D. (1992). Conceptions of teaching. *Adult Education Quarterly, 42*(4), 203–220.

Pratt, D.D. (in press). Ethical reasoning in teaching adults. In M. Galbraith (Ed.), *Adult learning methods* (2nd ed.). Malabar, FL: Krieger Publishing Co.

Smith, B. O. (1987). Definitions of teaching. In M. J. Dunkin (Ed.), *The international encyclopedia of teaching and teacher education.* Oxford: Pergamon Press.

CHAPTER 10

ANALYZING PERSPECTIVES
Identifying Commitments and Belief Structures

Daniel D. Pratt

By now, you will have gathered that perspectives are evident, and yet elusive entities. As though a lens, we look through our perspectives at what is visible (e.g., teachers' actions), and do not see the properties of the lens itself that determine what we come to believe is true—commitments and belief structures. However, captured within the "lens" of perspectives, teachers' notions of learners, content, context, and ideals, and what it means to teach, are interpreted and held in place by their commitments and belief structures. These notions both enable and limit what teachers think about their own teaching and the teaching of others. Only by excavating these underlying structural properties can we begin to understand the full range of perspectives on teaching.

In Chapter 9, I spelled out the analytical tools for digging deeper into perspectives on teaching. This chapter uses those tools to reveal the underlying structure of each perspective, specifically: key beliefs, specific focus within the General Model of Teaching, primary role and commitment, and power issues. In addition, some of the most common teaching difficulties associated with each perspective will be discussed.

Each perspective will be introduced with a snapshot—a skeletal outline of the most essential features of that perspective. The snapshots are only a superficial map of the underlying belief structures; they are meant to serve as a guide to the more detailed narrative analysis that follows. Because they do not portray the interactive nature of the beliefs, they are not an adequate or sufficient representation of each perspective. However, they are offered as an initial overview—an advance organizer and orientation—to the more complete portrait of each perspective.

Snapshot of
The Transmission Perspective on Teaching

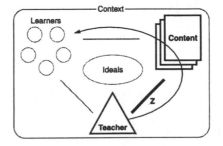

Key Beliefs

Central to this perspective is a belief in a relatively stable body of knowledge and/or procedures that must be reproduced by learners. The instructional process is shaped and guided by the content and it is the teacher's job to accurately represent that content and productively manage learning.

Focus within the General Model

- Dominant element/relationship: teacher's content credibility (line Z)
- Teacher's efficient and accurate presentation of content

Primary Role: Content expert and skilled presenter

Primary Responsibilities

- Set standards for achievement
- Specify course objectives
- Select and sequence readings and assignments
- Provide clear and well-organized lectures
- Make efficient use of class time
- Provide answers to questions
- Provide direction to reading and studying
- Clarify misunderstanding
- Correct errors
- Provide reviews and summaries
- Develop objective means of assessment

Primary Commitment

- Deep respect for the content, expressed through:
    - Accurate representation of content

- Enthusiasm for the content
- Encouragement of people to go on in the subject

Power Issues
- "Under the table"
- Located in knowledge/expertize of teacher
- Expressed as authority over decisions related to content and assessment of learning

Common Difficulties
- Adjusting to individual differences
- Empathizing with people who cannot understand content
- Using content as security/protection against "difficult" learners
- Anticipating where (in content) and why learners will have difficulty
- Shifting roles, e.g., from novice to more advanced levels of teaching
- Following this perspective when teaching "ill-structured" parts of a discipline

---

PORTRAIT OF THE TRANSMISSION PERSPECTIVE

It would be difficult to imagine that anyone has missed having an experience with a transmission teacher. As Boldt notes, our familiarity with this perspective can be attributed to its presence, indeed, its dominance in our schooling and formal training. In addition, virtually every study of models, conceptions, perspectives, or personal theories of teaching has recognized an orientation much like this one. It is safe to assume that most readers can recognize this perspective and its central tenets within their own experience, as learner if not as teacher; but not, perhaps, as articulated using the analytical tools just introduced. What, then, do they tell us about this perspective?

Key Belief Structures

Effective transmission teaching depends, first of all, on an objectivist orientation to knowledge as a commodity, existing independent of the learner and capable of being manipulated and structured for transfer to the learner. Teachers are expected to possess the knowledge that learners need. Indeed, it would be impossible, from this perspective, to be an effective teacher without having an exceptional grasp of the content to be taught.

Individual differences and difficulties in learning are accommodated through adjustments in the delivery of content (breaking the content into smaller pieces, changing the sequence of presentation, or using different media and methods for delivery). As Boldt points out in Chapter 4, if people are having difficulty with a particular section or content, teachers proceed in smaller steps, slow down the presentation, review more frequently, adjust the content or modify the learning environment. More often than not, however, such teachers assume that learners must adjust to the methods of delivery and presentation, and do the best they can.

Effective teachers must be able to manipulate their content in ways that can help people learn it with as little distortion as possible. Learning, then, is viewed as something that can be controlled by the teacher through manipulating the content and/or its delivery. This means teachers must find effective and efficient ways of organizing the content into manageable pieces or chunks that can be learned within a specific time frame.

It also means learning outcomes must be both observable and predictable. It is expected, for example, that content should be represented and taught in ways that allow for accurate measurement of learning. Consequently, it is common among those who have a strong commitment to content to also emphasize behavioral objectives and specific competencies which learners are to achieve. Vagueness in terms of what is to be learned is seen as a hindrance to learning and teaching.

Primary Role

More often than not, the popular media portray teachers as coming from this perspective, e.g., Anthony Hopkins in *Shadowland* or John Houseman in *The Paper Chase*. It would appear from these portrayals that teachers are, usually, passionate and articulate presenters with a lifetime of devotion to their discipline. Indeed, it would be interesting to know how deeply embedded and influential this image is within the psyche of teachers in adult and higher education. I think most of us have examples of memorable teachers that were some approximation of those movie images. However, I am certain that we also have examples where teachers were considerably less than articulate or passionate; perhaps they were not even particularly skilled presenters. The truth is, whether animated or boring, passionate or stolid, adept or inept, transmission teachers are devoted to their content.

As such, their primary role is to dispense and defend that content as accurately, efficiently, and completely as possible. To be good at this they must be able to plan, conduct, and evaluate learning in an objective, rational, technical manner. When this happens, the process of teaching is often characterized using a language of production and control, referring to modules, delivery systems, input and output, minimal competencies, and referring to learners as the target audience. While the raw materials (learners) may vary when they begin the process, it is assumed that it is the responsibility of the teacher to bring all learners to some minimum level of competence at the point of exit.

Failure to learn is usually attributed to either the learner's lack of motivation or the teacher's faulty delivery methods. As regards learners, it is not unusual to hear teachers talk about a lack of motivation and/or native ability in their learners. They suggest learners don't try hard enough, or are lazy, unmotivated, or going through the motions. Perhaps they are trying to get by without really being committed to the content, without applying themselves. In other words, when transmission teachers are faced with students' failure to learn, it is easy for them to assume it is the learners who are at fault.

Primary Commitment

As mentioned above, people holding this as their dominant perspective tend to have a deep respect for, and commitment to, the content they are teaching. They are enthusiastic, even excited, about the content and sometimes disappointed when students don't show the same enthusiasm (respect) for the material. Consequently, they may set high standards and expectations for their learners, just as they have for themselves, regarding learning and mastery of the subject matter.

Sometimes their respect and commitment go a bit too far when individuals ascribe qualities to their discipline that are, to say the least, contentious. Some teachers, for example, see themselves and/or their content as a guardian of academic or professional standards. As mentioned in Chapter 8, math teachers often refer to the inherent logic of mathematical reasoning as an argument for using it as a means of screening admissions to higher education, disciplining the mind of learners, and/or maintaining academic standards in a time of grade inflation. This usually makes about as much sense as assuming the inherent logic of Mozart's music should be used as the test of general ability to study engineering, chemistry, or medicine!

Power Issues

Power, within this perspective, is located in the knowledge and expertise of the teacher. It is embodied in the person of the teacher, which means that learners often come willingly to encounter this expertise, thus perpetuating an imbalance of power between teacher and learners.

As mentioned in Chapter 9, in the studies that led to this book, we found that those teachers who were predominantly aligned with the Transmission Perspective made little or no reference to power as part of their personal belief structure or goals for teaching. While it may have been important to them, it was not explicitly mentioned by them as something important in their teaching. On the other hand, for a great many teachers it simply never occurred to them that power might be part of their relationship to learners, content, or society. The process of teaching, and their roles, responsibilities, and relationships within that process, was understood to be more technical than personal, more objective than subjective, and more neutral than political.

Of course, power exists, even when not acknowledged; one or more of the four types of power mentioned in Chapter 9 is always present and influential in the process and outcomes of learning. Within the Transmission perspective the most apparent forms of power reside in the language or symbol system of content and the evaluation of learning. Individually, these are powerful means of control; together they can create substantial barriers to effective teaching and learning.

Language or Symbol System of Content

Even when teachers are not charged with the responsibility or authority to evaluate learning, as with most noncredit courses, they still hold considerable power over learners through their control of the language of discussion, readings, lectures, and so forth. Most disciplines, professions, vocations, and even leisure activities have a language of their own. The most obvious is mathematics, but even within the trades or professions the knowledge and skills to be learned are encoded in ways that can easily become a barrier to learning.

I watch new graduate students, coming from responsible positions of parenting and working, struggle with the jargon of education as they wrestle with the volume of reading that is required in the first few months. At first, it seems the volume of material is the problem. But when I look closer, it appears to be the combination of volume and language that is troublesome. These are, for the most part, good readers. But under these conditions, their reading speed is hampered by words and concepts that are not immediately meaningful. In class discussions some of these people sit silent, thinking they are the only ones who don't understand such words as "epistemology" or "ontology." The concepts are not difficult; it is, rather, the way in which they are encoded that makes them inaccessible. The knowledge of our field of study needs translation as much as any other.

When teachers do nothing, or very little, to translate key concepts, in lectures, discussions, or readings into the language of the learners, they maintain power over that content, and by extension over their learners. Whether intentional or not, this is one way in which many teachers maintain a sense of authority and status. Unfortunately, they also maintain a distance between the learners and the content. The key to yielding this form of power lies in a teacher's "bridging knowledge" or "pedagogical content knowledge." This bridging knowledge was highlighted in Chapter 6 (Developmental Perspective), but such knowledge is important in all perspectives on teaching.

For example, as in the case of "Jackson" in Chapter 7, statistics could have remained a distant and indecipherable language to Caddie T'Kenye and her study group. But Jackson chose to yield that authority and control by translating the concepts into the language of the learners. By doing this, he opened the door to yielding an even more potent source of power—control over evaluation of learning.

Assessment of Learning

When teachers have authority over the assessment of learning, in fact they have power over both learners and the curriculum; not only do they determine what is to be learned, and how it will be learned, they also determine the outcomes of a program. In effect, teachers become privileged actors in the discourse of education. Regardless of what the goals or objectives say, students will study and reproduce that which they think is going to be assessed. Thus, through this type of power, teachers determine what people will learn, what approaches they will take, and what will count as legitimate knowledge or skill at the end of a program.

It is not too difficult to understand why many teachers from this perspective use assessment as an extension of their authority. Consider the combination of epistemic and normative beliefs that are central to this perspective; objectivist orientation to knowledge, primary role as presenter of content, and a sense of responsibility and loyalty to the content. Transmission teachers may espouse goals of developing critical thinking and problem solving, yet many of them simply require people to reproduce a body of knowledge.

Common Difficulties

At its best, teaching from this perspective can be compelling and engaging because the content itself is gripping, or because the teacher is entertaining. Such teaching is evident in organized and enthusiastic lecturers that animate their subject, or individuals that are so committed to their craft or profession that we cannot but embrace and consider that commitment and the subject matter. This kind of excellence is evident in the Tai Chi master, English professor, or accountant who seem to bring the content to life and easily answer all our questions; or the physician, nurse, or pharmacist who is clear and systematic, never going too fast or too far in helping patients understand their conditions or medications. There is, in those who would teach effectively from this perspective, a sense of responsibility to be prepared, organized, methodical, and clear in presentations and explanations. Effective transmission teachers are truly dedicated and committed to that which they teach; there is never a sense that they are going through the motions of teaching to simply get to the end of the day.

Yet our collective experience suggests there are many teaching from this perspective who are not entertaining or engaging. I am sure that each reader has a story or two of teachers that showed too many slides, talked in monotone, lectured to the chalkboard, never knew your name, were disorganized, or trivialized the content and tested on matters that seemed arbitrary and disconnected to life. When teaching is reduced to covering a body of content, or achieving a set of predetermined, irrelevant, or nonproblematic goals, the result can be dull and tedious, regardless of perspective.

Many who teach from this perspective pride themselves on their expertise, knowledge, proficiency, and skill, much of which has become automatic to them. One of the most difficult aspects of teaching, for such people, is to empathize with learners who don't understand the content. For experienced practitioners, whether that experience is in math, carpentry, surgery, or piano, it is extremely difficult to put themselves in the place of learners. A third-year resident in orthopedics described her learning experience (and frustration) alongside a highly skilled and nationally recognized surgeon this way:

He [the attending surgeon] is a very good surgeon, one of the best in the country, but he does it so easily and so fast that he doesn't even think about it. He's telling me how to do step ten, when I'm strug-

gling with step two. He can't seem to understand that I need to learn
how to crawl before I can run, or even walk.

The surgeon is performing at a very high level of skill, and has virtually no understanding of the learner's struggle to do what he does so
naturally. He simply doesn't remember surgery being that hard. Even the
words of the resident, telling him that she needs "to learn how to crawl
before (she) can run, or even walk", are of little help. He is unable, or
unwilling, to empathize with her situation, in part because his own
learning of this skill has evolved over 20 years to the point where much
of it is automatic, done without consciously thinking about what he is
doing. His dedication to surgery, and expert performance over many
years, has blinded him to the stages of learning that even he traversed at
a time now forgotten.

For many teachers, this may be the only perspective they have ever
known. It might have been the dominant perspective governing their own
learning, or it may now be the dominant way of thinking about teaching
within their place of employment. In either case, they may have adopted
it without question. If this is the case, they have only fleetingly reflected
on issues of power or quality. They may never have questioned the power
that is inherent in their content expertise or the language of their instruction. They may not have thought about quality in teaching beyond the
expansion and refinement of a repertoire of techniques. Indeed, they may
not have even thought about whether there is any particular relationship
between teaching and learning, and what that might mean for their roles
and responsibilities. In other words, if this is the only perspective a
teacher has ever known it is very likely to be a difficult shift to consider
other perspectives as legitimate views of teaching.

Snapshot of
The Apprenticeship Perspective on Teaching

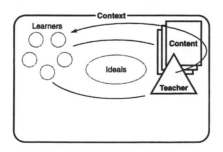

Key Beliefs
This perspective is based on the belief that expert knowledge is best learned in contexts of application and practice. To abstract the knowledge and wisdom from practice is to drain it of its most essential qualities.

Focus within the General Model
- Dominant elements: context, content, and teacher
- Knowledge, skill, and attitudes best learned using authentic tasks
- Impossible to separate content from the expert practitioner (teacher)

Primary Role: Role model and coach

Primary Responsibilities
- Teach for transfer of learning
- Provide conceptual models for thinking about application and feedback
- Locate content in authentic, relevant tasks
- Require learners to use their knowledge
- Provide for observation of expert practitioners
- Allow for legitimate participation in authentic forms of practice
- Provide coaching
    - Scaffolding of content . . . what can they handle right now?
    - Fading of direction and feedback . . . relative to progress and maturity
- Make thinking, uncertainty, and strategies visible
- Teach both domain and strategic content
    - Domain content: Facts, concepts, procedures, theories
    - Strategic content: Problem-solving heuristics

Primary Commitment
- To role and identity as practitioner
- To the standards of the community

Power Issues
- "Craft" knowledge (skill) is power
- Role in community determines authority
- Teachers are gatekeepers to practice

Common Difficulties
- Articulating craft knowledge
- Finding relevant and authentic tasks for classroom settings
- Teaching those who want quick access to practice
- Matching learner capability with authentic tasks

PORTRAIT OF THE APPRENTICESHIP PERSPECTIVE

For some readers, Chapter 5 may have given voice to familiar experiences, especially if you have been fortunate enough to learn from a "master," or to apprentice under the tutelage of an experienced mentor within a trade, profession, or community. For others, this may be a somewhat distant portrayal of their experience as an apprentice, a romanticized view of the servitude endured as part of becoming a journey tradesperson or professional. As with the Transmission Perspective, this orientation to teaching has a long history with mixed results. Ask anyone in medicine or a vocational trade about their apprenticeship and you will undoubtedly hear horror stories of virtual servitude and intimidation as well as stories of exemplary training. No perspective, unfortunately, is free of abuse. However, the Apprenticeship perspective is reemerging as a dominant force in professional and vocational education. It is also the basis for much exciting work on mentoring.

Key Belief Structures

For apprenticeship teachers, what is to be learned is often equated with experience and characterized as "craft" knowledge, or knowledge which is embedded in, and derived from, contextually authentic action. Knowledge is believed to be distorted and diminished when abstracted or separated from situations of its application. Indeed, to remove knowledge from social contexts of practice is to drain it of its most essential qualities.

On the continuum of personal epistemologies (Chapter 2), this perspective is located midway between objectivism and subjectivism. Compared to the Transmission Perspective, here knowledge is not a discrete body of skills, ideas, facts, procedures, and so forth, which can be learned in one context and applied in another. Instead, it is a set of competencies, skills, and way of relating, as well as performing, within the community. Knowledge is inseparable from the contexts in which it is practiced or applied. It reflects a commitment to its community's values and to acting with competence in the performance of community roles. Therefore, learning is best done within simulated or real contexts of application. Knowledge, role (identity), and context are inseparably entwined.

Primary Role

Teachers holding this as their dominant perspective are, first and foremost, expert practitioners. Individuals are given the responsibility for teaching others about their expertise, whether in kitchens, physics labs, or operating rooms. Experts are the role models and learners the observers of their expertise in action.

As learners spend more time observing, and gradually participating, the instructor continues to model more of what is to be learned, while also coaching learners and bringing them into more active roles as members of the community of practice. As Johnson and Pratt have stated in Chapter 5, coaching is a combination of demonstrating, scaffolding, giving feedback, and gradually fading support and direction as learners mature in their knowledge and expertise.

Primary Commitment

Modelling and coaching is a means of enculturating learners into a specific community, that is, into a social grouping with a common sense of purpose and clearly differentiated roles and authority. Remember we defined enculturation in Chapter 3 as "internalizing propositions of meaning and value as appropriate, significant, and true for you." Whether the community is a family, a trade or vocation, a profession, or cultural grouping, the process of learning (enculturation) results from intensive, diversified, and prolonged participation in the work and social relations of the community. The primary commitment of apprenticeship teachers is to the enculturation of novices into a proper understanding of the relationship between knowledge and the community. This manifests as commitment to a craft, that is, a specialized form of expertise that represents acceptable standards of practice within the community. This knowledge can only be learned in authentic contexts of practice, among the community of workers that make up one's colleagues.

There is a profound respect for the context of practice as the only legitimate site for learning and teaching. Effective teaching, for apprenticeship teachers, means knowing how and when to give learners more responsibility and more diverse roles, so as to push them toward their potential but not exceed it. Through this process, learners are expected to acquire not just the skills and knowledge of their community, but the commitment and confidence that comes with an identity of mastery. That is, they are not just to learn *about* something but to learn to *be* something. This unique quality of the Apprenticeship Perspective highlights some interesting points about the learning process and the role of the learner within this perspective.

The Learning Process

Learning is understood to be a process of socialization into the normative beliefs and values of the community. Learners are expected to work alongside their teachers, taking on different roles and experiencing different kinds of engagement in the work and business of a community. Eventually, learners must spend time in real, rather than simulated, situations of practice if their knowledge is to be credible.

Thus, the dominant conception of learning, within this perspective, is similar to the third conception of learning described in Chapter 2: *Learning is the acquisition of information and procedures so they can be used or applied in practice.* The difference between this view of learning and a transmission view is in the context, and consequently, the kind of knowledge that is valued. While the process of learning is additive (more experience equals more knowledge), the product of learning is a change in role and identity; learners must dwell in situations of authentic practice if they are to learn the knowledge that typifies that practice. Learning is not merely a condition for membership, but is itself an evolving form of membership and identity within a community (Lave & Wenger, 1991).

Individual differences among learners, therefore, are based upon experience, not prior knowledge. Learners are often referred to by their role, title, rank, or place within the hierarchy of experience, for example, child, adolescent, and adult; chef de par tie, sous chef, and executive chef; medical student, resident, and attending physician; colored belts and degrees of black belt; and so on. Thus, knowledge (and authority) is often equated with experience or time within the community.

The Role of the Learner

As is typical of many traditional apprenticeships, this occurs as a learner moves from the periphery to the center of a community's defining activities. For many teachers this means directing the content and process of teaching to an assumed standard within the community, such as to knowledge for third-year medical students. For more experienced teachers, it means teaching to each individual learner's zone of proximal development (Vygotsky, 1978), that is, to the distance between what a learner can do solo and what can be done under the guidance and direction of a more experienced person. Teaching is most effective when learners are engaged somewhere between the lower and upper boundaries of their competence, not exceeding but always pushing toward their upper limits. In practical terms, this means learners often start on the periphery, observing more experienced people, and are gradually assigned roles and tasks that allow them to participate in limited but valid ways in the work and social relations of the community.

A friend working on his third-year residency in orthopedics offers his story of starting on the periphery and gradually becoming an accepted and legitimate member of a community of medical professionals:

The journey from "recently graduated medical student" to "fully qualified surgeon" consists of at least 5 years of rotations through various surgical services. The rotations typically last 3 months and each progresses in a similar manner. Entering the surgical changing room at the start of a rotation is a bit like entering a foreign country. The surgeons and anesthetist that I meet will occasionally utter a suspicious greeting, but more often I am simply ignored. I am a foreigner in their world.

During the first few weeks the nurses and surgeons that I work with watch me like a hawk. The simplest act, such as putting on my surgical gown, is intensely scrutinized to ensure that I do it correctly. The nurses do not hesitate to inform me when my actions are incorrect. The surgeon has me watch him perform case after case. As a reward for my patience I am allowed to put the dressing on the patient's wound, an act which requires essentially no skill, but one which is nevertheless observed carefully.

Throughout this period of indoctrination I remain silent. Day after day conversations flow easily between the nurses and the surgeon as if I am not even in the room. My job is to watch and learn. If I pass these early tests I am given more responsibility. Soon it is my job to close the wound. Gradually the nursing staff becomes more comfortable with my presence. After a month I am no longer an unfamiliar face and some nurses have even learned my name. Occasionally the conversation during surgery will be directed toward me. I now partake in the conversations which occur, although I am very cautious of what I say. In a similar manner I am accepted in the surgical changing room. No longer a complete stranger, I am free to engage in superficial conversation with the surgeons and anesthetists I meet there.

Just as the extent of my interaction with the surgical staff increases, so too does my involvement in the operations. If all has gone well, after 2 months I am doing significant portions of many of the operations. Occasionally the surgeon will even leave me to do a very simple case on my own.

During the last month of my rotation I am no longer an outsider, I am one of them. I am included in the conversations and treated as a colleague by the staff. Operations are now more of a team effort between the surgeon and me. We work together to achieve a common goal. Although clearly the junior partner, I am not afraid to offer my own suggestions. At this stage, just as the 3 months are up, the training becomes enjoyable. But then, after saying my good-byes I am off to another service, at another hospital, where the process starts all over again. (Steve Pinney, personal communication, 1995)

Pinney's story is typical of many in apprenticeships, whether in professional schools, vocational or trade schools, or families. Even after 6 years of medical education at Harvard and 2 years of specialization, he starts on the periphery, observing and waiting for the community (particularly the chief surgeon) to decide he is capable of being given meaningful work.

Power Issues

Power, within this perspective, is housed in the accumulation of craft knowledge but teachers exercise power in two forms: *social role differentiation* and *gatekeeping*. Each form plays out in the relations between teacher and learner; they are borne of the nature of communities of practice and the status and authority accorded teachers as masters within those communities.

Beginners (even third-year residents!) are often assumed to "know nothing" and are relegated to a peripheral position and role within the community. Learners who have worked in legitimate roles and sites of practice are assumed to have accumulated a greater quantity of knowledge. If they have worked in specialized or higher status sites of the community's practice, they are also assumed to have taken on a different quality of knowledge. As a result, they are accorded greater responsibility and status. For example, Bingham (1995) describes an occupational first aid instructor's way of differentiating between students in his classes:

> [T]here are basically three kinds of students: newcomers with no experience; returning students that have no legitimate field experience (this category includes attendants in low risk, office environments where trauma calls are practically unheard of and those that have never had any field first aid duties); and legitimate field attendants . . . [they have experience not only in real settings but with trauma situations]. (pp. 5–6)

Bingham emphasizes that the "newcomers knew nothing, and the mis-trained—those trained by someone else—knew wrong" (p. 6). Those that had trauma experience had a different quality of experience and knowledge. Equally important, because the instructor represented the community of occupational first aid practitioners, his own level of expertise was the benchmark for assessing student achievement. Therefore, individual differences among learners was a matter of how close or distant they were to the teacher's expertise. Given that, the teacher could decide in which ways to allow particular learners to assume legitimate and peripheral roles within the community of practitioners.

Teachers working within this perspective also occupy a gatekeeping position for others wanting entry to practice. Entry is often closely guarded by those already inside the community. As Currey (1996) points out, withholding of expert knowledge is one strategy for maintaining power and reinforcing a sense of being irreplaceable. She quotes Pfeffer (1981) to show how expert power is parceled out as a means of controlling access to practice and positions within communities.

> Expert power, which is the power that comes from possessing specialized expertise, is eroded quickly if others can obtain access to the expert's information. Similarly, power deriving from the ability to solve critical organizational problems will disappear if others can acquire the capacity to cope with these contingencies. (Pfeffer, 1981, p. 113)

Apprenticeship teachers regulate gatekeeping through the permission they grant to learners concerning position and progression. Experienced practitioners first place learners alongside more seasoned practitioners somewhere on the periphery of practice, and then decide what learners will do, when they will do it, and to what standards. These teachers, in effect, set the standards against which learners are judged when they want to move from one role or level to another. Consequently, such teachers are in a position of "power-over" (Currey, 1996) their learners as they determine who passes through and progresses toward full and legitimate participation in the work of the community.

Common Difficulties

As with any view of teaching, this perspective has its heroes and villains. Again, I'm sure readers have their own horror stories of "masters" who held absolute power over their learning and their future progress and also made life generally difficult. Yet, there are probably many stories of "masters" who were extraordinary role models and who put their work on the line for people to observe, critique, and use as a benchmark for learning.

From the teacher's point of view there are some aspects of teaching from this perspective that are more than a little difficult. First, many are frustrated by their inability to put that which they know and do into words; they find it difficult to articulate their craft knowledge. Ask an experienced professional or tradesperson how they know what to do under difficult or complex circumstances, and most will fumble for words and ideas to represent actions and thinking that long ago became routine. They could easily justify what they do; it just isn't easy saying *how* they know that, or do what they do.

For those teaching in classrooms it is equally difficult to find authentic tasks for learners. Replicating the world of work within classrooms is one of the most difficult aspects of teaching from this perspective. Through simulations, case studies, problem-based learning, and role plays, they attempt to bring more reality into the relatively sterile environment of a classroom. Yet, even that is deficient, devoid of the whirl and pace of actual working environments.

Finally, teaching from a dominant perspective of apprenticeship requires an ability to scaffold or parcel out the work in ways that permit any learner to legitimately participate in the work to be done. For example, parents might teach their children to tie their shoes by starting with the pull of the bow, that is, the final act of tightening the bow. Each subsequent step is then added in reverse order so that, when they can tie the shoe unassisted, they will have worked backwards through many trials to the beginning. This backward chaining allows the learner to participate in the successful completion of the act while also seeing the completed tie each time they participate. Lave and Wenger (1991) have some additional examples in their book showing, for example, how apprentices in tailoring are first given the final task of sewing on buttons, because they can see the finished product and not cause any serious harm if they make a mistake. Yet, this is not easy; even when teaching in authentic contexts, it is difficult to dismantle the complex structure of one's knowledge and then scaffold it in ways that allow learners to participate at points of entry that are both meaningful and achievable. Many apprenticeship teachers choose the easier, and less successful, strategy of simply allowing learners to observe and find their own points of entry.

Snapshot of
The Developmental Perspective on Teaching

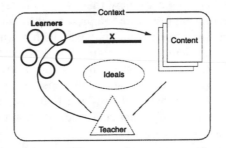

Key Beliefs
Fundamental to this perspective is the belief in the potential emergence of increasingly complex and sophisticated forms of thought related to one's content, discipline, or practice. The key to learning (and teaching) lies in finding effective "bridges" between present and desired ways of thinking.

Focus within the General Model
- Learners' prior knowledge or conceptions of content
- Use of content as means of developing thinking
- Line X as "conversational inquiry"

Primary Role: Guide and co-inquirer

Primary Responsibilities
- Assess or diagnose learners' prior knowledge
- Adapt content to learners' prior knowledge

- Challenge students' understanding of content
- Provide more questions than answers
- Encourage new ways of thinking about familiar concepts
- Foster deep approaches to learning
- Focus on structural changes in thinking
- Focus evaluation on ways of thinking and reasoning about content

Primary Commitment
- To learners' prior knowledge as starting point
- To desired ways of thinking as end point

Power Issues
- Allowing teaching processes to be influenced by learners' prior knowledge
- Allowing assessment to have regard for learners' ways of knowing

Common Difficulties
- Letting go of being the "expert"
- Asking good questions
- Refraining from giving answers
- Developing assignments and tests that are consistent with this agenda

---

PORTRAIT OF THE DEVELOPMENTAL PERSPECTIVE

Within North America this perspective is the most prevalent view of teaching and learning in any curriculum or program concerned with critical thinking and problem-based learning. In science education it is the dominant perspective in both public and private secondary schools. As pointed out in Chapter 6, it is informed by a constructivist view of learning.

You may have noticed that the narrative structure of Chapter 6 looks very much the way an effective teacher would teach in the Transmission Perspective. The authors have systematically structured the content in a clear and well-organized manner. The content is presented in manageable pieces or chunks, with an occasional review; the examples and language are familiar and easily understood; and the entire chapter is written in a rational and technical manner, much as Boldt recommends for effective Transmission teaching. Indeed, the narrative, or surface structure, of this chapter does resemble the advice of Chapter 4. However, it is in the deeper structures of beliefs and commitments that Chapter 6 departs from a Transmission orientation to teaching and learning.

Key Belief Structures

Fundamental to this perspective are two beliefs about learning. The first is that people perceive the world (and therefore any content they study) through personal, and transparent, templates or frames of reference which they have constructed from prior experience (Kelly, 1955). When confronting new content, learners project these ways of understanding upon the new content, attempting to find a reasonable "fit" between what they already know and that which confronts them. As Kelly says, the fit is not always very good. However, even a poor fit is better than none. For, without our templates, all learning would be like rote memorization of nonsense syllables.

This first belief about learning has direct consequences for a principle which is the platform for much of Chapter 6: *prior knowledge is key to learning*. In contrast to the Transmission Perspective, where learning is an "outside-in" process, in the Developmental Perspective learning is an "inside-out" process (Zehm & Kottler, 1993). Learners perceive and interpret new content in terms of their personal templates or existing sets of rules and concepts for understanding the world. If the content "fits" those personal rules and ways of understanding, it is assimilated into existing cognitive structures and schemes. If it doesn't, the learner has two choices: either construct a different template or set of interpretive rules and concepts, or dismiss the new information and retain the original ways of understanding the world. Either way, prior knowledge and ways of thinking form the basis of each learner's approach to any new content and provide a window into thinking.

The second belief is that the most important form of learning is a change in the quality of thinking and reasoning within a specific content, discipline, or practice. Individuals come to education with different conceptions of content, and with different levels of sophistication in their thinking about that content. However, they are not irrevocably captive of their prior conceptions and ways of thinking. Indeed, as comfortable as those prior conceptions might be, the primary role of a teacher is to challenge people's understanding and ways of thinking. To do this, teachers must be aware of, and able to relate to, a learner's current understanding of content; then they must challenge that understanding as a means of facilitating more sophisticated levels of thinking and reasoning.

The product of learning is new or enhanced understanding and cognitive structures that allow learners to move beyond their previous ways of thinking. Learning is a change in the *quality* of one's thinking rather than a change in the *quantity* of one's knowledge. Thus, learning is not simply a process of adding more to what is already there; it is, initially, a search for meaning and an attempt to link the new with the familiar. Ultimately, it is a qualitative change in both understanding and thinking. Thus, the dominant view of learning is similar to conceptions four and five in Chapter 2.

Primary Role

Effective developmental teachers act as guides or co-inquirers, building bridges between learners' present ways of thinking and more "desirable" ways of thinking within a discipline or area of practice. Bridging between these two forms of knowledge means teachers must be able to identify and then reconstruct essential concepts in language and at levels of meaning that can be understood by learners. In addition, learners' conceptions of knowledge and ways of thinking must be respected, even though they are incomplete or even incorrect. Thus, instead of working to pass along information or get information across, these teachers introduce learners to the essence of their content in ways that engage what people already know and challenge their ways of knowing.

Arseneau and Rodenburg (Chapter 6) present a clear set of principles which delineate the teacher's role and responsibility. Beginning with learners' prior knowledge, teachers are to make explicit the relationship between what people already know (or ways in which they understand) and what teachers want them to know. The "bridge" metaphor is a good one and captures the essence of what good teaching entails. From this perspective, a teacher's inability to bridge between his or her own knowledge and that of learners is a good indication of lack of teaching experience and/or lack of knowledge about the learners.

Primary Commitment

As a result, developmental teachers have a profound respect for learners' thinking and prior knowledge. Indeed, as can be seen in Arseneau and Rodenburg's chapter, they take that as the starting point for their work, proceeding from the known (learners' prior knowledge) to the unknown (more sophisticated forms of understanding and thinking). Effective teaching takes its direction from the learners' knowledge, not the teacher's: bridges are built *from the learner's point of view*. This is a significant shift from the more traditional Transmission and Apprenticeship Perspectives on teaching, even though it is still the teacher's perception of desired ways of thinking that determines goals.

Power Issues

The Developmental Perspective holds significant implications for the nature and distribution of power within teaching-learning relationships. In the Transmission and Apprenticeship Perspectives, power was located in the relationship between teachers, knowledge, and membership within communities of practice, respectively. Through this power, teachers could exercise control over both the process and product of learning.

Within the Developmental Perspective, the locus of power begins to shift from being predominantly with the teacher, to a sharing of power with learners in two ways. First, the process of learning (and teaching) is assumed to start with what the learner already knows, that is, prior knowledge or conceptions of the content. Therefore, learners may have some authority and voice in deciding how teaching should proceed and whether teaching is/was effective. (Note: this is not entirely unique to the Developmental Perspective; e.g., the Apprenticeship Perspective also has regard for what learners know or can do).

Second, because learning is assumed to be a change in understanding, learners must feel safe as they experiment and try out new ways of thinking. Thinking (out loud) in ways that are new, can be a risky business. It can be embarrassing, fearful, or just uncomfortable, depending on how people react. In particular, it can be risky if the person is confronted too quickly with errors or inadequacies, or if the person's thinking is contrasted with more sophisticated or complex ways of thinking. New ways of thinking, and ideas about the world, are in a very tender state when they are being born. Consequently, learners are at risk when they first try out their fledgling thoughts. This means developmental teachers must be cautious not to use the power of their own knowledge or ways of thinking in ways that would damage or curtail students' willingness to experiment. Teachers who are in the midst of a role transition, perhaps as part of a curriculum change, may see this as a particularly important power issue as they change from content expert to facilitator of ways of thinking. This is, in part, why Arseneau and Rodenburg stress the need for an ancillary Nurturing Perspective.

Common Difficulties

Within this perspective, it is necessary for teachers to explore people's current conceptions of content and then challenge those conceptions as a means of helping learners move to more sophisticated levels of thinking and reasoning. This is not always easy. A common tendency for beginning teachers within this perspective is to fall back into the role of "expert" and provide more answers than challenging questions.

But perhaps the most difficult challenge for teachers in this perspective is to develop means of assessing learning that are congruent with the beliefs and intentions of this perspective. While they may be able to bridge from the learner's prior knowledge to more desirable ways of understanding and thinking, they may not be able to develop critical questions, assignments, tests, and other means of assessment that allow learners to demonstrate how their thinking has changed, or how they can now think and reason like a professional.

Snapshot of
The Nurturing Perspective on Teaching

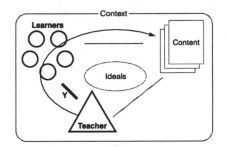

Key Beliefs
This perspective is based on a belief in the critical relationship between learners' self-concept and learning.

Focus within the General Model
- Regard for learner's self-concept
- Concern for fidelity of relationship

Primary Role: Facilitator and Friend

Primary Responsibilities
- Foster climate of trust and respect
- Engage empathetically with individual needs
- Promote/enhance learners' self-esteem
- Guide students through content to build confidence
- Promote success in learning
- Provide encouragement and support

- Encourage expressions of feeling
- Reinforce effort as well as achievement
- Focus evaluation on individual growth or progress
- Challenge people, while also caring about them

Primary Commitment
- To respect and nurture dignity and self-esteem of learner
- To pursue self-efficacy as the goal; achievement as the means

Power Issues
- Use of learners' language
- Elimination of institutional or social role titles
- Avoidance of dependency
- Assessment of congruence between competence and performance

Common Difficulties
- Assessing learning according to institutional expectations
- Setting boundaries between teaching and counseling
- Avoiding burnout
- Finding balance between challenge and caring
- Wanting (too much) to be liked

PORTRAIT OF THE NURTURING PERSPECTIVE

Readers who have worked in adult basic education, nursing education, self-help groups, parenting education, and a host of other "nurturing" occupations may have heard familiar echoes in T'Kenye's (Chapter 7) personal experiences and rendering of the Nurturing Perspective. While I don't hold the same disdain as she does for the term "teacher," I fully agree with her characterization of this perspective and its essential character. More than any other perspective, it resembles the andragogical image of an adult educator as portrayed in North America by Malcolm Knowles (1980, 1984, 1986). For anyone who has experienced or witnessed the kind of educational "wounding" T'Kenye describes in Chapter 7, this perspective offers hope.

Key Belief Structures

At first glance, this perspective seems similar to the Developmental Perspective in its beliefs about prior knowledge and experience. However, the prior knowledge and experience that is highlighted here, and is believed to most influence learning, is of a different character. It is more emotional than cognitive, and more central to the learner's self-concept than to his or her cognitive structure. When teachers from this perspective look at learners, they see a whole person who brings an emotional, as well as intellectual, past to the existential moments of learning. It is this view of prior knowledge—about self *and* about self as learner—that is the focal point of this perspective.

Thus, while the view of knowledge that prevails here is most often subjectivist, that is not the centerpiece of this perspective. Rather, it is the belief that learning is fundamentally influenced by the individual's tendency to defend and preserve one's self-concept against threat. Because learning is believed to be an emotional, as well as cognitive, engagement, the environment must be a place where people can express emotions as well as thoughts, fear as well as joy, uncertainty and confusion, as well as insight. Learners must never feel their self-esteem or dignity is under threat.

Consequently, there are three principles related to the learning environment. First, it must be a trusting and safe place where learners can take risks and not be humiliated or diminished for mistakes. Second, it must be a place where learners can attribute success to their own effort and ability, rather than luck or the sympathetic kindness of a teacher. Finally, it must be a place where the relationship between learner and teacher is both caring and challenging. Collectively, these beliefs bring the emotional aspects of the learner into sharp relief for the first time.

In our research, teachers expressing these beliefs talked about learners who came to them with a history of educational abuse, where teachers taught through intimidation, where challenge was perceived as more threatening than rewarding, and where students felt more diminished than nurtured. These perceptions were not limited to adult basic education students or "early leavers" from schools. Even "successful" graduate students talked about learning environments that left permanent scars and taught them how to pretend they knew when they really didn't for fear of being embarrassed or marginalized.

Primary Role

Nurturing educators, as T'Kenye points out, try to be both a friend and facilitator to their learners. As friend and facilitator, teachers have a delicate balancing act—they must be both caring and challenging toward learners. The balance can be abused by both teachers and learners. Teachers can sympathetically lighten loads or behave so as to be liked; and students can manipulate ties of friendship in lieu of attempting threatening or rigorous work. But equally, and perhaps more often, the balance can be struck.

For teachers standing most firmly within this perspective, the combination of caring and challenging gives direction to their role and responsibility. It also characterizes an effective relationship between teacher and learners. Rather than learning to shadow their teacher as a role model, students with a nurturing teacher learn to come into their own light through the mastery of content as a means, rather than an end.

However, because caring and challenging can be related to moral and ethical issues, the centrality of the learner-teacher relationship can be both a strength and a liability within the Nurturing Perspective. It is a strength when the relationship fosters growth in confidence and self-efficacy; it is a liability when it breaches personal values or boundaries. As such, it occupies a dominant position in the thinking of the teacher and opens one to greater risk. Whereas other perspectives may feel some justification in a relationship that is "at arms length," nurturing teachers see this as abrogating a central responsibility.

Primary Commitment

Within this perspective, teachers reveal a sense of personal regard for the welfare of learners, both inside and outside the formal learning environment. It is not derived from a sense of duty or obligation, nor from professional or institutional roles. Rather, it is derived from an ethic of caring, a form of commitment and genuine regard for the other.

Such teachers are clearly committed to the whole person, that has come to them as learner, and certainly not just the intellect of the person. Indeed, unlike the Apprenticeship Perspective, where content and practitioner are merged, in the Nurturing Perspective, content is merely the vehicle for learner self-efficacy; the emotional wholeness of the learner is primary. This has significant implications for how they interact with learners, what they consider legitimate conversation and discourse, and how they address power issues in their roles, responsibilities, and relationships with learners.

Power Issues

As with the Developmental Perspective, this orientation to teaching and learning seeks to empower the learner, both in the process and the product of learning. The process of teaching must maintain a genuine concern for the dignity and psychological well-being of the learner; neither self-esteem or self-efficacy is to be sacrificed on the alter of content achievement. Effective teaching environments must be, therefore, places where people feel safety and trust. As a result, the process of teaching can only be judged effective if achievement is the means and self-efficacy is the end.

Consequently, there is a shift from "power-over" based on the teacher's expertise (Transmission and Apprenticeship Perspectives), to "power-with," based on a caring relationship between teacher and learner (Currey, 1996). Nurturing teachers make every attempt to reduce the tendencies for their positions or expertise to imply or engender power that might undermine the growth and attribution of success to learners. T'Kenye illustrates this with Jackson's leveling of the hierarchy of power relationships:

We felt he appreciated our being there; appreciated our "trying hard" and our "stupid" questions; he indicated by his supporting language and his attitude toward us that he appreciated that we wanted to try. He behaved toward us as though we all were participants in a silent contract of mutual respect; he had his role and we had ours; but neither of us was set above the other. (Chapter 7)

One way in which Jackson leveled the power hierarchy was by translating the complex symbol system of statistics and the text into language that was meaningful and accessible to T'Kenye and her study group:

When my study group (one of several formed at Jackson's suggestion) met to do assignments from the text, we were usually astonished to realize that the data the textbook presented as intimidating symbol-laden formulae and complex word problems was the same material Jackson had translated into "our" language. (Chapter 7)

Language (or symbol systems), as mentioned in discussing the Transmission Perspective, is a powerful means of controlling access to content. Within the Nurturing Perspective that power is diminished and shared by demystifying and decoding the ideas into language and concepts that are already familiar to learners. However, even within this more egalitarian relationship, it would be wrong to assume there is an equality of power. To ignore the differences in responsibility and authority between teacher and learners is naive, especially as they relate to the assessment of learners and the responsibility of assuring safe practice.

For many nurturing teachers, their hearts are in conflict with their heads as they struggle to balance caring with challenging, supporting with evaluating, and wanting to be a friend while also carrying out the responsibilities of being a teacher. Roles, responsibilities, and relationships can collide in conflicting and confusing ways.

Common Difficulties

There are several difficulties associated with this balancing act, but three in particular are common to this perspective:

1. *Implementing assessment procedures that run counter to nurturing commitments and beliefs.* As with most of the perspectives, the evaluation of learning and learners can be problematic. Many teachers work in situations that measure learning according to pre-set standards, such as departmentally set tests or assignments, grade point averages, licensing or certification requirements, and so forth. Because these standards are often tied to socio-economic status and opportunity, learners (and teachers) tend to equate achievement with self-worth. As a result, teachers who care deeply about their learners struggle to meet external requirements, perhaps as a condition of keeping their job, while trying to ease the wounding that can come from yet another low achievement score on an important test.

2. *Maintaining the boundaries between teaching and counseling.* Because these teachers focus on the emotional wholeness of the person, they often slip into the role of counselor. In fact, the lines between teacher and counselor often are blurred in this perspective, which means some nurturing teachers succumb to exhaustion and burnout from trying to be all things to all people.

3. *Finding a balance between caring and challenging.* Perhaps the most difficult aspect of being an effective nurturing teacher is that of reconciling the apparent (though not true) contradiction between caring about learners while also holding them to reasonable expectations of work and achievement.

It is easy to misinterpret the name of this perspective and assume that caring means making things easy for learners, or crediting them for effort regardless of accomplishment. For example, novice nurturing teachers tend to assume that by reducing expectations or standards, whether in assignments or evaluation (challenges), they are showing that they care for their students. When discussing assignments or requirements, they easily give in to requests to lighten the load or raise someone's mark, or give credit for time on task, rather than what was accomplished. Indeed, in some circumstances this may be justified. However, more experienced nurturing teachers never confuse caring with rescuing learners from difficult situations or tasks. To do so could easily be perceived as a vote of "no confidence" in the learners' ability to do what they know they must eventually do.

Nurturing teachers don't ignore external standards; they simply don't accept that those standards are the most important indicator of dignity, worth, or even personal achievement. They also realize that self-efficacy is not raised through the gift of kindness but, rather, through personal effort and a sense of pride in one's accomplishment. As T'Kenye's statistics instructor demonstrated, finding a balance between caring and challenging means believing in your students and then helping them achieve what they must achieve.

> *In a subtle manner, he seemed to be challenging us: he didn't doubt in the least our capacity to grasp the material—his faith in our math capabilities far outstripped our own.*
>
> *But he spent a lot of time, especially in the early days, reminding us of our successes, not just in this class but outside, in our real lives. During our first class, he asked who we were academically and personally; but unlike most polite professors, he remembered what we'd told him and referred to it, often reminding us that we were his peers. He deferred to our knowledge base and looked to us for examples from our fields of expertise when clarifying points. He worked hard to make us "knowers" as well as "learners," and ot place himself beside us rather than above us, blurring the demarcation between our roles . . .*
>
> *We soon began to feel very close to him, to feel that he understood us. Jackson seemed to really care whether or not we did well, according to our own terms . . .*

Thus, effective nurturing teachers help learners set realistic and achievable goals, plan and work systematically toward those goals, acknowledge personal abilities and limitations that pertain to the achievement of those goals, and in doing this, constantly attribute success to the effort and ability of the learner rather than their own benevolence. In doing this, effective nurturing teachers find the delicate balance between caring (e.g., believing in peoples' ability and empathizing with their difficulties) and challenging (e.g., maintaining achievable standards that will result in a genuine sense of accomplishment and pride). While caring means understanding that this may not be easy, it also means never doing for learners what they can do for themselves. When this happens, teachers have lost sight of their role and responsibility while looking for approval and friendship from their students.

Effective nurturing teaching is, therefore, dependent upon a particular kind of relationship—one that is both challenging and caring. The crucial point here is that both must be present for either to be potent. Teachers that only challenge and demand without caring are usually perceived as insensitive; those that care but easily weaken in their resolve to challenge, are perceived to be "nice" but not helpful, and certainly not memorable (Pratt, 1987).

Snapshot of
The Social Reform Perspective on Teaching

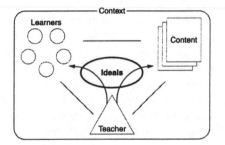

Key Beliefs
The most salient and dominant feature of this perspective is an explicit, well-articulated ideal. Although every perspective on teaching is an expression of an ideal, or an ideology, it is usually implicit, operating unconsciously to direct teaching. In this perspective, the ideals and ideology have emerged to a position of dominance and centrality.

Focus within the General Model
- Focus on ideal as social, political, or moral imperative
- Ideal deemed appropriate for all and necessary for a better society

Primary Role: Advocate for an ideal

Primary Responsibilities
- Authentically represent the ideal, in words and actions
- Clarify relevance of ideal in:
    - classroom
    - discipline
    - work/practice
    - society
- Demonstrate relationship and connection between ideal and content
- Justify and defend ideal against challenges
- Move individuals toward commitment and action
- Focus on the collective rather than the individual

Primary Commitment
- To ideal and/or ideology
- To collective social change rather than individual learning

Power Issues
- Pressure to conform to ideal or ideology
- Positional authority and expertise vs democratic facilitation

Common Difficulties
- Including those who enrolled for "content"
- Responding to those who object to the ideal
- Having patience with learners who assume content to be value-neutral
- Assessing according to externally imposed criteria for course content

---

PORTRAIT OF THE SOCIAL REFORM PERSPECTIVE

This is the most difficult perspective to analyze; it has no single, uniform characteristic set of epistemic, normative, or procedural beliefs. The "radical educator" described in Chapter 8 is a good example of teaching within this perspective. Yet, it is not completely representative of the range and diversity of social reform educators. For example, social reform teachers can be found in community development, women's health, Native education, AIDs awareness, Mothers Against Drunk Driving, the civil rights movement, environmental education, labor union education, religious education, and even within such established occupations and professions as automotive repair and medical education. Those who are social reform teachers have a unique sense of mission which directs and defines their teaching. That "mission" is the implementation of a well-articulated ideal, which social reform teachers assume is necessary for a better world. It is the clarity of a specific ideal and a missionary sense of purpose that give rise to each form of the Social Reform Perspective.

Virtually all social reform teachers make three assumptions: first, that their ideals are appropriate for all; second, that they are necessary for a better society; and third, that the ultimate goal of teaching is to bring about social reform, not simply individual change. It is the collective, not the individual, that is the object of change—thus, the name Social Reform Perspective.

Apart from this, effective social reform teachers have much in common with effective teachers in other perspectives. They are clear and organized in their delivery of content; they gradually and appropriately bring learners along with them as they perform complex duties in a community of practice; they ask probing questions and use powerful metaphors that help learners bridge between prior knowledge and new concepts; and, many work hard to respect and promote the dignity and self-efficacy of their learners.

However, these are not indicators of the essential belief structures of social reform teachers; they are the means by which they work toward a particular set of ideals. It is the ideals that are central to their commitment and ultimately the basis on which they judge the effects of their teaching. Effective social reform teachers articulate and integrate their ideals and content in ways that illuminate both, while making clear the place of each within the social order. Thus, it is essential to clarify first, the specific ideals, and second, the belief structures related to those ideals, if we wish to accurately interpret and understand a particular social reform teacher's intentions and actions. To illustrate, I will analyze the ideals and belief structures of radical educators as an example of the Social Reform Perspective. In doing this, I will draw upon the material in Chapter 8 and the work of Ira Shor and Paulo Freire, two of the most renowned radical educators in adult education.

Key Belief Structures

First, as identified in Chapter 8, radical educators generally hold to at least three key beliefs:

1. no education is ideologically neutral (not even mathematics)

2. educational systems reflect the views and interests of those in possession of social, economic, and political power

3. all knowledge is socially-constructed

Radical educators use education as a means of creating a more just and humane society. Whatever the nature of an injustice, a central belief is that power lies at the heart of much of what is unjust in society today. Thus, if education is to redress injustices, based on issues of power, radical educators must always be conscious of the role and significance of power: who has it and who does not. Thus, to the initial three beliefs, I would add three more:

4. all education is infused with issues of power

5. injustice is intimately linked to issues of power

6. education can only redress injustice if it addresses issues of power

By drawing attention to power within the classroom and society, radical educators use education as a means of changing society. However, while education may be a means toward that end, radical educators believe that the individual learner is only an instrument of change, not the object of change. It is social change—not individual growth, development, empowerment, or learning—that is the ultimate measure of success. Thus, goals and concepts such as "individual empowerment" and the development of "personal autonomy" are not usually representative of this perspective; they assume a hierarchy of power that places the teacher in a higher position, as dispenser of power. They also suggest that independence and learner autonomy are the ultimate destination of learning and education. From a radical education perspective, such individual independence and autonomy may be viewed as useful intermediate goals, but they are not enough to catalyze the necessary political transformations within a society.

Radical educators operate from positions of inclusion and recognize forms of knowledge independent of the usual hierarchies of expertise and authority. For example, in organizations with several layers of positional authority radical educators don't assume that someone in a superior position has more knowledge. Indeed, it may be just the opposite; depending upon what knowledge is needed, it may be the workers on the line that have more knowledge to change things. Thus, the epistemic beliefs that buttress this perspective are firmly rooted in a subjectivist, *egalitarian* view of knowledge; it is a view that assumes experience is as good a teacher as texts, and that participants are rather well educated in matters pertaining to their future needs.

You might ask, "Are we still talking about content that is part of a program? Can this really be a legitimate view of knowledge in a college, university, or even a hospital ward? What about curricula or subjects we are required to teach?" Radical educators agree there must be a curriculum. They are not anti-curriculum, per se, only opposed to the authoritarian and elitist ways in which it reproduces injustices in society. The challenge, for radical educators, is one of clarifying the underlying values embedded within the content and curriculum which serve to perpetuate injustices. As noted by Nesbit, within any curriculum, even one based on numbers and formulae, there are issues of power, control, and elitism which act as gatekeepers to much of the formal educational system, and silence learners into passivity and a sense that they have no right to challenge preexisting forms of knowledge and learning.

Rather, radical educators believe the curriculum, as a body of knowledge, is both received and reconstructed within the bounds of language, culture, and historical time and place. Learners are understood to be situated within a set of values that influence both the process and product of learning. The emphasis is on the interdependence and co-determination of individual, social, historical, and cultural knowledge. Consequently, radical educators know they are neither the owner nor the sole author of any content they are teaching.

The type of learning that parallels this personal epistemology is similar to the fifth conception of learning in Chapter 2: *a complex interpretive process aimed at understanding reality and self as co-determinant.* Starting with problems or issues within learners' lives, radical educators use content as a means of exploring and challenging problems and the "givens" in their lives. Math, English, art, physics, nursing, or economics are (re)located in the problematic and social contexts of people's lives.

In contrast, recall that the Apprenticeship Perspective places learners in real settings, occupying legitimate roles so as to learn the tangible and intangible aspects of work, interaction, and relationship. From this point of view, learning is understood to be a process of *enculturation into* the norms and practices of a particular role, group, setting, and set of relationships. From a radical educator's point of view, learning must critically examine those norms and practices, entering the lives of learners at the nexus of injustice, if it is to be meaningful.

Radical educators believe, then, that learning is a process of transformation, a fundamental change in perceiving the world, and "discover-[ing] vulnerable points for breaking through. Simply recognizing that we are surrounded by political membranes is an advance. Then, finding means to go beyond its limits is a social action goal [of this perspective]." (Freire and Shore, 1986, p. 105)

Primary Role

Radical education's agenda may be social change, but its immediate goal is to get people to look more closely at what they know and examine more carefully their common sense understandings about the content. Within this process the primary role of the educator is to first draw out what learners know. However, the agenda that drives this perspective is linked to collective social structures, not just an individual. Thus, it goes further than the "bridging" that is a feature of the Developmental Perspective. For example, teachers within the Developmental Perspective might begin an encounter with new content by exploring learners' conceptions of the content as a means of gauging a starting point, and then build bridges to more sophisticated forms of understanding, reasoning, and application of that content.

In contrast, radical educators who are committed to bringing about social change through developing learners' cognitive and *political* insights, are interested in what kinds of political, as well as conceptual, ideas are operating, and how those are related to larger social structures. Thus, an activity starting with students' experiences and/or conceptions initiated by a radical educator would be:

> ... directed toward the learner, not as an individual, but as a representative of social structures and networks of power and privilege, class and gender, economy and ethnicity, and so forth. Instructional content and processes are not abstracted from peoples' lives. (Freire and Shore, 1986, p. 106)

The primary strategy, then, of the radical educator is to locate a dialogue about any content in the experience, language, and culture of the learner. Learning and teaching begin with the experience and knowledge of participants, and highlight the ways in which content interacts with social structures in the lives of participants.

In this perspective the teacher is trying to, first, discover with the students that which is most problematic about their perception or understanding. As Freire says,

> we don't only look at the familiar, but we try to understand it socially and historically. The global context for the concrete, the general setting for the particular, are what gives students a critical view on reality. In this way, situating pedagogy in student culture does not merely exploit or endorse the given but seeks to transcend it. That is, the themes familiar to students are not thrown in as a manipulative technique, simply to confirm the status quo or to motivate students. (Freire and Shore, 1986, p. 104)

From the vantage of the ideals espoused by a social reform teacher, his or her primary role is to pose problems or, in the language of radical educators, to make problematic that which is taken for granted. By posing problems educators expect learners to eventually interrogate their own assumptions and beliefs and to learn how to ask deeper questions and research thoughtful answers as a means to action. Therefore, the role of the teacher is one of "democratic facilitator" wherein the teacher is concerned about developing critically aware people equipped to recognize and actively, thoughtfully resist injustices.

Primary Commitment

Radical educators, like most social reform teachers, announce their ideological partisanship as an integral part of their teaching agenda. It is up front and acknowledged to learners and colleagues alike as an expression of commitment. In the early sessions of teaching, they make clear their political, moral, or social commitments and their relationships to the process and outcomes of teaching and learning. This clarity may be verbalized; most often it is revealed through teachers' actions. In any case, these teachers are not only clear, but very often unyielding in their commitment to their ideals, which are an essential aspect of who they are as people and teachers.

Power Issues

As you might have guessed, radical education is about power, and making explicit that which is usually implicit—people's values and ideals. It is also about challenging the status quo and changing social structures that perpetuate injustices in society. Therefore, it should not be surprising that its teaching is often in conflict with other established (and often nonexplicit or assumed) values or ideals. As learners are invited to peer behind the hegemonic veils of power, they discover their own unconscious submission to the status quo; they also unveil the values and ideals of others whose "good life" depends on maintaining the status quo. This is fertile ground for at least two kinds of conflict that are rooted in issues of power: how to use a teacher's expertise, and how to manage competing values and vested interests.

First, learners may see the teacher as the expert, but may eventually resent and challenge the very status (power) they have accorded him or her. This is both a power issue and a common difficulty for radical educators. In order to build the educational agenda from the lives of their learners, expressed in their language, and from their point of view, radical educators must neutralize, but not abandon, their own expertise. The transition from teacher to "democratic facilitator" is not an easy one, as it requires a delicate dance of making available, but not imposing, legitimate "expert knowledge."

Second, most educational groups contain competing values and vested interests based on power. Some of those differences may be based on gender, as in the power to shape the informal rules for a group discussion; others may be based on positional authority and role, for example, when different levels of a hospital staff meet in the same instructional setting. Indeed, they are so common that mainstream adult education literature abounds with ideas for handling "difficult situations" or "troublesome learners." However, radical education reframes both the difficult situation and troublesome learner as natural and necessary occurrences in the life of a working group. Instead of finding ways to avoid or resolve these power struggles, so as to get on with the agenda, radical educators try to have participants focus on the nature of the conflict as it relates to issues of power and privilege in the group. Instead of seeing conflict as a stumble along the path to the content, it is experienced and examined as part of the destination. It affirms conflict in groups, rather than avoiding it, as something that is natural and necessary for working collectively toward common goals.

Common Difficulties

I'm sure many readers have experienced the missionary zeal of radical reform educators. To the extent that we have agreed with their ideals we may have been more tolerant of their approaches to teaching. If, however, we have been presented with a teacher advocating an ideal that we oppose, we are likely to have had a different impression of the quality of teaching.

In addition, if the most important goal is to change society, and not just the individual, then evaluation of learning and/or teaching is more than a little difficult for several reasons. First, the most relevant test of student learning and teacher effectiveness lies beyond the bounds of the immediate teacher-learner relationship and context for learning; second, the most important evidence of social change will, very likely, be delayed in occurrence beyond the boundaries of course or program time limitations; and third, many of the reforms sought by radical education teachers would require changes in the organization that hired the teacher and may now be asking for evidence of effective teaching. For these reasons, most radical educators accept evidence of their effectiveness that is more closely aligned with individual changes in awareness, belief, and commitment.

Perhaps the most serious difficulty within this perspective is for radical educators to maintain a high degree of consistency and congruity between their espoused ideals and teaching behavior. It is one thing to champion an ideal; quite another to live that ideal. Teaching is in grave trouble when there is a disparity between the teacher's words and actions. It is all the more unsettling when the words advocate a moral or principled high ground and the actions are not so virtuous. Here too, many readers will have experienced someone's teaching that seemed at odds with an espoused set of convictions or values.

FROM TOOLS AND ANALYSIS TO EVALUATION

This chapter has taken you into the heart of each perspective, revealing the essential belief structures that define and differentiate perspectives on teaching. At this point you should have a clearer picture of five qualitatively different ways of thinking about, and enacting, what is simply called "teaching." Yet, a most difficult and important task remains: how to evaluate teaching within and across perspectives on teaching. The final chapter will do this, by building a strategy for evaluating teaching that respects the plurality and diversity of each perspective on teaching.

REFERENCES

Bingham, W. (1995). Adult Education Term Paper—ADED 519, The University of British Columbia, Vancouver, Canada

Currey, I. (1996). *Teaching, power, and curriculum change*. A major paper submitted for the masters of education, The University of British Columbia, Vancouver, Canada.

Freire, P. & Shore, I. (1986). *A pedegogy for liberation: Dialogues on transforming education*. South Hadley, MA: Bergin and Garvey.

Kelly, G. A. (1955). *A theory of personality: The psychology of personal constructs*. New York: Norton & Co.

Knowles, M. S. (1986). *Using learning contracts: Practical approaches to individualizing and structuring learning*, San Francisco: Jossey-Bass.

Knowles, M. S. (1980). *The modern practice of adult education: From pedagogy to andragogy* (pp. 40–62). Chicago: Association Press, Follett Publishing Co.

Knowles, M. S., & Associates. (1984). *Andragogy in action*. San Francisco: Jossey-Bass.

Lave, J. & Wenger, E. (1991). *Situated learning: Legitimate peripheral participation*. Cambridge: Cambridge University Press.

Pfeffer, J. (1981). *Power in organizations*. Cambridge, MA: Ballinger Publishing Co.

Pinney, S. (1995, September). Electronic message, Vancouver-Hong Kong.

Pratt, D. D. (1987, May). A study of memorable teachers. Address given to the annual meeting of the Newfoundland and Labrador Association for Adult Education.

Vygotsky, L. S. (1978). *Mind in society: The development of higher psychological processes*. Cambridge, MA: Harvard University Press.

Zehm, S. J., & Kottler, J. A. (1993). *On being a teacher*. Newbury Park, CA: Corwin Press, Inc.

CHAPTER 11

EVALUATING TEACHING
Approaches That Are Equitable and Rigorous

Daniel D. Pratt

At the start of this text, you were introduced to a General Model of Teaching and the commitments and defining attributes of five perspectives on teaching. These five perspectives were then illustrated by authors who hold one of the five as their dominant perspective. In order to detail the diverse belief structures and commitments which comprise these perspectives, several analytical tools were introduced and discussed. These led, in turn, to a summary "snapshot" and more detailed profile for each perspective. Now we must address the problem of judging quality across that diversity. The purpose of this chapter, therefore, is to produce guidelines and principles for evaluating teaching.

There are three goals to designing effective evaluations that honor the perspectives illustrated in this text. First, the process of evaluation must be thrown open so as to reduce the anxiety and increase the dialogue about what constitutes effective teaching. Second, evaluation procedures and criteria must go beyond generalized and superficial approaches to teaching. Finally, evaluations must be both rigorous and equitable—rigorous so as to make visible the substantive aspects of teaching, and equitable so as to not promote or impose one perspective over another when making judgments about the quality of teaching.

The chapter begins with three questions that must be addressed if the process is to be more open and less anxious. Following that, surface and deep approaches to evaluating teaching are compared, and some specific and practical ideas are given for making the evaluation process more equitable and rigorous. The chapter ends with seven principles for evaluating teaching.

OPENING THE PROCESS OF EVALUATION

Anyone whose employment or promotion has ever been dependent (even slightly) on the evaluation of their teaching knows the tension that accompanies that experience. Even when colleagues are a part of it, the process is often filled with anxiety. Why is this so and how might we reduce the anxiety while increasing the rigor? First, I think much of the anxiety comes from uncertainty. Evaluators seldom negotiate or even discuss the grounds for their evaluation. Nor are teachers reassured that their teaching will be patiently and deeply understood before it is judged.

Second, because the evaluation process and criteria are not usually open and negotiated, there can be a mismatch between the perspectives of those doing the evaluation and the person being evaluated. This causes incongruities to go unexamined and unspoken, as if they didn't exist. Consequently, there is an increased risk that judgments are about differences of perspective rather than levels of effectiveness in teaching.

Third, evaluation is a process of judging—it sets the value and appraises the worth of something. However, the process is seldom impartial or balanced in power. It involves values and vested interests, with evaluators always in a more powerful position vis-à-vis those values and interests. Evaluators are not required to reveal anything about their own teaching, including their beliefs, intentions, or actions, or results of previous ratings and evaluations they might have had. They may be good teachers; or they may not be good teachers. Nevertheless, it is their opinion and judgment about the quality of teaching that counts.

If we are to reduce the anxiety, while also increasing the rigor of evaluations, we need to find ways to open the process and allow better communication between those being evaluated and those doing the evaluating. Assuming people know why an evaluation is being conducted (students, teacher, and evaluators alike), and how the information from the evaluation will be used, there remain three important questions that are seldom asked and which can form the basis for an open and collaborative process of evaluation:

- WHO is being evaluated?
- WHO are the evaluators?
- WHAT is to be evaluated?

Who Is Being Evaluated?

When evaluating teaching, we look through the lens of our own beliefs about teaching. If evaluation is to be open, we must try to step outside that lens and ask, "Who is this person? How do his or her beliefs differ from my own? And, how might that influence my evaluation of this person's teaching?" These questions highlight the central tenet of this chapter: evaluation of teaching must have regard for the underlying beliefs of those involved in the process, particularly the person whose teaching is being evaluated.

Perspectives on teaching are an extension of individuals within their social, cultural, and political contexts. Too often the view of teaching held by those in positions of power and authority is accepted, uncritically and unconsciously, as the best or only view of teaching. Such hegemonic assumptions regarding correct or best ways of teaching violate the central premise of this book—that perspectives on teaching (and therefore evaluations of teaching) are inherently pluralistic rather than monolithic. To re-establish a more appropriate, thoughtful balance in evaluation, those teachers being evaluated must have the opportunity to consider and reveal their beliefs and intentions.

Who Are the Evaluators?

Equally compelling is the question of who is evaluating, and therefore judging, a person's teaching. Again, it is necessary to see the evaluator as both an individual, possessing a dominant perspective on teaching, and an extension of the institution which may have its own dominant view of effective teaching. Both the person and institution have commitments and values which will be played out in the evaluation process; both should be made clear in the evaluation process.

The most essential foundation for evaluation is that both the evaluator and teacher clarify their commitment(s). It would be wrong to assume that only the person being evaluated need clarify commitment; to do that is to increase the imbalance of power that already exists by giving one party (evaluators) information which can be used in the process, but denying the other party (teacher) information to use in negotiating the meaning of what is observed, reported, and used in judgment.

Granted, it may not be realistic to expect that evaluators will be as thorough and revealing in expressing their perspectives on teaching as will the person being evaluated; most often, they have the choice of whether or not to even engage in this dialogue. However, there is room for the teacher being evaluated to probe these values and positions before the process begins so as to be in a position to speak about differences in perception, interpretation, and evaluation as they emerge.

What Is to Be Evaluated?

Most instruments and procedures for evaluating teaching in adult and higher education are designed for efficiency and breadth of application. They start from a conception of teaching as a generic set of skills and duties, not substantively influenced by one's beliefs about content, context, or the characteristics of the students taught. As a result, they most often take a surface approach to evaluating teaching by focusing on duty and/or technical skill.

Yet, if evaluation of teaching is to be rigorous, it must look beyond duty and beneath technique to examine the deeper belief structures associated with variations in what is taught, why it is important, and how it can best be taught to "these people, in this setting, and at this time." Evaluation must look at the substantive aspects, rather than just the most common attributes, of teaching. This is the focus for the next section of this chapter, where we will explore not only the differences between surface and deep approaches to evaluation, but also how to make the substantive aspects of teaching visible for evaluation while remaining fair to each of the perspectives in this book.

SURFACE APPROACHES TO EVALUATION

Focus on the Duties of a Teacher

In these times of educational accountability, one approach to evaluating teaching that has gained considerable attention is what Michael Scriven calls the "duties-based" approach. This approach cuts across perspectives (and styles) and suggests that the best we can do, in the midst of philosophical and cultural diversity, is ask whether or not teachers are fulfilling their duties. Duties, as prescribed by those who take this view, are concerned with fair treatment of students, preparation and management of instruction, and evidence that students learn what is in the objectives when they do the set activities. In response to a question about how to evaluate teaching while respecting and tolerating diversity, Scriven said:

> In the recent teacher evaluation literature, there is a point of view which can handle the problem you raise, namely the "style-free" approach. On this view, the only thing you can require of a teacher is the performance of duties, e.g., fairness in the treatment of stu-

dents, effort in the preparation and management of instruction, and successful learning by students that do the prescribed activities. So the style [perspective] of teaching, e.g., didactic vs. inquiry, is totally irrelevant to teacher evaluation, and hence you can honor divergence while requiring success. The success is measured in the usual ways, with heavy but not exclusive use of student ratings at the pos-sec level. (Michael Scriven, personal communication, May 2, 1995)

He goes on to explain that he is the author of this duties-based approach and that the K-12 version has been through more than 40 revision cycles, using feedback from several thousand teachers and administrators. There is, he said, a less well worked out version for college-level teaching, though no source was given.

This approach seems to take the position that we cannot, in any morally and intellectually honest way, acknowledge all possible forms of good teaching; there are too many possible variations on the "good" of teaching. Thus, the only recourse for evaluators of teaching is to identify those who are negligent in the performance of duty.

Some may say this is one way to be fair to all five perspectives; yet, I doubt that we could get the authors of Chapters 4 through 8 to agree on what are the most essential duties for a teacher. In fact, this approach ignores the very essence of each perspective—the belief structures and commitments—and imposes a set of instrumental values that might be more amenable to one perspective than others.

In addion, "duty" is a socially constructed notion. One's sense of duty is inextricably bound up with one's cultural heritage. In China, for example, one's sense of duty as teacher involves the establishment of a lifelong relationship with students and a responsibility to develop their moral character as well as their professional competence (Pratt, 1991, 1992; Wong, 1996). Many teachers in such societies would be insulted to have the notion of a teacher's duty circumscribed in such limited ways as spelled out by Scriven. Furthermore, while Scriven's notion of duty may seem expedient and even appropriate for some institutions in North America, it perpetuates the belief that the quality of teaching cannot, and therefore should not, be part of determining who is retained, promoted, or given merit increases. Unless we can rigorously and reliably differentiate between poor, adequate, and exemplary teaching, there is no way to reward people for the quality of their teaching.

Focus on Technical Aspects of Teaching

Another popular approach to evaluating teaching within adult and higher education is the assessment of the technical aspects that cut across disciplines, contexts, and philosophical perspectives of teaching. The workshop described at the beginning of Chapter 2 is an example of one type of faculty development activity popular in higher education. Because such approaches to the improvement and evaluation of teaching are campuswide and conducted through a centralized office their focus is, primarily, on the technical aspects of teaching—planning, setting objectives, giving lectures, leading discussions, asking questions, communicating under difficult circumstances, and providing feedback to students. These are important and, though not sufficient, are a necessary part of what makes an effective teacher.

Yet, their strength is also their weakness; in their generality they lose specificity and substance. When one looks only at the technical aspects of teaching, it matters little whether one is teaching English literature, mathematics, music, or automotive mechanics. For example, I watched a friend in China teach for two hours in a language I didn't understand. At the end of the lesson, she asked for feedback on her teaching. Though I understood neither the language or the content, I was able to say something about the technical aspects of her teaching. I could see how often she asked questions, to whom she directed them, and what patterns of response occurred. I could see how much the discussion centered around the teacher and how much of it spread horizontally to involve the students in the far corners and back of the room. I could comment on her use of the chalkboard and overhead projector, e.g., that she seemed to talk to the board more than to the students. In general, I could say something (apparently) useful to her about her class, without having understood a word of what was said.

As common as these technical aspects are to teaching across disciplines, contexts, and even cultures, there are problems with taking this approach to evaluating teaching. First, we must agree on what technical aspects are universal and necessary to be a good teacher. Chapter 4 (transmission) suggests these should include: review and check of previous day's work, presenting new content/skills, guiding student practice, checking for student understanding, providing feedback and corrections, allowing for independent student practice, and giving weekly and monthly reviews. Chapter 5 (apprenticeship) emphasizes several key stages of learning and parallel roles for a teacher: modeling, scaffolding, fading, and coaching. Chapter 6 (developmental) takes yet another view and emphasizes seven principles that the authors think are appropriate across disciplines, learners, and contexts. While these are not all of the same technical character implied earlier, they are, nonetheless, assumed to be universal aspects of teaching, applicable across disciplines, learners, and contexts. This assumes that the role and responsibility of a teacher to represent and transform a particular body of knowledge to a particular group of learners is the same, despite the subject or the group of learners. This not only ignores the obvious differences between disciplines and professional fields of study, it also dismisses the differences between novices and advanced learners, laboratories and lecture halls, and teaching one student vs. one hundred students. Even the most generic of skills must bend to the conditions of who, what, and where the teaching is being done. Thus, we might have some difficulty reaching agreement on what should constitute *the* technical aspects against which all teachers should be judged.

Both surface approaches—duties-based and technically focused— impose a particular set of values and yet, implicitly deny that values should be a part of the evaluation of teaching. In the duties-based approach, for example, the most essential responsibilities (duties) of teachers sound very similar to the primary responsibilities listed in the snapshot of the Transmission Perspective on teaching (Chapter 10). While this view of duties may be acceptable to some, it would be unacceptable to others. It would not, for example, be the most crucial duties for teachers holding the opinion that education is the foundation for a democratic society and must, therefore, challenge those aspects of society that reproduce injustice and inequality (Chapter 8). Those duties may be part of one's responsibilities, but for radical educators, among others, they are not the most essential duties.

Finally, both of these approaches skip over questions of commitment, and the relationship between beliefs about knowledge, learning, and instructional roles and responsibilities. When those questions are omitted, evaluation threatens to be an exercise in assessing what is easy, rather than a process of judging what is essential—what teachers think constitutes knowledge and learning.

Clearly, one cannot be a good or effective teacher without concern for duty and the technical aspects of teaching. These are necessary and important aspects of teaching. But, if teaching is more than duty and skilled performance of technical aspects, how can it be evaluated? We must shift from the generic to the specific, from universal to contextual, and from technical to substantial aspects of teaching.

DEEP APPROACHES TO EVALUATION

The essential ingredient left out of both surface approaches above is the very essence of most adult and higher educators' identity—their content. There can be no teaching without content; something (and someone) must be taught. Whether they teach in universities, colleges, trade schools, or evening adult education programs, most faculty think of themselves as a member of a profession, discipline, or trade, rather than as a teacher (Becher, 1989). More often than not, they introduce themselves in terms of those associations, as historians, chemists, nurses, librarians, carpenters, and so forth. Their content is a pivotal aspect of their identity as teachers. As a result, if evaluations are to be credible, the substantive aspects of what is taught must be considered. The decisions teachers make—what is included/excluded from a course, what is emphasized/minimized, and what is assessed as evidence of learning—give some indication of the deeper structures beneath their fulfillment of duty and performance of techniques. Without an evaluation of the substantive aspects of teaching, evaluators are likely to elevate duty and technique to a distorted sense of importance and omit that aspect of teaching upon which people build a life time of identity.

Where to Look

Any good teaching evaluation process must consider at least three substantive aspects of teaching, regardless of one's perspective: *planning, implementation, and results.* Within planning, teachers should be able to articulate their intentions and beliefs (justification and/or commitment) related to the subject and their teaching. Colleagues (within one's institution) and peers (external to one's institution) are the best judges of intentions and beliefs related to the content, including the history, purposes, and policies surrounding a course or someone's teaching.

Within the implementation of that planning, there should be evidence of a match between espoused beliefs and intentions, and the enactment of those beliefs and intentions. Colleagues and learners should provide evidence of implementation effectiveness. Colleagues can look for the match between espoused and enacted beliefs and intentions. However, learners are also an important source of data; they have a more complete picture of a person's teaching and can judge as to whether it was responsible and respectful as well as meaningful.

Results, refer to learning outcomes. Alongside an evaluator's scrutiny of the results of formal evaluations of learning (tests, assignments, projects, etc.), there should be an assessment of progress on the stated goals, and the extent to which people learned things incidental to those goals, but important nonetheless. Good teaching very often reaches beyond assignments and tests for its impact. Indeed, for some of the perspectives presented in this text, evidence in the form of tests and assignments may be incidental to more important outcomes of teaching, e.g., an evolving sense of identity as a member of a community, or having developed more complex ways of understanding one's discipline, or feeling an increase in self-efficacy. These may be more significant kinds of learning than the formal results of examinations, yet they are virtually invisible in traditional means of learner assessment and teacher evaluation. Thus, for a broader, more encompassing estimate of the results of teaching, learners must be given the opportunity to assess their own learning as well as the relationship between their learning and someone's teaching.

In summary, then, effective teaching must have some evidence of clear and significant intentions, which are enacted or carried out in ways that are consistent with those intentions and respectful of learners. Teaching then results in learning outcomes which are related to the teacher's intentions and are evident to the learners. To illustrate how planning, implementation, and the results of teaching can be evaluated in substantive ways that are equitable and rigorous, a few specific examples are presented next.

SOME PRACTICAL EXAMPLES

Planning: Peer Assessment of Intentions and Directions

There are, at least, four questions to be answered about a teacher's planning. They address a combination of intentions and beliefs that, if clarified, give insight and meaning to the teacher's actions. They also provide a foundation upon which the next two aspects of teaching can be judged—implementation and results.

- What is s/he trying to accomplish? (Intentions)
- Why is that important? (Beliefs/Justification)
- What (and whose work) is included and excluded? (Intentions)
- Why? (Beliefs/Justification)

These are questions and assessments that can only be addressed by those familiar with the content area of instruction—usually one's colleagues (within the same institution) and/or peers (outside one's insitution). One procedure for evaluation of a teacher's planning that holds promise to be both equitable and rigorous is what Shulman and Hutchings call the "reflective memo" (1995). Although it is intended for higher education, it could also be used in adult education.

The Reflective Memo

When someone's teaching is to be evaluated, s/he is asked to select a course and the most important assignment for that course. With the course syllabus and assignment in mind, the teacher writes a reflective memo that discusses the instructional and intellectual goals for the course, and how the assignment will contribute to those goals. Prior to any observations of teaching, the instructor meets with the evaluators and discusses all three parts: syllabus, assignment, and reflective memo. The purpose is to address the questions raised at the outset of this chapter about "who" and "what" is being evaluated. The documents are used to open the evaluation process by probing and revealing information about the deeper intentions and beliefs of the teacher and the evaluators, and clarify just what is being evaluated.

In preparation for this, teachers are given a set of questions to consider and use as prompts to guide them as they compose their reflective memo. They are not expected to respond to each question. Instead, they are to select questions that engage them in critical reflection on their planning. Because this is a reflective memo, it is recommended that instructors be given the questions well in advance, to allow time to think about them before composing the three to five page memo that elaborates upon underlying intentions and beliefs.

Neither the documents or the reflective memo alone is as revealing as the combination of them. The teaching plan and assignment allow colleagues to review actual samples of teaching materials; the reflective memo supplies underlying thinking, and provides a context and framework for interpreting and judging substantive aspects of planning.

The entire exercise is an example of how the evaluation of teaching can incorporate reflection on key commitments and belief structures. Incidentally, it also allows the evaluators to make explicit their own beliefs and commitments related to teaching and learning, providing a conversation among the peer evaluators and the teacher about what constitutes good teaching.

The questions below are a sample of what might be included in the directions to teachers. Because the original questions proposed by Shulman and Hutchings were biased toward one or two perspectives, I have replaced them with a more neutral set of questions. They are grouped according to epistemic, normative, and procedural beliefs to illustrate the link between substantive aspects of teaching and underlying belief structures. However, when using them it may not be appropriate to group or label them this way. For convenience, all questions are written in the language of a "course" but are appropriate for other forms of teaching as well.

Epistemic Beliefs: Questions about Knowledge

- What do you want people to learn in this course? Why is that important?
- What crucial issues, key arguments, debates, and authors are to be considered?
- Whose work (authors, critics, practitioners, artists, etc.) is most central to the way you have developed this course and its content? Why?
- Whose work (authors) have you intentionally omitted? Why?
- How does your course link with or lay a foundation for other courses?
- How does it complement or contradict learning from other courses?

Epistemic Beliefs: Questions about Learning

- What do learners find particularly fascinating about your course? Why?
- Where do they encounter their greatest difficulties in understanding or motivation? Why?
- Where do they do best in the assignments or examinations? Why?
- Where do they have the greatest difficulty in assignments or exams? Why?
- Does your course build on people's prior knowledge or experience? How?

Epistemic Beliefs: Questions about Evaluation

- What is the most important assignment in this course?
- Why is it important and how does it reflect your overall intentions?
- How does it reflect your notions of what learning means?
- How does it reveal differences in learners' thinking, acting, or believing?
- How does it get at the key concepts or skills in your course?
- What standards do you use in evaluating peoples' work on this assignment?
- How would your standards change if you were teaching a more advanced or introductory course on this topic?
- How have your standards for this course changed over time? Why?
- What have you learned about improving this assignment, your course, or your teaching as a result of learners' responses to this assignment?

*Normative Beliefs: Questions about Roles, Responsibilities,
and Relationships*

- What is your primary role in this course? Why?
- What do you and your students do as the course progresses?
- How has your teaching role been successful for you in the past?
- How has that role been difficult or less than successful?
- Why do you think your role has/has not been a particularly successful for you?
- What is the role of students or learners in this course? Why?
- How do you know when you're successful as a teacher?
- What is the nature of your relationship with students?

Procedural Beliefs: Questions about Tactics and Procedures

- How does the course begin? Why does it begin as it does?
- How can you tell when things are going well?
- Think back to a recent episode that didn't go well. Describe it and explain why you think it didn't go well. What would you do different next time? Why?
- What does it require to be really good at teaching your subject?
- What do you think is the relationship between teaching and learning?
- What do you plan to do next, to improve your teaching in this course?

As I said, it is not intended that all questions be used; they are offered as a range of possible questions that will allow a teacher to reflect and reveal the deeper structures of his or her beliefs and commitments related to teaching. Some kind of reflective activity is necessary if teachers wish to communicate their perspectives to evaluators. It is also necessary if teachers are to become critically aware of their own perspective(s) on teaching, and if the process of evaluation itself is to promote the improvement of teaching. In so far as the exercises invite reflection on tensions, questions, problems, and educational issues the teacher may be struggling with, they may also prompt a more convincing account of teaching excellence. Furthermore, these means can certainly supplement, and perhaps replace, existing sources of data that treat teaching as unproblematic, skilled performances.

Peer Review in Higher Education

For some, this close scrutiny of teaching may run against assumptions and traditions of academic freedom, especially in higher education. Yet, it seems ironic that academics are willing (and expected) to go public with other kinds of scholarly work, but close the door on their teaching. Teaching is, even more than other forms of scholarship, a public act within a community of students and colleagues that affects all members of that community. To protect it from the same kind of scrutiny given to research or publication is to promote its continued marginalization within academic settings. Teaching must be accountable to the same standards of evaluation as other forms of scholarship, and this must involve colleague and peer review.

Because judgments about teaching often have regard for the history, purposes, policies, and articulation with other program requirements within a department or institution, colleagues are usually asked to assess the quality of planning documents (Centra, 1993). This is not an unusual occurance. However, to increase their rigor and credibility, judgments must be perceived to be impartial and of high standards. One way to accomplish this is to have the same planning materials, and reflective memo, sent out for peer review by a respected academic, at arms length, involved in similar work/teaching at another institution, much as is done with the review of academic writing.

The entire exercise is an example of how the evaluation of teaching can incorporate reflection on key commitments and belief structures. Incidentally, it also allows the evaluators to make explicit their own beliefs and commitments related to teaching and learning, providing a conversation among colleagues, peer evaluators, and the teacher about what constitutes good teaching.

Still, this exercise does not absolutely guard against unfair judgment of a teacher. To do that, evaluations of planning and intent must focus on the individual's representation of a perspective, not the perspective per se. As Brookfield points out, this can be a source of conflict when evaluating teaching.

> The evaluative criteria by which we decide that some educational directions are more just, humane, or equitable than others are, at root, value judgments. Teachers always have an agenda, a direction in which they wish to take their students that they believe is better than other directions. (1990, p. 134)

As part of this, evaluators must look beyond planning to the implementation of plans and intentions as another source of data on someone's teaching. The most common form of data gathering for this aspect is observations by colleagues and learners. The next section offers some practical guidelines for the conduct of teaching observations.

Implementation: Peer and Learner Observations

Classroom observations, as they are usually conducted by colleagues, take only a snapshot of teaching and tend to focus primarily on technical skills of presentation, questioning, responding, and so forth. As such, observations have a poor record and limited potential for the evaluation of teaching. As French-Lazovik reported in a review of literature on classroom observations in higher education:

> The general finding is that it does not provide a sound method of evaluating the teacher's in-class activities. A few classroom visits by one colleague cannot be expected to produce a reliable judgment . . . Even when the number of colleagues is increased to three, and each makes at least two visits, the reliability of resulting evaluations is so low as to make them useless . . . (1975, p. 75)

This is not a surprising finding, given the usual way of conducting classroom observations, at least in higher education. An observer (usually a colleague) enters the room armed with his or her personal and private "yardstick" of good teaching against which this person's work is to be assessed. During the visit the observer may scribble notes or sit passively but, under the usual rules of engagement, neither the notes or the thoughts of the observer are presented to the teacher as a way of explaining what was seen, what was considered important (or not), and what value was placed on the process and content observed. After the instructional session is completed, the observer may offer a word or two of re-assurance to the teacher, or even set a time to discuss the observation, before exiting. Sadly, classroom observations are too often driven by the perception that teaching need only be adequate, because it doesn't occupy an important place in the reward system anyway. As a result, the usual process of observing a colleague is neither democratic nor compassionate; more over, the product is often neither helpful to the teacher or reliable to the evaluator.

The American Association for Higher Education (AAHE) *Peer Review of Teaching Project* (1995) offers several guidelines for improving observations by colleagues. They are presented below, with some additions and modifications, as part of a strategy for reducing the anxiety and increasing the reliability associated with gathering implementation data.

- *Avoid "parachuting" into a class*, making your observations, and then exiting to make judgments without consulting with the teacher.
- *Make observations part of a consultation process which includes both a pre-visit and a post-visit meeting.* The pre-visit meeting should establish the purpose of the observation, the goals for the class, and how those goals fit within the overall agenda for the course. The post-visit meeting should be a de-briefing to discuss what the observer saw. As well, the teacher's own assessment of the session should be included in the discussion.
- *Link observations to reviews of teaching materials, the reflective memo, and discussions of these materials.* Colleagues' observations and meetings with students should assess the internal consistency of a teacher's espoused and actual beliefs and intentions. Planning, implementation, and results should be complementary.
- *Conduct several observations*, distributed across the entire term of a course, rather than a single snapshot look at one session.
- *Combine observations with other information about the person's teaching*, including interviews with students, review of course materials, examination of assignments and samples of student work.
- *Use a team approach*, in which colleagues pair up or work in small groups to visit one another's classes over the term of a course.
- *As observers, be open to learning* about different approaches to teaching while judging the quality of another's teaching.
- *Let students know what is happening and why*; tell them the purpose of the evaluation and the role of observations in the process.

Notice that this method of peer observation is not the same as the glimpse one would get through one or two observations of someone's teaching; nor is it entirely dependent upon colleagues' opinion of teaching. Learners in this aspect of evaluation are an important source of data and opinion. By being clear in purpose and procedure to learners and teachers alike, this method offers a more open process of evaluation that can, potentially, reduce anxiety and increase the likelihood that observations will focus on substantive aspects of teaching. Most importantly, this approach is meant to complement the review of course materials and the teacher's reflections on plans and assignments.

Substantive approaches to evaluation of teaching also require assessment of a third aspect—the effects of teaching. For data on that, evaluators must turn to learners and *their* assessment of the effects of teaching on *their* learning.

Results: Assessment of Learning

Overall, there is no more widely used source of data for evaluating teaching than learner opinion. Learners are perceived by many to be the most reliable source of data about the relationship between teaching and learning on the grounds that they are witness to the teaching across time and the best judge of its effects on their achievements (Cashin, 1988; Kahn, 1993). Learner opinion is considered a necessary, and sometimes sufficient, source of evidence on which to judge the quality of teaching, even across diverse groups of learners, disciplines, and cultures (e.g., Marsh, 1986; Marsh, Touron, and Wheeler, 1985; Watkins, 1992; Watkins, Marsh, and Young, 1987; Watkins and Thomas, 1991).

Yet, most learner evaluations focus on the process rather than outcomes of teaching. For example, they often ask to what extent the teacher clarified goals and objectives, was organized and prepared, used time wisely, emphasized key concepts, provided timely feedback on assignments, was enthusiastic about the subject, and treated learners with respect. While this may be useful information for the improvement of teaching, it is not very useful for assessing the effects of teaching. For example, it does not address what was taught and what was learned, the value of that learning, or the effects of teaching upon student learning. If learner evaluations are to be credible, the data must reflect issues clearly related to the effects of teaching; and learners must be a logical source of that data.

In order to make learner evaluations equitable to all perspectives on teaching, they must be designed with a broad conception of what effective means, including both intended and unintended outcomes. Learners, too, bring perspectives to the task of evaluating teaching; they know what is effective for their class and for their learning. Therefore, unlike the evaluators, learners *should* be invited to judge the effectiveness of teaching from their point of view; it is *their learning* that is a measure of the teacher's effectiveness.

In addition, while examinations, assignments, lab work, and even portfolios of students' work are important evidence of learning, they may not be accurate or sufficient indications of the relationship between teaching and learning. We all know people and circumstances where achievement was not due to the teacher but to diligence and determination on the part of the learner. Thus, for information about learning to be equitable and credible, it must be related to the *perceived effects* of teaching, not the personal diligence or attributes of learners.

This requires another note of caution: opinions about a teacher must not be confused with opinions about a subject or course. It is possible to value a course or subject, but not the teacher; it is also possible to appreciate an instructor but not the subject or course. For example, learners may have taken a particularly critical course that opened new vistas of thinking; yet, their teacher may have been only marginally effective and not at all central to their awakening. Conversely, a teacher may have been critical for an individual, or even a group of students, but the subject or course may have been only incidental to that impact. In both cases, if the evaluation of teaching is to be rigorous and equitable it is important not to mix the perceived value of a course with the effectiveness of a teacher. For an evaluation to be credible, it should differentiate between evaluations of courses and instructors, and between levels of effectiveness ranging from poor to exemplary teaching.

With these conditions and cautions in mind, the literature on *summative ratings* of teaching suggests that learners can provide reliable information on the following topics:

- *An estimate of progress on course goals*
- *Information on additional learning (beyond course goals)*
- *An overall assessment of the value of a course*
- *An overall rating of the instructor's effectiveness*

Each topic is presented below, as part of a *sample learner evaluation form* (Figure 11.1) with appropriate response scales and related open-ended questions. The order is important to this process—beginning with an assessment of personal learning, followed by an assessment of the course, and concluding with a rating of the effectiveness of the instruc-

Student Evaluation Form

This evaluation form asks you to provide information on the following:

PART A: An estimation of your **progress on course goals**
PART B: Additional **learning** (beyond course goals)
PART C: The overall **value of this course** to you
PART D: An evaluation of the **instructor's effectiveness**

Your responses will contribute to an evaluation of the instructor's teaching. In addition to your opinion, there will be an assessment of the course readings, assignments, and content by the instructor's peers. The instructor will also be asked to provide information related to the teaching of this and possibly other courses.

PART A: PROGRESS ON GOALS—Using the scales below, rate your progress on each of the goals listed. These should be the same goals you were given at the beginning of the course. Then, comment on what was helpful and what else would have facilitated your progress related to these goals.

1. Rate your progress on each of the course goals listed below: (circle a number for each goal)

Goal (a) _____
Rate your progress: 0) none 1) little 2) some 3) average 4) good 5) excellent 6) extraordinary

Goal (b) _____
Rate your progress: 0) none 1) little 2) some 3) average 4) good 5) excellent 6) extraordinary

Goal (c) _____
Rate your progress: 0) none 1) little 2) some 3) average 4) good 5) excellent 6) extraordinary

Goal (d) _____
Rate your progress: 0) none 1) little 2) some 3) average 4) good 5) excellent 6) extraordinary

Goal (e) _____
Rate your progress: 0) none 1) little 2) some 3) average 4) good 5) excellent 6) extraordinary

2. What was particularly HELPFUL to your progress on these goals?

3. What else could have been done to FACILITATE your progress on these goals?

Figure 11.1   Sample Learner/Student Evaluation Form

PART B: ADDITIONAL LEARNING—If you can, identify any additional learning from this course or instructor that was particularly important to you. If you cannot think of any, leave this section blank and go on to PART C.

4. *Within this course, was there something else you learned (in addition to the goals above) that was particularly important to you?*

5. *Why is that important to you?*

PART C: VALUE OF THE COURSE—On the scale below, rate the value of the course. Then, comment on what was particularly valuable and what could be done to make the course more valuable.

9. *Provide an overall rating of the VALUE of the COURSE: (circle one)*

0) none 1) very 2) some 3) average 4) more than 5) far exceeded 6) an excep-
little   most courses   most courses   tional course

10. *What was particularly VALUABLE?*

11. *What could be done to make the course MORE VALUABLE?*

PART D: EFFECTIVENESS OF THE INSTRUCTOR—Using the scale below, provide an overall rating of your instructor. Then, comment on the ways in which your instructor could be more effective. Notice that the highest ratings are reserved for those instructors perceived to be among the most effective in your program or in your experience as an adult learner.

12. *Provide an overall rating of the INSTRUCTOR: (circle one)*

0) poor 1) marginally 2) sometimes 3) usually 4) always 5) one of my 6) an exceptional
effective   effective   effective   effective   most effective Instructor

13. *What did the instructor do that was PARTICULARLY EFFECTIVE?*

14. *What could the instructor do to be MORE EFFECTIVE?*

Figure 11.1 Sample Learner/Student Evaluation Form *(contd.)*

tor. By asking about the effectiveness of the teacher last, people have had a chance to vent any negative or positive feelings they might have that could confound the rating of the instructor (e.g., a required course or a favorite subject). Furthermore, this sequence allows them to consider their learning separate from the teacher's effectiveness.

In PART A, students are asked to rate their progress on a number of key goals related to the course/instructor under evaluation. The sample form allows for five goals; the number will vary, but probably shouldn't exceed ten. Goals that are rated should be the same as those given to learners at the beginning of a course. Prior to receiving the results of the evaluation the instructor gives a weighting to those same goals as an indication of intention and emphasis within his or her teaching. Student learning (progress) can then be compared with an instructor's intentions, as indicated in the weighing of his or her goals (Cashin and Downey, 1995).

Notice that the scaling for PARTS C and D is different than most rating forms, allowing for course and instructor to be evaluated in four categories: poor (0), marginal (1–2), adequate (3–4), and exemplary (5–6). This is to counter the tendency with most evaluation forms to rate the majority of teachers at the higher end of the scale, thus loosing the ability to identify those who are "uncommonly" effective. If learners' evaluations are to be rigorous and credible, evaluators should be able to differentiate between poor, marginal, adequate, and truly exceptional teaching. Thus, as is mentioned in the instructions to learners in PART D, the highest ratings are reserved for teachers who are perceived to be among the most effective—in a program, an institution, or the learner's adult experience. In addition, there is allowance for comments that give more specific feedback about what was valuable, helpful, and effective, as well as how the learning, course, and teaching could be improved.

In summary, students are asked to tell evaluators to what extent their course is valuable, their instructor effective, and that they are making progress on goals that are deemed important by a faculty member and his or her peers. In terms of an evaluation's credibility, these are questions that must be addressed; they are also questions that only students can answer.

It would be difficult to reconcile a difference of opinion that said a teacher was uncommonly effective, yet people learned very little; or if people said a teacher was only marginally effective, yet they learned more than in most courses. Yet, evaluators must know what part the instructor played in the learning that resulted from a course. One would hope there is agreement between these questions; but if there isn't, it is a clear indication for the need to inquire as to why there isn't.

Self-evaluation: The Teaching Portfolio

A source of information about teaching effectiveness left out of this chapter is the self-evaluation. Teachers are increasingly being asked to prepare documentation that substantiates their efforts and accomplishments in teaching. This approach is called the *teaching portfolio* and holds great promise. It had its start in Canada, under the sponsorship of the Canadian Association of University Teachers (CAUT) and was intended to expand the body of evidence administrators could consider when making personnel decisions. According to the original guide called *The Teaching Dossier*, it is a "summary of a professor's major teaching accomplishments and strengths. It is to a professor's teaching what lists of publications, grants, and academic honors are to research" (Shore, 1986, p. 1), a kind of "extended teaching resume . . . a brief but comprehensive account of teaching activity over a defined period of time." (AAHE, 1991, p.3). A great deal has been written on the subject (e.g., Foster, Harrap, & Page, 1983; King, 1990; Seldin, 1991; Stark & McKeachie, 1991; Vavrus & Collins, 1991) and does not need to be repeated here.[1] However, if teaching portfolios are to be taken seriously, they must be perceived as rigorous pieces of evidence about teaching. How can that be accomplished?

One way in which teaching portfolios can be more rigorous is to incorporate reflection as part of the substance upon which judgments are made. Rather than judging the volume of work submitted, or the sheen of its lamination, evaluators might ask teachers to provide evidence of growth and change, success and failures, plans and aspirations, with reflective comments/memos that take the reader/evaluator deep into the substance and reasoning of the teacher's evolving thinking and approaches. In other words, much of what has been said thus far, applies as well to self-evaluations of teaching. They must be rigorous and go into substantive aspects of teaching if they are to be credible.

Being Strategic: Involving Key Individuals

Finally, we must consider the costs and benefits associated with this more elaborate approach to the evaluation of teaching. Clearly, the time and resources needed to assess and document the quality of teaching in the ways described here go well beyond the usual learner evaluations and colleague observations. In many institutions there will not be support for such an expenditure of diminishing resources on the evaluation of teaching. Yet, this is a catch 22. Until such time as the evalution of teaching is rigorously and credibly documented, it will not be considered a legitimate scholarly activity; but, until it is valued alongside the more traditional scholarly activities, resources will not be spent in documenting its substantive nature. Therefore, we must be more strategic in the development and implementation of evaluation procedures.

One way in which to begin the process is by focusing on helping the person who writes the report that goes forward within the institution. Too often, the work of evaluation has been focused on helping the faculty member document his or her teaching, without giving enough thought to the person that must take the recommendations forward on behalf of the candidate who is up for review. For example, in most of higher education the key person responsible for making a case for reappointment, tenure, or promotion is the department or division head. He or she is responsible for taking the evidence (and possibly a personnel committee's recommendation) to the next level in the institution. In effect, this individual becomes the chief advocate for the person who is under review. Evaluation criteria, procedures, and evidence should facilitate this person's work. Indeed, without this strategic concern, evaluations are at risk of being ignored or dismissed, thus perpetuating the catch 22 of teaching not being valued because of the ways in which it is conceptualized and documented, yet not being rigorously documented because it is not highly valued.

SUMMARY

The challenge of this chapter has been to suggest guidelines and principles that honor the diversity of teaching perspectives while also increasing the rigor of evaluating teaching. It would be relatively easy to offer evaluation guidelines that are equitable but which do not concern themselves with rigor. Surface approaches based on duties and/or technical aspects of teaching do this. Yet, good teaching is rigorous; to be less than that in its evaluation is to be unfair, not in the sense of promoting one perspective over another, but in not seeing what lies at the core of that which is uncommonly good about truly effective teaching. To be rigorous in the evaluation of teaching requires a fundamental change in approach—one that shifts the focus of evaluation from surface features to deeper structures, and one that asks "why" more than "how." Without this crucial shift in approach, teaching will continue to be seen as a relatively mechanistic activity, devoid of the most essential ingredient—one's professional identity.

And yet, the very diversity of perspectives, coupled with the inherent structural imbalances in the process of teacher evaluation, seem to present a formidable barrier to changing evaluation. As such, this chapter began with some suggestions about how to open the process to perspectives on teaching that are different from those that predominate within a group or an institution. The use of reflective memos as an artifact around which to discuss and negotiate ideas about good teaching in a collaborative exchange of views allows the assessment of teaching to also become a means by which the community improves its teaching.

Indeed, the evaluation of teaching should not be an end in itself, but a vehicle for educational reform or improvement. To that end, I invite those who are charged with the evaluation of teaching to recognize and acknowledge the lens through which they view and interpret another's teaching. At the same time, I ask that evaluators not succumb to the entrapments of efficiency and anonymous representation of that which is intensely personal—one's teaching. In the end, we must be careful not to enter the realm of evaluation looking for reflections of ourselves.

The benefits, therefore, from equitable, credible, and appropriately respectful evaluation processes are legion. It simply makes sense, from the learners', the teachers', and the institutions' points of view to embrace evaluation methods that attend to substantive rather than surface aspects of teaching. With that in mind, I close this chapter with a list of seven principles which, if used to guide evaluation, support both the reality of multiple, legitimate perspectives about excellence in teaching, and promote its continuous thoughtful improvement.

Principles for Evaluating Teaching

Principle 1: *Evaluation should acknowledge and respect diversity in belief structures and commitments.*

Principle 2: *Evaluation should involve multiple and credible sources of data.*

Principle 3:   *Evaluation should assess substantive, as well as technical, aspects of teaching.*

Principle 4:   *Evaluation should consider planning, implementation, and results of teaching.*

Principle 5:   *Evaluation should be an open process.*

Principle 6:   *Evaluation should be concerned with the improvement of teaching.*

Principle 7:   *Evaluations should be done in consultation with key individuals responsible for taking data and recommendations forward within an institution.*

CONCLUSION

If this book has persuaded you that the diversity of teaching is not accidental but is rather a manifestation of deeply held beliefs applied to a vast array of learners, subjects, and contexts, it will have half succeeded in its intent. Acknowledging the legitimacy of multiple perspectives, comprehending how to analyze those perspectives, and relishing the different ways they approach teaching and learning, is, after all, still confined to mental exercises. But teaching is visceral. It changes and challenges each participant every time the class starts. It is full of thought provoking moments; indeed, it is one of those rare professions that can grow immensely more interesting over time. This book will really succeed when it not only comes off the shelf of your library, but off the shelf of your own self-expectations as a teacher. Once you find yourself practicing, observing, evaluating, and discussing teaching in full enjoyment of its many faces of excellence, then you will have made this text your own.

ENDNOTE

1. A concise and useful brochure on the use of teaching portfolios is available from the Educational Technology Centre at the Hong Kong University of Science & Technology. This four page flyer gives practical advice on developing a portfolio around nine elements, three of which are essential to all disciplines and fields. It then describes five steps to creating such a porfolio (Wong, 1995).

REFERENCES

American Association for Higher Education (AAHE) (1991). *The teaching portfolio: Capturing the scholarship in teaching*. Washington, DC: Author.

American Association for Higher Education (AAHE) (1995). *From idea to prototype: The peer review of teaching—choosing from a menu of strategies* (pp. 4–5). Washington, DC: Author.

Becher, T. (1989). *Academic tribes and territories: Intellectual enquiry and the cultures of disciplines*. Milton Keynes: SRHE and Open University Press.

Brookfield, S. D. (1990). *The skillful teacher.* San Francisco: Jossey-Bass.

Cashin, W. E. (1988). *Student ratings of teaching: A summary of the research*. Idea Paper No. 20. Manhattan: Center for Faculty Evaluation & Development, Kansas State University.

Cashin, W. E., & Downey, R. G. (1995). Disciplinary differences in what is taught and in students' perceptions of what they learn and of how they are taught. In N.Hatva & M. Marincovich (Eds.), *Disciplinary differences in teaching and learning: Implications for practice* (pp. 81–92). New Directions for Teaching and Learning, No. 64, Winter, San Francisco: Jossey-Bass.

Centra, J. A. (1993). *Reflective faculty evaluation*. San Francisco: Jossey-Bass.

Foster, S. F., Harrap, T., & Page, G. C. (1983). The teaching dossier. *Higher Education in Europe*, 8(2), 45–53.

French-Lazovik, G. (1975). *Evaluation of college teaching: Guidelines for summative and formative procedures*. Washington, DC: Association of American Colleges.

Marsh, H. W. (1986). Applicability paradigm: Students' evaluations of teaching effectiveness in different countries. *Journal of Educational Psychology*, 78, 465–473.

Marsh, H. W., Touron, J. & Wheeler, B. (1985). Students' evaluations of university instructors: The applicability of American instruments in a Spanish setting. *Teaching and Teacher Education*, 1, 123–138.

Kahn, S. (1993). Better teaching through better evaluation: A guide for faculty and institutions. *To Improve the Academy*, 12, 111–126.

King, B. (1990). *Linking portfolios with standardized exercises: One example from the teacher assessment project* (Technical Report). Stanford, CA: Stanford University, School of Education, Teacher Assessment Project.

Pratt, D. D. (1991). Conceptions of self within China and the United States. *International Journal of Intercultural Relations* (USA), *15* (3), 285–310.

Pratt, D. D. (1992). Chinese conceptions of learning and teaching: A Westerner's attempt at understanding. *International Journal of Lifelong Education* (UK), *11* (4), 301–319.

Seldin, P. (1991). *The teaching portfolio: A practical guide to improved performance and promotion/tenure decisions.* Boston, MA: Anker Publishing.

Shore, B. M. (1986). *The teaching dossier: A guide to its preparation and use* (Rev. ed.). Montreal: Canadian Association of University Teachers.

Stark, J. S., & McKeachie, W. (1991). *National center for research to improve postsecondary teaching and learning: Final report.* Ann Arbor, MI: NCRIPTAL.

Shulman, L. & Hutchings, P. (1995). Exercise I - teaching as scholarship: Reflections on a syllabus. In P. Hutchings (Ed.), *From idea to prototype: The peer review of teaching—a project workbook.* Washington, DC: The American Association for Higher Education.

Vavrus, L., & Collins, A. (1991). Portfolio documentation and assessment center exercises: A marriage made for teacher assessment. *Teacher Education Quarterly, 18*(3), 13–39.

Watkins, D. (1992). Evaluating the effectiveness of tertiary teaching: A Filipino investigation. *Educational Research Journal, 7,* 60–67.

Watkins, D., Marsh, H. W., & Young, D. (1987). Evaluating tertiary teaching: A New Zealand perspective. *Teaching and Teacher Education, 3,* 41–53.

Watkins, D. & Thomas, B. (1991). Assessing teaching effectiveness: An Indian perspective, *Assessment and Evaluation in Higher Education, 16,* 185–198.

Wong, M. (1996). A study of traditional Chinese apprenticeship: A look at five Chinese masters. Unpublished master's thesis, The University of British Columbia, Vancouver, Canada.

Wong, W. (1995). Use of teaching portfolio to capture your scholarship in teaching. *Teaching-Learning Tips,* Issue 10/95. Educational Technology Centre, The Hong Kong University of Science and Technology: Clear Water Bay, Kowloon, Hong Kong.

AUTHOR INDEX

283

SUBJECT INDEX